D0440447

MAD MAN IN WACO

MAD MAN IN WACO

BRAD BAILEY & BOB DARDEN

WRS
PUBLISHING

A Division of WRS Group, Inc.
Waco, Texas

First published in the United States of America in 1993 by WRS Publishing, A Division of WRS Group, Inc., 701 N. New Road, Waco, Texas 76710
Book design by Kenneth Turbeville
Jacket design by Joe James and Talmage Minter
Front jacket photo credit: World Wide Photos, Inc., N.Y., N.Y.

10 9 8 7 6 5 4 3 2 1

Library of Congress Catalog Card Number
Bailey, Brad
Darden, Bob

ISBN 1-56796-027-8

Dedication

This book is dedicated to my wife
Mary Landon Darden, who endured the scorched earth,
no-holds-barred, take-no-prisoners, 90-day-and-night
writing siege that produced *Mad Man in Waco*.
—Bob Darden

Acknowledgements

Bob Darden would like to thank:

Kent Keeth, Ellen K. Brown, Kathleen Hinton,
and the staff of the Texas Collection of
Baylor University; Janet Sheets and the staff of
Moody Memorial Library of Baylor University;
Lois Myers and the staff of the Institute of
Oral History of Baylor University; Dr. Glen Hilburn,
Dr. Dan McGee, and the staff of the Department of
Religion of Baylor University; Ann Page,
Pam Schreiber, and the staff at WRS Publishing,
Alan Nelson, and various friends, neighbors, educators,
doctors, lawyers, judges, clergy, and others—
named and unnamed in the manuscript—who
graciously and unselfishly offered their
insights and information.

Foreword

When we first tackled this project, it was still a siege on the heels of a shootout. With no great intelligent foresight, we authors blindly stumbled on what we now—with hindsight—believe was the perfect approach.

In the uncertain days following the shootout on February 28, 1993, as we began planning how to tackle this subject, we realized that there was absolutely no way on earth that we *could* plan for it. No way in the world—not and do a good job.

If, as we began our planning on Day Three, we had decided to focus on current aspects—the siege, the players in the Now, tactics—well, fine... but what if Dave had come out on Day 5?

It would have been wonderful news, much better news than we all ultimately got—but a book? Five Whole Days of Purest Heck, with photos? We realized that the siege alone was by no means the whole story, that its roots and "reasons" lay farther back along the time line; at least as far back as the 1920s, demonstrably as far back as 1833, arguably as far back as about 90 AD to John the Divine, and thence to be the Christian Year 1 and the birth of Jesus—of whom Koresh claimed to the Second Edition. And then, philosophically, if not from the standpoint of narrative, all the way back to the first human ever to hear his name being called by the wind.

So, do we therefore bury our noses in the history? But... what if the siege itself began to take on a life of its own, motives of its own, pressures of its own, passions of its own—and all of it suddenly boiled over into an unforeseeable outcome of its own? And we were just caught sitting there with our noses covered in History Dust when it happened?

After about five minutes of sheer panic, we decided to cover our bets. It fell thusly: Darden would totally immerse himself in Davidian Past, a subject with which he was already well acquainted, and do it with no distractions from the present. And then he would write it.

Just in case the siege petered on out to die with a whimper.

Bailey would totally immerse himself in the Present, a subject which couldn't *completely* elude even him, especially with no distractions from the past. And then he would write it.

Just in case the siege became overheated enough to die with a bang.

As it turns out, both were the right ways to go.

With most publications, dual authorship can be taken to mean, "two writers sat down and wrote one book."

Here, it means, "Two authors each wrote two separate books, leaving it to some fairly brilliant editor to put them together." It could not have been otherwise, with so many strange doings in both the ever-unfolding present and the now-set-in-stone but Time-obscured past.

Because both past and present, as it turned out, were stranger than we could have imagined. Both also had far more to do with each other than we could have imagined. Though we worked independently of one another, heading toward a sort of imaginary "golden spike" where the two lines of work would hopefully link, we were amazed at how smoothly in fact the linkage was. The past so clearly foretold the present, and the present—as it was in April, 1993—was so fully the culmination of the past that we realized we had been incredibly lucky. We had stumbled upon truth.

It is no walloping great observation to realize that yes, the Past does lead to the Present, and, yes, the Present always leaves a Past behind it. But in the case of the Davidians, the Past seems to have led them so inexorably, so... well, for want of a better word, so *perfectly* to that awesome ending in the fields of Elk, Texas. And the ending in the Present was such an elegant, illustrative embodiment of the folly of Davidianism's past.

Because the story of the Branch Davidians and David Koresh is only the latest exposition of something us "enlightened" modern folk believed we'd left behind (as have "enlightened" men so believed, erroneously, throughout history). That most dangerous and seductive combination: Narcissistic Egocentrism, coupled with an unshakable belief in a higher power.

We all suffer from it, to some extent. Each individual constructs his concept of God in such a way that he can go around believing that God is optimally shaping his life, and always for the benefit of that individual. It is for this reason that people followed David Koresh—not that he was a great leader. They were egotistical enough to believe, in spite of all the evidence to the contrary, that they were themselves among the Chosen.

The example of David Koresh (and the earlier men and their beliefs which led to him) is the ultimate cautionary tale about the dangers this belief holds both for individual men and for Mankind. It is a very seductive trap. Anyone can fall into it.

And so here we go, into the trap: we have to wonder if our fortuitous division of labor (and the vast amount of support we received from our publisher) was Providential.

We have to wonder the same thing about our editor, Margaret Leary, who was fortuitously there not only to stitch together what we each said, but hear what we were both saying, and then make us say it together.

Knowing the difference between the two piles of paper we handed her and the one pile she handed us back after weeks of sleepless nights, it must have been Providence—whoa!

Warning! Davidian Logic! Does not compute:

Margaret Leary was born in Australia not that long ago, and much, much more recently, 76 people got burned up in Elk, all so we could have a pretty good *book*?

This is Koreshian reasoning at its finest.

And you'll run into a lot more of it in the pages that follow. After a while, it may stop seeming quite so funny. Your laughter may take a turn toward the nervous. In fact, it may start to scare you. Because, more to the point, David Koresh didn't have any kind of patent on this kind of thinking.

It's all over the place.

Next door. Up the street. Sitting in the McLennan County Jail, waiting for trial. The man staring at you in traffic.

There are, in fact, large organizations—some call them cults, some call them churches—that are bent on encouraging this brand of reasoning.

Those people are crazy?

Yes—but only as crazy as us. Only as crazy as you.

Point is, perhaps, that we humans will never know very much of anything about *ourselves*, much less our ultimate outcomes and net effects—and much, much less about any "Higher Intents" for us.

Stumbling blindly around down here as humans is always dangerous. But the biggest danger of all may lie in *thinking* that you know. *Thinking* that you are not blind; *thinking* that you *can* see.

Because people who are every bit as sightless as each and every one of us in this land of the blind just might *believe* that you can see, and follow you, hoping.

Follow you, in fact, God only knows where.

And on second thought, our hindsight concerning this being the perfect approach is of course also wrong. It was just *an* approach; it happened to be the one necessity forced us to take.

Though there may be an infinite number of other approaches, and even an infinite number of better ones, this one worked out well enough, and we are therefore grateful. To ascribe more to it than that, to believe that there is *only* one way, is, in a word: Davidianism.

Maybe the best we can do, both as men and Mankind, is to thank whoever we think we need to thank, for whatever good that comes our way (for whatever reasons, Divine or merely mechanical, circumstantial or random), and then just hope—but never assume—that maybe someone actually hears us saying it.

So in the immediate sense, to Margaret Leary, Doc Spence, and all the WRS folks who got up early and stayed late to help us produce this book, thanks.

And in the larger sense: for all the order and disorder, pain and pleasure, strife and harmony, predictability and unknowable outcomes, just *thanks*.

Thanks for letting us see some of it—whoever You are, whatever You are, wherever You are.

We hope You heard that.
But, for our sake, please, don't tell us if you did.
Because then, we might *think* we heard you telling us *other* things...

—Brad Bailey and Bob Darden

Introduction

The sad, sick story of David Koresh and the Mt. Carmel massacre of April 19, 1993, doesn't begin with the ATF raid of February 28. It doesn't begin with the birth of Vernon Howell, who later became the self-styled "Sinful Messiah." It doesn't begin in the halls of the Bureau of Alcohol, Tobacco, and Firearms. It doesn't even begin in Waco, Texas.

To believe this story begins with the death of four ATF agents in the fields of a rural Central Texas farm is to believe that a single politician has a single idea that can balance the budget, that there's one answer to the violence in Bosnia—that there's a simple, easy answer to any problem, no matter how complex. Worse than being merely simplistic, it is to be deceived.

And if the events near Waco, Texas, teach us anything, it is the danger of allowing yourself to be deceived.

This is not a simplistic story. It can't be told in a simplistic manner.

To reduce this story to just another example of unwarranted, terroristic governmental excess, an exploitative, ultimately murderous attack on a peaceful religious commune is worse than simplistic, it is an affront to the memory of the four agents who died on the rolling hills outside Elk, Texas.

To reduce David Koresh into a paranoid madman, a subhuman demon who raped babies and killed for pleasure is worse than simplistic moral expediency, it is to spit on the graves of 17 tiny children in their ash-filled coffins.

This story has no such agenda; we're not here to present our version of the entire sordid affair. We'll let the survivors and the National Rifle Association and the FBI do that. Professional spin doctors had been at work here long before we got involved writing this book.

Instead, our goal from the beginning has been to present the most complete account and context possible.

The world knows the main players. Now the time has come to set the stage, to introduce the supporting cast, to provide the motivation, to script the action.

Without George Roden, there could have been no David Koresh. Without Benjamin and Lois Roden, there could have been no George Roden. Without Florence Houteff, there could have been no Benjamin and Lois Roden. Without V. T. Houteff, there could have been no massacre in Waco.

The events of February 28 and April 19 could not—and do not—exist in a vacuum. They were, in a sense, pre-ordained, almost predictable. Certainly hindsight is 20-20—but only if you know where to look.

Events since the 1920s have been moving inexorably toward the events of 1993—and beyond. Before David Koresh, there were self-proclaimed Davidians and Branch Davidians who practiced polygamy, who married women 35 years their junior; there were shootouts with a staggering array of modern automatic weapons, there were graves disturbed, there were Messianic claims by people even less likely than David Koresh. In Koresh, these events found their spearpoint; they narrowed and were refined and given shape and focus. Koresh could have no more created these actions and beliefs out of the sheer fabric of the air than he could have remained untouched in the roaring inferno he may or may not have instigated on April 19.

To be ignorant of the past is to be doomed to repeat it. To ignore the past is to be liable for the consequences of repeating it.

Ultimately, this is a cautionary tale, a re-telling and re-creation with the sole purpose of making these events known so they won't be repeated. So they can't be repeated.

Along the way, you'll meet a colorful cast of characters unmatched outside of the most imaginative science fiction and fantasy novels. You'll travel to Australia, Israel, Bulgaria, California, Canada, Washington D.C.—and Waco, Texas. You'll hear about religious beliefs beyond the abilities of L. Ron Hubbard to create and implement. You'll be exposed to weaponry and firepower little seen or heard or experienced outside of the battlefields of Kuwait or Herzegovina.

And if it wasn't all true and documented in meticulous detail, you'd believe we made it all up.

Chapter 1

Here we stand, in one of several hells on earth created by David Koresh, amid the rubble of what's left of the end of the world, amongst the remains of Ranch Apocalypse and the fate of all mortal things: Dust to dust, ashes to ashes.

Wraiths of smoke still rise from the ruins carrying the miasmic stench of decomposition and incinerated flesh. Dozens of grim-faced forensic workers silently sift through the debris. They lift shovels full of ashes—of flesh, of wood—and pour them through a sieve.

They are looking for pieces of people.

Over the piles, tiny orange flags sprout like grisly carrion flowers, their traffic-cone color shining in bright, artificial contrast with the deathly, ashen rubble.

Everywhere a flag sprouts, there's a body—or what's left of one—buried in the ash. Temperatures inside that column of orange flame at the peak of the fire at noon, April 19, 1993, reached nearly 2,000 degrees.

At those temperatures, the bodies were cremated; if it had lasted much longer, there wouldn't have been enough for an urn. As it is, in many cases, only skulls and torsos remain. Some of the people inside at the time, experts concede, will probably never be found.

Here, a pile of slag, bones and ash that used to be a man. There, a blackened, saddle-shaped object that had been a woman, curled in on herself, warped, carbonized, buckled by the weltering heat of the blaze. Entwined with it, with what is left of her, a smaller, heat-hollowed black object that used to be her child. Mother and child, once again commingled.

Entanglements like this are among the biggest logistical hassles facing the policemen and forensics experts who comb and sift and sieve their slow way, inch by inch, over the scene where large numbers of Davidians had concentrated during the fire. The bodies are inseparable, their bones interlaced and intermingled.

These masses of charred humanity must be pried loose and shipped to Fort Worth to be further separated, examined, catalogued, autopsied, and, with luck, identified.

The only good thing is, the bundles are easy to lift. They don't weigh much. And it is good also that some are being found with finger bones still clenching handguns and with evidence of bullet wounds to the head, so the odds are good that many of them didn't suffer much.

The flames did their work on the flesh after the owners were gone.

Except for the children. There were no guns found in their hands—when their hands could be found.

And somewhere in that pile, already assigned a flag but with the identity unknown, is a heap of faceless bone with yet another new name, at least the fourth name attached to this particular piece of protoplasm since it came into existence: MC-DOE-8. It will be his last name-change—unless, as some fear, a religion springs up around him.

Vernon Wayne Howell.

David Koresh.

Yahweh Koresh.

And now MC-DOE-8.

MC-DOE-8 took the easy way out, a bullet to the forehead. With the bullet in the center of his skull, just above his brow ridge, it's going to be difficult to say for certain whether he shot himself or had someone shoot him, execution-style. It's not an easy position in which to hold a gun, but nor is it an impossible one.

What's left of MC-DOE-8's shattered skull is grinning—the same all-knowing, I've-got-a-secret grin that compelled friends, repelled enemies, infuriated authorities, and thus had much to do with propelling Vernon Howell/David Koresh/Yahweh Koresh/MC-DOE-8 to where he is today.

It is easy to imagine him smiling that smile, grinning that cocky, all-knowing, Messianic grin at the last of his followers, smiling through the wind-whipped smoke and flame as he—or a follower, carrying out orders—pressed the pistol to his head and started to squeeze the trigger. Smiling especially if, at that point, he still had an audience.

Watch me. Watch me have the last laugh. Anybody got a light?

The whole compound is like one of those "What's wrong with this picture?" puzzles.

The first problem is that the rambling, ramshackle, beige compound which had become so entrenched, so enlarged, so nightscoped and telephotoed into the American imagination, is now utterly, completely, irresurrectably gone.

Its absence leaves a discomforting vacuum in the mind.

Thoughts return to that absence like the tongue to the hollow where a tooth has been pulled.

As with its Branch Davidian occupants, all the Branch Davidian compound's soft parts have been burned away, leaving only skeletal remains: The rusted water tank that Koresh and his followers had used as a storage facility still stands at the west end of the compound. And in the middle of the rubble is the concrete vault which formed the base of the three-story observation tower. It survived relatively intact to entomb both the dead and the deadly. Inside it are thousands—by some accounts, millions—of rounds of unspent ammunition, and another layer of charred and intertwined ash and bone

If onlookers' eyes are confined only to the inside of the compound's perimeter, it is indeed the end of the world—the late afternoon of The Day After.

It's a world of rubble, with only ruined reminders of human habitation: a set of bed springs, oxidized; a stove, or perhaps a metal kitchen pantry, blackened and twisted by the heat and the falling debris as the burning bones of the building and the bodies buckled down from above.

And, stacked against the vault, a piece of evidence that the Davidians, at one point, at least, had every intention of remaining among the living: hundreds of gallon-sized cans of fruit and vegetables, labels torched away—cans of food that would have allowed the Branch Davidians to last months, maybe years, under siege. The cans of food now, in the remaining heat, continue to explode, forcing the startled, ash-covered workers to hit the deck— or the dirt, or the ash, or the bodies—wherever they happen to be when one of these last spastic blasts occurs.

And then the fruit and vegetables, scattered and spattered over the ashes by the explosions, proceed to cook awhile, and then to rot, mingling their own sickly sweet,   rotten-peaches aroma into the already stifling air.

Clouds of flies and insects smell the rotting food, the decomposing bodies, the burned flesh, and come. Their sonorous buzz counterpoints the deathly silence.

And underground, in Koresh's subterranean realm, worse horrors await: In utter darkness, five skulls grin wider with each passing day, as the flesh of the five bodies killed in the initial shootout rots and putrefies in the muddy darkness of these yet unsealed and water-filled tunnels.

This is a kingdom of worms and flies—the domain of Death— the new world headquarters, the home office.

Death and Dave did a good day's work at Ranch Apocalypse. And no one who sees it can fail to feel that dark, eternal presence.

John Cabaniss, McLennan County Justice of the Peace, was on the scene almost from the moment those ashes cooled enough to allow the first tread of living feet—and that was three days after the fire.

Cabaniss and the other McLennan County JPs had the grimly ironic but nonetheless necessary duty of pronouncing these still-smoldering hunks of humanity "dead," for official purposes, three days after they died.

Cabaniss is no wimp when it comes to Death. With 37 years' tenure in office, it's not atypical for him to see as many as three bodies in a single day—a suicide, a murder, and "the natural death of a man my age. I can go see a body in a field that is rising and falling with maggots and still eat rice for supper."

But this place got to him.

"Here is the blackness and the grayness of an area that once was life, and now, it's just rubble. Absolute rubble. And yet it's all surrounded by the beautiful rolling countryside. And you think of the beauty of all those children that are dead, some of them in the ashes around you there, that at one time were playing and laughing and looking out at that lake, the rolling hills, the greenness of life—and there's nothing here any more but the grayness and blackness of death. That is the way it hit me.

"It was almost like a physical presence. I'm not talking about angels or demons or spirits flying around, anything like that, but the awful, awesome presence of many deaths. That is almost like an entity in itself. It's an awe of the reality of death, I guess you'd have to say.

"It doesn't stay with you the whole time you're out there. Like anywhere else, you get hot, you get tired, the smoke is still coming out of the place there; a can of food blows up and you damn near jump out of your hide. But it keeps coming back to you—that awful presence of many dead people."

As Cabaniss and the others picked their way through the hidden pitfalls of the ashes—hidden cisterns and other holes, ammunition, weakened underground structures—he was conscious of the danger, but more conscious of each corpse: Am I standing among the children?

And, of course, you start thinking, and wondering how their last moments were.

"I've heard this, I don't know it for sure, it may be something that someone made up, but I've heard that they injected them with something, and that they probably died before the fire. I don't know if someone just made it up, but it's a nice thought. I hope they were. I hope they had something so that they didn't have to realize the horror of a fiery death."

There is no small talk in a place like this; the only conversation is that which is relative to performing one's official duties. There is a lot of silence.

As Cabaniss put it, "Everyone had some awe over the situation. Every man was preoccupied with his own thoughts. You'd see all those canned goods and the ration-type meals, 50,000 of them, I heard. Strangest thing I saw out there was a page out of a cookbook, relatively intact—how to fix potato soup or some such.

"The thing that preoccupied me about this level mass of awful debris is that underneath it, just a few days ago, there was some kind of habitation for living beings, with food, and places where they ate and slept and talked to each other, no matter what their crazy ideas. And yet they were about a type of life that bound them to their leader in such a way that they would follow him to death.

"It was like David Koresh had put on a *play*. He had Armageddon in it. He outlined what the characters would do. He had in his own mind some kind of ending: 'I won't be with you next year.' And he followed it through. It's unbelievable."

The property outside the compound's demarcation only adds to the mystery, the "What's wrong with this picture?" feel. It's a strange, ash-blurred line between hell on Earth and just another pretty day in April, and it serves as a reminder that each of us indeed lives in our own little world, and that these worlds come to an end precisely both as we do, and when we do.

Ranch Apocalypse has fulfilled the goals of its owner: it has excised itself from the world.

Just to the west of what's left of the end of that world—the end of 76 (or more) worlds, in fact—back out here in the world that so mundanely and undramatically kept on going, there is a pretty little pond.

Over its surface glide a mated pair of the most blissfully unconcerned little ducks God ever made, going about their ducky doings in their own watery little world, oblivious to the possibilities of becoming duck dinner.

Not too far from the pond, just up the bank, there's a jet-ski, its luminescent green paint gleaming in the spring sun and looking as if it's just waiting for someone like David Koresh to hop on and scoot off across the water.

A few hundred feet away, an old but serviceable-looking Silver Eagle bus stands waiting for Koresh and the gang to come hop on and go do the Guns N' Davidians World Tour.

And over by a stand of mesquite trees sits David Koresh's vintage muscle car, the black Camaro which had been such a source of concern to him as the government tanks rumbled over his property, his once-sovereign state, in the days before the fire.

It still runs. It won't be running for Dave.

Dave's play is over.

With so little to see outwardly and so much to consider inwardly, the Home of the End of the World is less a place to see and more a focus for flashbacks.

Koresh's realm has left our world to become instead a Kingdom of the Imagination.

As the forensic specialists tag, bag, and remove the bare bones and pitiful scrapings of what's left, the mind cannot help but try to rebuild, in memory, the physical details of the Madman's Paradise that David Koresh created here. The mind goes sifting through rubble of its own for clues to comprehending a monstrosity of this magnitude and to begin to come to terms with it.

In the week or so following the fire, for those newsmen and lawmen intimately involved with the compound for the two months of the "Waco Standoff," there has been a dull feeling of numbness—a time of averting the raw horror of what happened here, simply because there are aspects of it that the mind can't encompass.

A purely unintentional, accidental fire of this severity, speed, and size, with such a scene as this remaining to memorialize its victims, would under better circumstances have brought out the best in human nature.

Humane organizations and individuals would be trampling all over each other in the rush to provide aid—financial, physical, and emotional—to the few survivors of the Great Tragedy.

The survivors of this one were, for the most part, unceremoniously plunked into the McLennan County Jail.

Under better circumstances, politicians and pundits and preachers would be busting a gut to be the first to declare it a Great Day of National Mourning. Instead, they are dodging blame—or accepting and then reapportioning it, per Bill Clinton and Janet Reno.

If it had been a pure accident, reporters and TV newsies would be swarming all over the survivors to pester them with questions concerning how they were able to make it to safety, rather than asking, "When you last saw David, what was he doing?" and "Did you really *believe* that stuff?"

And, invariably, under more sympathetic circumstances, by now a survivor would have said—and a reporter would have diligently and soberly reported—that it was God who rescued him from the inferno.

And Mankind could begin to hug himself and give himself warm snugglies about Strength in Adversity and how God works in mysterious ways.

But unless God works in some *truly* mysterious ways and has a far darker sense of humor than anyone's ever given Him credit for, that is not the case here at Ranch Apocalypse. And that is what is numbing.

The process of society's confronting its worst nightmares, darkest fears, and direst tendencies starts gradually, incrementally.

As grim unsmiling men begin sifting the ashes for the last bits of bone, elsewhere, in bars and restaurants across the country, the first dark jokes are tentatively tested.

Guess who just stopped smokin'?
David Koresh.

Haw haw. Yep—Heard they found him next to his favorite wife.
Who's that?
Ashley.

Haw. What do Don King and Dave Koresh have in common?
Their initials?
Nope. They're both black.

Haw. You know how to pick up Branch Davidian chicks?
Yep. Dust-Buster.

You know why Dave didn't become a priest?
He wanted to be a FRIAR?

Haw. What were God's first words to David Koresh?
Well done!

These jokes are perhaps not as inhumane as they appear. Rather than serving as evidence of further inhumanity to man, humor usually marks the first efforts at dealing with such inhumanity.

Turning such dark horrors into sources of humor provides temporary emotional distance, a buffer zone, time to absorb. Laughter helps to dissipate the emotional charge.

And the charge surrounding Ranch Apocalypse and the Branch Davidians is as huge and dark and foreboding as the giant arm of smoke that smote the compound that day, and it is a cloud of smoke laced both with lightning from above and with hellfire from below.

If Dante were alive today, he'd have to call for a rewrite:

"I see calling it 'David's Level,' and, get this, we change the sign on the door from 'Abandon hope, all ye who enter here' to read, 'Hope *put* you here, you sucker.'"

Because here is where the world got turned upside down.

Here, right is wrong. Love is hate. God is Satan.

Hope leads to horror. Faith in God leads straight to a crackling cremation in a godforsaken inferno.

Suffer the children to come unto me to suffer molestation, followed by a horrible death.

Here, faith kills, and there is salvation only for those who lack it.

Here, Jesus raves.

He who believeth in me shall be cooked at 2,000 degrees for three days, or until done.

God is gonna get ya.

Have a nice day.

Some people who witnessed the fire that day are now "in the care of health-care professionals." And if a psychiatrist could put the entire country on a couch, after a brief interview, he would have to conclude, at the very least, that there are issues here.

The first of these is Guilt. In most suicides, the counselors hasten to tell the survivors that such guilt is misplaced, misdirected, and wrong, even stupid: "You didn't do it," they say.

True. We didn't do it. We didn't start the fire.

But we did do this: We watched.

And the question we will never quite answer as individuals or as a nation is, if we hadn't been watching, *would he have done it?*

We held up the world's biggest mirror so that an immature narcissistic psychopath could caper and preen and pose and admire himself.

David Koresh had desperately desired, all his life, in fact, even more than life itself, his own Warholian 15 minutes of fame, and America handed it to him—and him to the world—on a silver satellite dish.

And he used that satellite dish to scoop himself up out of mere pop culture and *People* magazine and pour himself into a more rarefied realm: that of history.

And if immortality lies not in Heaven but in proportion to how long one is remembered, we gave old Dave the best of that deal, too.

While he was alive he made the nightly news and the front page every day. And, dead? Day-long newscasts, non-stop. And boy, would Dave have just loved the picture on the cover of *Time*: his face, staring toward Heaven, smiling, exultant, superimposed over the rising fireball he believed (or said he believed) would take him there.

There's even a wonderfully dire quote from Revelation—the many dire warnings of which were Dave's stock in trade:

"His name was Death, and Hell followed with him."

Hot stuff. We watched it. We watched it over and over again. We *like* to watch.

Of course, the corollary question is even better: Could we have *not* watched?

On a certain level, it seems that it just had to happen, couldn't *not* happen. All accusations, counteraccusations, investigations, recriminations, allegations, explanations, and expostulations aside, it had to happen.

Whether or not God *willed* it to happen, God only knows.

But men were sufficiently *convinced* that God willed it. And so, it had to happen.

As mindless as the flames that licked away the robes of Joan of Arc, as relentless as the Spanish Inquisition, as insensible as the Thousand Year Reich and the Holocaust, as intractable as a Papal Bull and as compelling as Holy Writ, men thought it was the will of God, and believed that the will of God requires some helpful enforcement at the hands of men, and so it happened.

REV. 1:7 *Behold, he cometh with clouds; and every eye shall see him, and they also which pierced him...*

The news accounts never quite made clear the eerie other-worldliness of that final day in the fields of Central Texas. It was, in fact, a nice day for the end of the world.

Except for the gritty wind scouring the landscape at 40 miles an hour—fast, strong, and hard even for Texas—April 19 was an Easter Sunday/Second Coming kind of day. Recent rains had left the sky an almost holy, robin's-egg blue. The fields, whipped by that wind, were an ocean of succulent alfalfa, fast-rolling waves of grass breaking around the plodding hooves of the ever-present Black Angus cows that had been milling and grazing over the surface of this dark-green sea for the fifty-one days of the siege.

In this sea of grass, three islands—geographically only miles distant from one another, but in terms of separate times, differing purposes, and variant realities, worlds apart—were separate universes, sovereign kingdoms, each an unresolvable mystery endlessly fascinating to the other.

If aliens ever come to this planet, their first staging area may well resemble the assemblage of strange dished and antennaed craft which materialized almost overnight after the events of February 28, 1993, east of the city of Waco near the town of Elk.

And the main purpose of the aliens will also be much the same as that of the humans in the strange craft: The entire colony, which came to be known as Satellite City, had, as its whole reason for being, the observance, in the minutest possible detail, of its other two neighbor-islands two miles away, and then the broadcasting of this knowledge back to the inhabitants of its "world."

Satellite City's inhabitants, as they twiddled knobs and peered into banks of glowing screens inside their craft, all spoke the language of the technological future which has become the present—foot-candles, lux, nightscopes, heat-vision, millimeters, satellite packets, dubs, microwave feeds. They spoke fluently the cynically sterile arcana of the global mass telecommunication complex, which amounts to the Planetary Eye.

That Eye, with all its powers of resolution and magnification, all its ability to see in the dark and the rain, all the parabolic microphones capable of picking up rumors among field mice at 300 yards, had finally found a mystery it could not penetrate—and thus the Eye and its keepers and its viewers were endlessly fascinated: compelled, obsessed, enthralled with the visible yet mysterious kingdom of Koresh two miles over the fields and maybe 2,000 years back in time.

What the Eye *could* see only contributed to the mystery, further romanticized it.

Physicists easily dismiss the phenomenon as "scintillation" or "heat shimmer." Those differences in the temperature of columns of air rising from the ground that account for the dance and waver of distant objects, particularly those seen through high-powered television cameras.

But though the cameramen carped endlessly about the heat-shimmer and prayed to the gods of physics that it would soon dissipate so they could get some "good clear shots," those shimmering veils of capering, spirit-like evanescence dancing between the electronic eyes and the mystery on the hill only enhanced its enigmatic, other-wordly appeal, and served to enhance the gulf between David Koresh's charismatic, apocalyptic Kingdom Apart and the rest of the "civilized" world.

And the distortions—both of fact and of photography—only served to make the world peer and ponder that much harder.

Fifty-one days, in the grand scheme of things, is not much time at all. But lives are not lived in the grand scheme of things; humans must wade slowly and linearly through the tedium of the seconds that add up to minutes that make up the hours that become the days and weeks and months... It is, subjectively, all the Time they have, at the time. It is one quarter of a year, of which only threescore and ten are allotted to the span of man. It is winter into spring, dry branches into a green tree.

Satellite City, plus the no-man's land of the green fields and the distant beige castle/fortress of Ranch Apocalypse, plus the arcane and intimidating doings of the powerful third kingdom, the Kingdom of the Law, had in those 51 days become the subjective, de facto world for each of us.

Those hundreds of cameramen, editors, sound men, print reporters, still photographers, as well as the hundreds of highway patrolmen, ATF agents, and FBI men charged with "protecting public safety" and limiting media access to the compound (and thus only enhancing the mystery), had come to subconsciously think of themselves as "living" within this world.

There was a phrase in popular use among them: *It's Groundhog Day.*

Early on in Satellite City there had been, naturally enough, given that this was a very sardonic crowd, the joke about David Koresh coming out at Easter, seeing his shadow, and there thus being six more weeks of winter. The reference was more often aimed at the Bill Murray movie then just released, in which Murray, a TV newsman sent to cover rodent-of-note Punxsutawney Phil, wakes up day after day after day on February 2, with the same events occurring over and over again, with no foreseeable end in sight, world without end.

The same wake-up call in the same motel. The same route to the 10:30 news conference at the Waco Convention Center. Then, Waco Police Public Information Officer Malissa Sims, in her usual helmet of blonde hair, laying the same ground rules yet again, which by mid-siege most of the media had memorized.

Some scribes and recorders would silently and sarcastically mouth it along with her: "Speakin' this morning will be FBI Special Agent Bob Ricks, that's spelled bee-oh-bee are-eye-see-kay-ess. He'll speak for a few minutes and then he will allow some questions. One question and a follow-up. No shouting; if you shout, you will be ignored."

Then the FBI cult's high priest of PR would say the morning mass and deign to answer the politer questions from those he would convert.

And then amen. Thus it is written. Thus will it be.

And then, if there were no other religious nuts or right-wing zanies picketing in front of the convention center for the scribes and recorders to interview en masse, they could maybe grab a quick cup of coffee at the Hilton. And then head off east on 5th Street, north on I-35, west on Loop 340 past the Wal-Mart (unofficial clothier of the Waco Siege), thence to Holy Hill and the T-shirt sellers, thence to the ATF press identification checkpoint—and then drive another five or so miles down to the press area.

There, it was park the car at the end of the long, long row of magical vehicles; grab the cell-phones, the laptops, the tape recorders, and other weapons and accoutrements of the Second Kingdom; walk the half mile down to the last checkpoint, beyond which none but the givers of the Law were allowed. And then get a cup of coffee from the Salvation Army truck; shoot the breeze with whoever was running it—Joe Roberts, Jay Walker, the little Czech lady, faces becoming as familiar over time as those of family.

Then find an unoccupied lawn chair.

Then settle in for another day's tedium; another day's Hurry up and Wait.

And always, becoming with the progression of the season every bit as constant as the sun to farmers and the moon to sailors at night: that compound. Ranch Apocalypse. That beige, towered, crazy, blue-flagged presence on the horizon, always taken for granted but nevertheless instinctively checked with a glance every few minutes during the endless ennui of those twelve-hour shifts in the big middle of nothing on the Central Texas prairie.

By day, cameramen and reporters played golf in a nearby cow pasture, tossed footballs back and forth, napped, sunned themselves in lawn chairs and chaises. By night, under strong studio lights powered by huge, gas-guzzling generators, cards were dealt, horseshoes pitched, beers consumed, margaritas mixed, over and over.

And still old Dave did not emerge to see his shadow.

Groundhog Day after Groundhog Day after Groundhog Day— fifty of them, long enough for fields to turn from dun yellow and brown to full, lively green; long enough for bare, wintry trees to give way to leaf-laden bowers; long enough for bluebirds to build nests, lay eggs, raise their young.

And no foreseeable end in sight. In fact, the plethora of possible ends provided an endlessly absorbing topic of conversation.

One of these conversations keeps coming back to haunt those who were there to hear it.

Esquire writer Ivan Soloaroff had sprawled his big Russian frame into a small lawn chair where he was drinking Salvation Army coffee and amusing himself by asking the newsies not "How do you *think* it will end?" but, "How do you *want* it to end?" with the implication being, Hey, gang, tell me what'll be best for *bidness.*

And the answer kept coming back: Well, *violent* would be nice. A shootout, or a suicide, or something.

And Soloaroff, who consistently writes much better than he talks would say: "Yeh. Hey, you know what you want? You want Da Big Heat. You know: Cagney. Da Big Heat. Dat's what you want."

Hindsight is the mother of Prophecy.

And on the morning of April 19, Day 51, Groundhog Day gave way to Apocalypse Now, Da Big Heat.

A watchful cameraman, who'd been watching next to nothing for nearly two months now, finally hit paydirt. There was finally something to see through the huge telephoto lens of his camera.

Hell.

There is one more thing wrong with the picture out here at what's left of Ranch Apocalypse, and it doesn't hit most visitors until well after they're gone. It is a subtle thing, in a way, and yet is large in its obscenity, when reconsidered.

Flags. Not the tiny plastic squares, the little carrion flowers the

Davidians got, but the big ones on the big pole, flying proudly over the compound at half-mast.

The U.S. flag, long may she wave.

The flag of Texas our Texas.

And the flag, bearing one star for each agent killed in the initial raid, of the U.S. Bureau of Alcohol, Tobacco, and Firearms.

The tragedy here is not merely that these foolish and gullible followers after God thought the end of the world had come. People have thought that many times before, and done many foolish things because of it.

The tragedy was that the U.S. government was going to such great pains to confirm it for them. And thus the government has put itself in a truly ironic bind. If it refuses to acknowledge that it pursued its apocalyptic, paranoia-confirming course on purpose, that leads to a far larger area of concern, because it means that the government pursued the course outlined in Revelation by accident.

There are only two possible takes on that. The panicked, apocalyptic spin: That, since there's no such thing as an accident, the government's action was foreordained and outlined by John the Divine in Revelation, and we aren't out of the woods yet. Tribulation times are a-coming.

And the secular spin: That, if this was an accident, the country has at the helm a star-studded constellation of truly amazing bunglers.

And we still aren't out of the woods yet.

Because now, here's the government going out to Ranch Apocalypse and proving yet again, in spite of the benefit of hindsight, just how useless, hidebound, puffed up, and blustery it has remained determined to be. Before, during, and now after.

There are at least eighty-one dead people here, seventeen of them children.

And the government still seems to be under the impression that this was a war, a war with a separate, sovereign kingdom, and a war it had won—and comes galloping in to play "plant the flag."

This last big bungle is the best one, because at least it contains a built-in answer.

The question is: What caused this horror to happen?

The answer is: From start to standoff to fiery finale, it was all just an attitude thing.

Chapter 2

The attitude thing on the Davidian side of the fence really began in Raikovo, Bulgaria, in 1886, when Victor T. Houteff was born.

What little is known about the early life of Houteff (pronounced HOT-if) comes from one of his followers, George Saether. Saether, who would later live and study under Houteff for nearly 20 years, remembered with remarkable clarity the events of Houteff's life.[1]

Houteff—who had only a third-grade education—and his cousin opened a shop in Turkey, just across the border from the Bulgarian village where his family lived. Houteff's business prospered, apparently because he lowered his prices and undercut the local market. The other dealers, who were also Bulgarians, were enraged, and threatened the budding capitalist. When their warnings and threats failed, they began throwing bricks and stones through the windows of Houteff's store and firing guns into the air to scare off customers. Alarmed, Houteff and his cousin turned to their Orthodox priest and archbishop in Bulgaria for relief.

"Why are these members of my church doing this to me?" Houteff asked him.

"Well, they like your cousin," he replied, "but you're too competitive, and they want to get you out of there."

Houteff was hurt and disillusioned by this failure to come to his aid, which he considered a betrayal by his church. The incident proved to be a pivotal moment in his life—and faith. Disillusioned, he emigrated to the United States in 1907.

(According to the official Seventh-day Adventist (SDA) account of his life—which was rarely sympathetic—Houteff was actually "violently expelled from the country of his birth.")

Like most immigrants, Houteff, who spoke little English, landed in New York City. Once there, he got a job in a restaurant, and rose to become assistant cook before leaving for Milwaukee to join his brother Nick, who had recently arrived in America.

A world-class penny pincher, Houteff saved enough to eventually leave Milwaukee and buy and operate a small hotel in Rockford, Illinois. There, in 1918, Houteff first became aware of SDA teaching. One night he was out walking along the street when he heard music coming from a tent. He went in, found a seat, and started listening to the speaker. The sermon struck a chord with Houteff, who came back to the tent on several occasions, and finally became an Adventist on May 10, 1919.

The fact that he felt he had gotten a raw deal from the Greek Orthodox Church probably predisposed him to respond to the Adventists, whose faith—in its present form—dates to 1844. That year, the Great Disappointment occurred on October 22, when founder William Miller's prediction of the Second Coming of Christ failed to materialize. Miller had a pretty bad record in that area, having missed three earlier dates for the end of the world over the previous year and a half. His followers, in white ascension robes and standing by open graves, waited expectantly all day and all night for the heavens to open up and the trumpet to sound. When midnight passed and all were still standing by their graves, the group (at one time his followers numbered 100,000) splintered into smaller sects or drifted away completely. The Millerites were disappointed—but some were not disappointed enough.

One group of disheartened Millerites, amongst whom was 17-year-old Ellen Gould Harmon, continued, in spite of being 0 for 4, to meet in Washington, New Hampshire. Influenced by teachings of the Seventh-day Baptist Church, the Adventists began keeping a Saturday Sabbath. Soon Gould's visions and teachings began to dominate the group. Ellen, who in 1845 married an Adventist preacher named James White, was promoted to a prophetess, and proceeded to rehabilitate Miller's prophecy, there being, apparently, no such thing as "just wrong."

White interpreted the October 1844 date as the cleansing of the heavenly sanctuaries mentioned in Heb. 8:1–2, rather than as the Second Coming. Only after the cleansing was completed, she said, would Christ return to earth.

As the Whites' movement grew, they began publishing *The Review and Herald*, a paper that served to knit the fragmented Millerites into a cohesive denomination. In 1860, those who accepted the Saturday Sabbath and Ellen White's other teachings[2] adopted the name of Seventh-day Adventists.[3]

Fundamentally Protestant, the SDAs accept the Bible as their rule of faith, although White's writings continue to play a pivotal—some critics would say dominant—role in determining questions of faith and morality. Strongly evangelical, SDAs believe salvation is available only through grace and a belief in Jesus Christ as a personal savior. They are single-mindedly millennialist and from the beginning have taught that Christ's return is "imminent," though they never crawl far enough out on the limb to say precisely when. Through White's influence, most Adventists also adhere to Old Testament health laws regarding "clean" and "unclean" meat.

Like many small groups that emerged in the mid-1800s, White's followers were mainly the poor, who had little chance of advancement in the world's social order. Because of this they were perhaps more open to White's teachings, which are dominated by a belief that the Apocalypse is fast approaching, and that only a tiny remnant will secure a place in the glorious afterlife to come—and that they're *it*.

Houteff was an enthusiastic convert, embracing all the tenets of his new-found faith and shutting down his business each Friday evening in recognition of the Sabbath. Despite—or perhaps because of—this, and his allowing church members to stay in the hotel from Friday night until Sunday morning without charge, the hotel prospered. In time, Houteff helped the Rockford SDAs build their own spacious sanctuary.

Eventually, however, because of a physical problem and the presence of several SDA sanitariums in southern California, Houteff sold his hotel and moved to Los Angeles, which has been described[4] as "the most celebrated of all incubators of new creeds, codes of ethics, philosophies... a breeding place and a rendezvous of freak religions" and which proved to be a perfect match for the little man from Bulgaria.

Houteff started looking for work immediately, and applied for a job as a washing machine salesman at an appliance store. The sales manager was less than enthusiastic, telling Houteff that, with his limited English, he'd be a hopeless salesman. But the plucky Houteff persuaded the sales manager to give him a chance, and soon became their top salesman. Salesmanship remained Houteff's gift for the rest of his life, whether selling washing machines or eternal life.

He also became an active member in the city's only SDA church (which became known as Tabernacle Church). Soon, Houteff decided to seek relief from his physical ailments at the Glendale Sanitarium, an SDA health-care center near Los Angeles.

Although Houteff was obviously ill, officials at the sanitarium required a $25 deposit, which Houteff paid with a check. This meant a delay of several days, during which time the gravely ill Houteff waited at the sanitarium. He was given only water, and no doctor or other medical professional checked his condition. Once the check cleared, a doctor finally saw Houteff and treated him, but the event forever changed Houteff's perception of the SDAs. Houteff would often refer to the event, considering it proof that the SDA Church had lost its initial purity of vision and purpose.

(The official Adventist biography claims that "disaffection came early in the man's experience, for, dissatisfied with the care given him at one of our sanitariums, he was tempted with doubt... [and] a root of bitterness sprang up in his heart.")

Once released from the sanitarium, Houteff threw himself into Bible study. Despite his lingering difficulties with the English language, he began teaching a Sabbath School class at the Adventist church in Los Angeles in 1928. He eventually became the assistant school superintendent of the Sabbath School, where one of his duties was to preview the upcoming lessons.

During a study of the 54th chapter of the Old Testament book of Isaiah, something happened to Houteff, something profound and life-changing, something that would still be felt around the world more than 60 years later: Houteff further thinned the ranks of the elect with the truth—as revealed to Victor Houteff.

He received a revelation, believed it, and began teaching it with typical enthusiasm. His students became so interested they told others, and soon Houteff's Sabbath School class had grown to 60 people, a sizable percentage of the church's membership. Alarmed, church authorities told him he should hold his class in the afternoon.

He did. But people still flocked in.

Seeing this, authorities claimed that the young people of the church now needed the auditorium where Houteff's class had been meeting. Houteff was forced to find another room for his Bible lessons. Soon there was such a demand for his studies that Houteff had them printed up each week.

Frightened by the sweeping nature of Houteff's teachings, the leaders of Tabernacle Church finally barred him from the church building completely. A woman in the class offered her large home for Houteff's next Sabbath Day lesson, but soon buckled under pressure from church elders and withdrew her offer.

After that, the elders told church members that anyone who studied with Houteff, read his literature, or attended his meetings would be disfellowshipped.

Many did, and many promptly were.

The differences between the teachings of Houteff and those of mainline Adventists appear trivial to non-Adventists, but to Houteff and the mainliners, they were literally of life and death importance.

By now it was 1929, the early days of the Great Depression,

and Houteff began to circulate hand-copied versions of what he called *The Shepherd's Rod, Volume I.* He claimed that the messages contained in *The Rod* were the result of two years of intensive Bible study.

Houteff then presented his primary reason for compiling the various studies that comprise the book, which was to unlock the "long concealed mystery concerning the ever challenging and much discussed subject of the 144,000 (Rev.14:1), with the central object in view of bringing about among God's people that 'thorough reformation' foretold by the Spirit of Prophecy."

Houteff considered the truths revealed in the book as divinely revealed and of supreme importance to the church, which was about to undergo "trying, sifting circumstances... Being vital concerns to salvation, they call for decided action from ministry and laity alike to separate themselves from all worldliness and to anchor themselves on the Solid Rock by obedience to all the truth known to the Church, if they would escape the forthcoming ruin that is to take every sinner." In other words, everyone who didn't heed Houteff.

The dominant theme was the correct understanding of "the remnant," the 144,000 who would be delivered at the Second Coming while all sinners perished. Houteff believed that the SDAs had been used by God since 1844, that they alone had the secret of the "sealing of the 144,000," and that his teachings were to aid and abet their work. Houteff wanted to reform the Church from within: His message was aimed solely at practicing SDAs, and thus he set himself above them. This feature would be repeated: Branchings were never forks in the road, but a matter of leaving the unenlightened at a lower level.

"The Shepherd's Rod," he wrote, "takes its name from Moses' rod, the instrument through which the Lord manifested His power in the deliverance of the children of Israel. 'The Shepherd's Rod,' the only Rod that has ever spoken, is predicted and recommended in Micah 6:9: 'Hear ye the Rod, and (Him) Who hath appointed it.'"

The Shepherd's Rod rested on two disparate sources to which Houteff gave equal authority: The Bible, and the teachings of Ellen White. To Houteff, each one "proves" the other. The verses and citations fly furiously by at such a rate that only a prodigious Bible scholar can keep up.

Sixty years later, David Koresh would use exactly the same technique, speed-referencing a bewildering array of sources in the staccato manner of a veteran auctioneer, not giving his audience time to think or reflect, but only to blindly accept.

Finally, the appearance of *The Shepherd's Rod* was seen in itself as fulfilling prophecy, and justifying the interpretations it would make. Houteff reminded his readers of Ellen White's vision of the 144,000, which supposedly signaled the ascent of the "sealing angel" from the East. After this, the saints were waiting for his arrival until the Lord announced His arrival to the SDA denomination through Houteff's Sabbath School lessons. "Then," he wrote, "the scroll began to unroll and the angel's presence to be felt by many of those who were agonizing for truth and righteousness."

Houteff asserted that the Old Testament stories of the Bible were actually historical road maps that predicted coming events. He argued that, "while leading His people to the Kingdom eternal, He employs for light on their way even *typology*—the lives of men who have gone before and the experiences through which they have passed—and decrees that their defeats and victories should be the saints' stepping-stones over every pitfall." God, he seemed to be saying, was neither powerful enough nor straightforward enough to just say what was on His mind. He had to put it in code—code which conveniently only Houteff could interpret.

The concept of the "antitype" would also dominate the pronouncements and actions of every Shepherd's Rod prophet from Houteff to David Koresh. It enabled prophets to justify any action, "prove" any theological utterance, and endow themselves with god-like power and wisdom.

To make his typology work, Houteff divided the Bible into Types and Antitypes. For instance, he said, Cain typifies the Sinners, Abel typifies the Martyrs, and Seth typifies the Saints. "It is also clear," Houteff said, "that Hagar's rebellion against Sarah forespoke the rebellion of the rabbis against the Christian Church, and that Ishmael's persecution of Isaac pointed out the Jews' persecution of the Christians."

Clear only if you'd walked a mile in Houteff's moccasins.

Houteff also explained the elaborate numerical system he used to justify his movement and to predict the end of this world, often conveniently forgetting certain years and shifting dates to fit his needs:

"...Moses at the age of 40 attempted to deliver Israel, but failing, he ran away. Adding these 40 years to 1850 a.d., we arrive at 1890, the time the Seventh-day Adventist Denomination organized the National Religious Liberty Association, which likewise failed to fulfill its purpose.

"Forty years after his first attempt to deliver the children of Israel, Moses was finally sent back into Egypt and was then enabled to break the Egyptian yoke. Adding these 40 years to 1890 a.d., we are brought to 1930, the year in which *The Shepherd's Rod, Volume 1* was first published."

With a hand-drawn chart to further prove his handily self-serving thesis, he concluded that the work of *The Shepherd's Rod* is "Divinely foreordained and as timely in our day as was Moses' work and his rod in his day. One is consequently overwhelmingly compelled to acknowledge Providential design and foreknowledge of the reader's eternal welfare for thousands of years."

Admittedly, Houteff's reasoning didn't strike *all* of his readers as quite that compelling. Still, his growing popularity and the widespread dissemination of *The Shepherd's Rod* finally prompted the SDA hierarchy into action. Houteff was genuinely surprised, since he had thought the "sheer logic" of his message would win immediate converts among the Adventist elect.

After forbidding members to attend Houteff's classes, the church elders had Houteff physically barred from attending services.

Eventually, a task force of Adventists met with Houteff at the Olympic Exposition Park church. Wirth[5] claimed that although Houteff was allowed to present his views, "they were so fanciful that they did not take them seriously."

Undeterred, Houteff continued to spread his message.

A number of official meetings followed, culminating in the decision to disfellowship Houteff.

In 1932, Houteff published *The Shepherd's Rod, Volume 2*, another 304 pages of his writings, and SDAs redoubled their efforts to get Houteff to recant.

Several publications disputing *The Shepherd's Rod* were released in 1932, but in 1933 Houteff published *Volume 3*, and released a revised version of *Volume 1*. He seemed puzzled by the vehemence his writings provoked, since he was completely convinced that the Bible and the works of Ellen White "supported *The Shepherd's Rod* one hundred percent."

An Adventist booklet, *The History and Teachings of 'The Shepherd's Rod,'* details the "heresy" of the teachings found in *The Shepherd's Rod*. But, unlike similar Adventist publications, it provides relatively clear-cut summaries of the arguments against Houteff. It outlines major areas of significant doctrinal difference from *The Shepherd's*

Rod, and uses the writings of White and selected quotations from the Bible to establish their authority.

One of the most interesting disagreements concerns Ezek. 4:9. *The History and Teachings* accurately summarizes Houteff's interpretation, then offers what is apparently—by Adventist standards anyway—a stinging and irrefutable rebuttal:

"Mr. Houteff says, in comment on Ezek. 4:9, that the wheat is the doctrine of justification by faith as taught by Martin Luther; the barley is the doctrine concerning the Holy Spirit as taught by John Knox; the beans are the doctrine of grace as preached by John Wesley; the lentils are the doctrine of baptism by immersion as taught by Alexander Campbell; the millet is the doctrine of 2,300 days as taught by William Miller; and the spelt is the doctrine of the Sabbath in connection with the sanctuary as revealed through Ellen G. White.

"Many other such fanciful plays on figures and symbols found in the Scriptures appear in Mr. Houteff's writings.

"And where is any proof presented for any of this fancy? The author of *The Shepherd's Rod* gives none, but merely presents his fanciful and private interpretation of Scriptures, against which we are warned in 2 Peter 1:20. The following timely counsel from the pen of Mrs. White should be heeded by all who would not be led into error:

"'In order to sustain erroneous doctrines or unchristian practices, some will seize upon passages of Scripture separated from the context, perhaps quoting half of a single verse as proving their point, when the remaining portion would show the meaning to be quite the opposite. With the cunning of the serpent, they entrench themselves behind disconnected utterances construed to suit their carnal desires. Thus do many willfully pervert the word of God. Others, who have an active imagination, seize upon the figures and symbols of Holy Writ, interpret them to suit their fancy, with little regard to the testimony of Scripture as its own interpreter, and then they present their vagaries as the teachings of the Bible."[6] As if she hadn't done the same herself!

But again, an almost eerie parallel exists between these charges and those leveled against David Koresh 60 years later.

Other SDA groups joined in condemning Houteff's teachings, and the national organization began publishing another series of pamphlets warning against the heresy of *The Shepherd's Rod*. Houteff, for his part, considered the committee dishonest, and in referring to one disagreement, said that "if *The Shepherd's Rod* is wrong in this, then they [find] fault with Christ as well." Bold words from the little immigrant from Bulgaria!

Houteff was not shy about drawing other parallels with Jesus Christ, either, in his correspondence with an unnamed SDA elder:

"You know that if you should arise to declare the message in *The Shepherd's Rod,* or one similar to it, the same charges that they have poured on me would also be poured upon you. The same would prove true with any one individual that would dare tell the straight Truth. The class that lived in the days of Christ is also here today, and if He failed to convince them, it is not likely that I can do it now.

"...it is impossible to tell you my experience, but it will suffice to say that if *The Shepherd's Rod* is not inspired, I would not have said that it is. Your doubt in this fact does not only discredit God, but it also leaves you destitute of His power, and robs the fruit of your labor."

Houteff's detailed response to most of the charges brought against him by the Adventist examining committee was eventually published in *The Great Controversy Over 'The Shepherd's Rod.'* To an untrained eye the charge and counter-charge are virtually interchangeable. Houteff's followers, for the most part, remained unmoved by their former denomination's accusations. But the attacks did have some impact. Houteff responded to them in *The Symbolic Code, Volume 6*:

"Thus both the type and the testimonies of the prophets, as well as history, identify the Shepherd's Rod message as the only one ordained to lead the church, freed from sin and sinners, into the land of Promise, when 'the times of the Gentiles be fulfilled' (Luke 21:24)."

But for the moment, the "land of Promise" was definitely not Los Angeles. Perhaps spurred on by the active opposition from the SDAs, Houteff's emerging theology was leading him to believe that he needed to move to a more rural setting—one far away from Los Angeles. Because of the prophecy of Ezek. 4:1–3, Houteff believed his new home must be a "camp," a way station for God's elect since, he believed, the 144,000 would shortly be gathered together and transferred to Palestine to become God's literal, theocratic kingdom of David, with a human king—presumably Houteff—ruling over them. From their new kingdom in the Holy Land, Houteff and his followers would then proclaim their gospel to the entire world. And, having accomplished that task, the living righteous would be gathered in Palestine for immediate translation into heaven with the Second Coming of Christ.

Houteff began searching the Bible for a new location to house his fledgling body of believers. A number of factors impacted his decision, primarily Isa. 19:24—"In that day shall Israel be the third with Egypt and Assyria, even a blessing in the midst of the land." By quite a stretch, Houteff somehow interpreted this to mean Texas, since this was the "third" and only place between both North and South America and would thereby provide a convenient base from which to spread his message to the rest of the world.[7]

So, in January 1935, Houteff, E. T. Wilson, and M. L. Deeter traveled to Texas to investigate possible sites. The men carefully examined rural areas outside the cities of San Antonio, Dallas, Houston, and Waco, ultimately choosing Waco because of its central location.

The property they selected was about five miles from the center of town, and about two and a half miles from the city limits. It had originally been part of the giant Rich Field, an Army base established during World War I. Some of the base's hangars still stood just outside of the property line.

The choice of Waco wasn't unanimous[8]. The plot of land at Waco was rocky and not particularly conducive to growing crops. However, it did overlook a small lake, which in later years became Lake Waco.

The owners of the property, the Darden family, were reluctant to let go of the highest spot in the land, saying they planned to build a retirement home there some day. They would, however, allow the men to buy the rest of the parcel, which would form a U shape around the crest of the hill.

Houteff and his group decided to go back to their motel and pray, asking the Lord to let them know if this were the property they were to buy. If it were to be, they said, they would like the lady selling the property to agree to sell at the price they had discussed—about eight dollars an acre—and to do so before they began any discussion. When they returned the next morning, the lady said she had decided to sell and the price would be the same. (One of your more minor miracles here.) So Houteff borrowed the $1,000 down payment needed to secure the property, and purchased it, deciding to erect the first building in a small clearing frequented primarily by goats.

Houteff considered the 189-acre tract of land[9] —mostly cedar brake and almost impassable—far enough from the city to be away from the world and its evil environment. And because it was outside any city limits, the new colony would also not be subject to city zoning and health regulations. They wanted enough land to build a church, a school, and living quarters.

Houteff searched the Bible for an appropriate name. In explaining his choice of Mt. Carmel Center, Houteff explained:

"...the naming of our 'camp' 'Mt. Carmel Center' came about in the same way as the naming of our publications *The Shepherd's Rod,* for we did not know beforehand that it was in prophecy until after our attention was called to Micah 7:14 and Amos 1:2. In the prophecy of Amos we read: 'The Lord will roar from Zion, and utter his voice from Jerusalem; and the habitations of the shepherds shall mourn, and the top of Carmel shall wither.'"

Houteff followed this with several arcane conclusions drawn from the passage, once again "proving" that the selection of Mt. Carmel was divinely ordained, even giving a nifty spin to the final phrase, "...and the top of Carmel shall wither," which most theologians would have interpreted as a less than affirming sign!

Houteff failed to mention an earlier reference to Mt. Carmel in I Kings 18, where Elijah challenged the 450 prophets of Baal. The prophets of Baal fail in their attempt to persuade Baal to consume a bullock on the altar. Elijah then douses the altar in water, prays to God, and a fire utterly consumes the altar. The people watching the spectacle on Mt. Carmel then take the 450 prophets of Baal and slay them.

Nearly 60 years later, another "spectacle" would draw crowds to Mt. Carmel, with equally horrific results.

But between Houteff and David Koresh would be many others who would claim to be leaders, or prophets, and who would pave the way for the man who claimed to be the Lamb of God.

·

[1.] Saether shared them in lengthy oral memoirs with Dr. Dan McGee of Baylor University. Without Saether, Houteff would forever remain a shadowy enigma, a rarely seen prophet without portfolio. Saether makes him come alive. In return, Houteff gave meaning to Saether's life.
[2.] White, who died on July 16, 1915, at the age of 87 wrote at least 24 books amounting to 100,000 pages, as well as 4,600 periodical articles, more that 200 tracts, and thousands of other pages of letters and general manuscripts.

3. The denomination finally codified in 1863.
4. The late Carey Williams, widely regarded as an expert on the state's history, described California in this manner.
5. W. G. Wirth, a Bible teacher at the College of Medical Evangelists.
6. *The Great Controversy*, p 521.
7. More worldly concerns may have entered into the decision as well. Texas is centrally located, and the climate is milder.
8. Bonnie Louise Smith, "Oral Memoirs": "They didn't want that one in Waco, because the ground was so hard, and there was nothing there to grow much on."
9. The initial purchase of land was 189 acres, but a subsequent purchase from Southwestern Life Insurance Co. gave the group a total of 377 acres.

SOURCES

Some Teachings of the Shepherd's Rod Examined, published by the Committee on Defense Literature of the General Conference of Seventh-day Adventists (March 1956). The booklet purports to quote from a number of sources, including various issues of V. T. Houteff's *Timely Greetings*, the Church Record Book of the Seventh-day Adventist Church of Rockford, Illinois, Houteff's *Latest News for 'Mother";The Great Controversy Over 'The Shepherd's Rod'* and other sources.

George W. Saether, "Oral Memoirs," Baylor University Institute for Oral History. Most interviews conducted by Dr. Dan McGee.

Glen Webster Green, Sidney Albert Smith, and Bonnie Louise Smith, "Oral Memoirs," Baylor University Institute for Oral History. Interview conducted by David Stricklin and Dr. Bill Pitts.

The Shepherd's Rod, Vol. 1, That the First Fruits May Stand On Mount Zion, Second Edition, 1930, 1945, V. T. Houteff.

The Symbolic Code, Vols. 10–11, Victor T. Houteff's Sermons, Taken from the Symbolic Codes, From May 1955 to October 1956.

The History and Teachings of 'The Shepherd's Rod.'

Mary Elizabeth Power, M.A. Thesis, "A Study of the Seventh-Day Adventist Community, Mount Carmel Center, Waco, Texas," 1940. Baylor University.

Waco Tribune-Herald, February 6, 1955, pp. 1–2.

Waco Tribune-Herald, February 27, 1955, pp. 1, 11.

Mary Elizabeth Power, interview, May 16, 1993, Waco, Texas.

Chapter 3

After buying the land in Waco, Houteff sent out a call to all of those who followed the "Shepherd's Rod" to join him in Waco, promising free transportation to the families who responded. Those who couldn't—or wouldn't—go, were asked to support the new venture financially with what Houteff called "The First Tithe." Twelve people (including Houteff) from seven families committed to the venture. Houteff happily interpreted both numbers as yet more signs from God of the righteousness of his vision.[1]

The trip took seven days—to Houteff another encouraging sign. The group arrived in Waco on Sabbath eve, Friday, May 24, 1935, a day riddled with heavy storms.

Seven of the original 12 took rooms in a Waco hotel and the remaining five stayed in a trailer house until the first temporary buildings could be completed. Even after the purchase of the land, Houteff still had a fairly large war chest amassed from donations from Davidians in Los Angeles, so construction work began almost immediately.

Those who followed Houteff to Waco included some real characters, as did those who followed in the weeks and months to come. The first wave included John Berolinger, Mr. and Mrs. Charboneau, their daughter Sophia Hermanson, their grandson Oliver, aged 13, and granddaughter Florence, aged 15 (about to turn 16).

Oddly, "Dad" Charboneau was not a Christian, much less an Adventist. When his house was completed, he'd sit on the porch smoking a cigar, which was strictly forbidden. Still, he was well-liked in the little community, since he was not antagonistic. He had also advanced Houteff $1,000 toward the down payment on Mt. Carmel, which may have secured his place in the community. (Other Davidians whose relatives were not of the fold were not welcomed, since Houteff felt that space should be reserved primarily for Davidians.)

The early inhabitants of Mt. Carmel considered it a "wilderness," and felt that Mt. Carmel was only their "camp" before they were to move to the Holy Land in the near future. Houteff believed their stay in Waco would be only a year. He wrote other wavering Seventh-day Adventists, urging them to come quickly, saying they would stay there until their mission was completed, but hinting that the completion was near at hand.

By August 1935, another 15 people—mostly from California and a few from North Carolina—had joined the original group. By November, Buildings 1 and 2, both residences, were virtually complete. During the first year, water had to be hauled from artesian wells in downtown Waco. Later, wells were dug on the Mt. Carmel grounds.

But even before the first buildings were completed, Houteff began holding regular Sabbath services at sundown every Friday night and again on Saturday afternoon. Almost without exception, Houteff was the speaker. And, from the beginning, Sophia Hermanson's daughter Florence tried to transcribe all of Houteff's sermons/Bible studies so they could be saved for posterity.

Beginning Friday night, members threw away their newspapers, turned off their radios, and put away everything worldly until Saturday evening, when the Sabbath was over. Houteff insisted that everyone at Mt. Carmel spend their time in prayer, prophesy, or Bible study.

All meals were held in the communal cafeteria, which was another of the first buildings constructed. All were required to be vegetarians. Those in charge of the food tried not to combine vegetables and fruits at the same meals. Meat, especially pork, was strictly verboten. Great theological debates were held over whether honey was "animal" or "vegetable" because it came from bees. Graham flour was used whenever possible.

Shepherd's Rod Adventists always drank their fill of water before eating. They believed that eating till they reached a sensation of fullness led to a number of physical, moral, and mental problems.[2]

Other believers began to trickle in from across the country. Glen W. Green, 20, came in the summer of 1937 after reading the first two volumes of *The Shepherd's Rod*. Bonnie Louise Smith came from California in 1936. Sidney Smith arrived in 1939, while George Saether, of Madison, Wisconsin, was first invited to join Houteff in 1936. Houteff himself helped Saether and his wife Romana move in late August 1937. They arrived in Waco in early September, bringing the number at Mt. Carmel to about 75.

Despite his food-service background, Saether quickly found himself in charge of the construction crews. Construction on the rocky ground of Mt. Carmel continued non-stop for nearly 20 years, with the group using hand tools to clear the thick brush that covered the land.[3] Eventually they bought a bulldozer, and built a water system.[4]

The settlers' goal was to become as self-sufficient as possible, and part of that self-sufficiency meant coining their own money. Blue-colored money could be exchanged for regular U.S. currency, but green-tinted bills were valid only at Mt. Carmel. Houteff even had tender—made in amounts of 5 cents, 10 cents, 25 cents, and 50 cents—created out of cardboard to duplicate hard currency.[5] The green money could be used only at the mercantile department for necessary personal items or deposited at the grandly named Mt. Carmel Bank of Palestina. This was done in part to keep the residents from being unnecessarily tainted by the "outside" world. Trips to Waco were limited to authorized business transactions.

Pay was pretty skimpy, even by Depression-era standards, and everyone was expected to tithe to the First Tithe fund. Children over the age of four were expected to work, attend school, and tithe.[6]

In addition to their four hours of classes at Mt. Carmel Academy (which included agriculture, cooking, household economy, and other practical courses), each child had four hours of physical labor each day. Children under the age of four were kept in a day nursery, which allowed their mothers to join the men in the fields or doing construction, or in the printing operations.

But the work at Mt. Carmel Center did not go entirely without incident. At one point, while Saether was directing a large work gang during a particularly difficult excavation, Mrs. Hermanson took offense:

"'Brother Saether, you're telling everybody else on this hill what to do, but I'm telling you one thing, you aren't telling me what to do.' I was so amused I just laughed right out.

"That was the idea and Florence had that, too. But she was smarter than her mother and kept it under [her hat]. The Hermansons were smart people. They must have got it from their father."

In 1937, Houteff, now 52 years old and apparently long separated from his first wife, found himself increasingly drawn to Florence, a "tall and pretty [teenager] with very long hair, like all of the women who lived at Mt. Carmel."[7] Despite the more than 30-year age difference, they were married sometime during that year. The couple had no children.

The original group at Mt. Carmel still had no formal name, although SDA publications generally refer to them as "Shepherd's Rod adherents." Houteff finally addressed the issue in late 1937 when he organized the group under the name of "The General Association of the Shepherd's Rod Seventh-day Adventists."

But the title was ungainly, and eventually the group became known as "Davidians" because of their unceasing message that they would someday establish a "Davidic" kingdom in Palestine.

Houteff often railed at the lack of financial support the Davidians received from their members elsewhere. Despite Houteff's penny-pinching ways, Mt. Carmel remained on financially shaky ground. Finally, when it became obvious that the First Tithe money was not enough to support the growing community, Houteff instituted a "Second Tithe" for all Davidians, whether they lived in Waco or not. That tithe, which began in January 1938, was roughly nine percent of earned income. Saether said that numerous free-will offerings were also expected.

To receive the annual certificate of membership as a Davidian, members were required to tithe 100 percent of both the First and Second tithe. For this, all members received medical care. The Davidians had no medical insurance, but had a small dispensary on the property. More serious illnesses were treated at Waco-area hospitals, with the Davidian organization assuming all expenses.

Believers continued to trickle into Mt. Carmel. Among the later wave of arrivals was the 6'4" M. J. Bingham, a fearless fellow, especially when it came to expounding on Shepherd's Rod theology—and his own agenda.

Saether remembers "...he could outtalk about anybody you ever heard. He was a student of words. He doted on that. When he'd talk, he'd get new words and see how many times he could use that new word in his sermon or talk."

E. T. Wilson also quickly emerged as one of the leaders of the group, although he too was not of the original 12. Whenever Houteff was absent from Mt. Carmel, Wilson led the daily Bible studies. But Wilson spent most of his time on the road as the only field worker, whose job it was to spread the Shepherd's Rod message among SDAs in the United States and Canada.

After a few years, a definite tension emerged between Wilson and Bingham, and both began to draw adherents from among the faithful. Since Wilson was appointed by Houteff to lead the flock when he was out of town, Wilson took over Houteff's official duties when Houteff visited his ailing mother in Bulgaria in 1938.

It wasn't long before Bingham began to chafe under Wilson's leadership. (The California contingent apparently always considered themselves something special.) Bingham was bright, Saether recalled, and as the person in charge of the education system, had a natural constituency, many of them teenage boys. Finally, some of them rebelled and went off into the woods where they made a hideaway.

Since Bingham was disabled, his wife, Genevieve Bingham, led the group when they were away from camp. Despite the loss of manpower during construction and the breakaway group's pilfering of supplies from the kitchen, Wilson apparently wasn't aware of the "rebellion" until weeks later.

When Houteff returned to Waco after about a four-month absence, however, he found the two groups openly vying for control of the camp.

Houteff almost miraculously patched the rift, though Wilson and Bingham remained bitter enemies.[8]

The group had grown to 120–125 people during Houteff's absence, partly due to Wilson's untiring missionary efforts. Wilson had visited hundreds of Seventh-day Adventists and invited many of them to join the Davidians at Mt. Carmel. Houteff was not pleased with this and told Wilson so. But the people stayed, though finances remained tight—so much so that whenever Houteff visited Davidians in California, he'd sleep in his old car to save money.

Houteff was subject to normal human emotions, most notably the sometimes imperious manner of people who think they have a direct pipeline to the Divine Ear. He was tempestuous but not sanctimonious or arrogant, according to Saether. He could be courteous and polite, but he didn't stand on ceremony.

Mary Elizabeth Power, who wrote her Master's thesis on the group, remembers him as "gracious, polite, and gentle. He was especially gentle and loving toward the children. He was also very gentle, very kind to Mrs. Houteff."

Still, the combination of Houteff's personality and the Spartan life at Mt. Carmel meant the actual membership was in a state of flux at any given time.

"Brother Houteff was a hard-handed ruler sometimes," Green said. "He was the president and things were to go his way. And sometimes people didn't like to do that."

Green's mother and brother joined him at Mt. Carmel in 1941, and Green met his wife at the compound. In time, the couple had six children, but the rugged lifestyle and strict system of rules eventually forced his wife to leave, taking the children. Green remained, faithful to Houteff's teachings.

Following Houteff meant that many SDAs were

disfellowshipped from their churches once they became Davidians. From the beginning, Houteff had tried to remain a member in good standing of the Seventh-day Adventist Church, but after World War II began, the Davidians formally split from the mother church.

Actually, the Davidians were probably among the last Wacoans to hear about the war. Power said that Houteff strictly controlled *all* outside news entering Mt. Carmel. Only elders and teachers were permitted to review selected "worldly" events during the communal noonday meal. So, when the United States finally entered the war after the bombing of Pearl Harbor, the surprised young men at Mt. Carmel were forced to go to the nearby small town of Speegleville to register for the draft. SDAs had traditionally been either conscientious objectors or noncombatants—but in 1941, the national Adventist organization refused to support requests from members for either the conscientious objector status or ministerial credentials.

At that, "Houteff hastily organized, issued membership certificates, and distributed ministerial credentials. A formal theocratic organization was created, with Houteff as its leader, and, in 1942, the name of the organization was changed to the Davidian Seventh-day Adventists."[9]

The Davidians chose, whenever possible, to enlist as noncombatants who would look after the sick and wounded, drive ambulances, or carry stretchers. They also asked to take the Sabbath off from regular duty, although they agreed to care for the sick on that day. Their vegetarian diet also posed problems for them. Mess halls and K-rations didn't cater to vegetarians.

Construction continued during the war, although at a slower pace because of the scarcity of materials. *Tribune-Herald* writer Chris Whitcraft said that residents continued building work anyway:

"Residents used rock and clay from the hills, ingenuity, and hard physical work to carry on.

"Most live in family groups in homes clustering about the center's four main buildings. These are a cafeteria, administration building, rest home, and dispensary, a new publishing building of tile and stucco, and the Davidic Levitical Institute, a ministerial school.

"The buildings have a strange, appealing architecture all their own. It is hard to describe, except that they are solid looking, different, unusual, a blend of many different heritages."

During this period, Bingham suggested that the boys and girls of the community live in separate dorms apart from their parents. Previously, school-age children had lived at home and attended Mt. Carmel Academy, where the Bible, and knowledge of God and the work He had sent them to do, were the basis of much of their education. But Bingham had grander goals.

"He was the head of the school and by having them in the dormitory, he could control them day and night," Saether said, "in the school and out of the school, except when they worked... But then, his lieutenants also controlled the work squads and different things, especially the students."

Not everyone liked the new arrangement. Some of the parents, like Saether, objected to the almost Svengali-like influence Bingham was exerting on the young people. And some of the children had problems as well.

Saether said that at the time he lived with his wife in Building B-6, there were four rooms on the floor above the Saethers' floor, and four rooms on the ground floor.

"One day I heard a big commotion upstairs and I was going up anyway, but I had to go up around the outside of the building," Saether said. "When I got there, the screen door opened and my girl (daughter Marian) was backing out and she had a girl by the hair, a younger girl, but heavier than Marian. I thought that was funny.

"She had a determined look on her face. She wasn't talking. She just pulled this girl out the door. I said, 'What's the matter?'"

"Before replying, Marian kept pulling until the hapless girl was outside the building.

"Gwendolyn just wouldn't leave my things alone and I just put her out. And I'll do it again if she bothers my things again."

Obviously, the SDA doctrine of pacifism didn't reach all the way down to the teenage girls!

The girls' room had three double bunk beds, six girls to a room. But the conflicts among the children and pressure from the parents finally forced Houteff to rescind the order and re-unite the families after a year or two.

It would not be the last time a leader at Mt. Carmel separated the sexes.

During the dormitory experiment, Houteff instituted a ministerial school in the evenings. Many of the men would work all day in the fields or in construction, then spend their evenings in intensive Bible studies.[10] Naturally, Bingham taught the first classes, but it wasn't long before his overbearing ways caused conflict in the ministerial school as well. As Saether said:

"I said to Brother Houteff one day, 'I want to talk to you about this school, this ministerial course. In order for a person to be a good speaker, he has to have some practice. Well, Brother Bingham takes up all the time. He talks the whole time himself and the rest of us don't have a chance to say anything. We're not given the opportunity...

"Brother Houteff never said anything. He just never made a comment on it. Nothing came of that for a while. Then one day, as I understand it, Oliver Hermanson told him the same thing that I'd told him.

"Then Brother Houteff put Bingham's wife in as the head of the school and my! that sure rankled Brother Bingham. He never got over that. That turned him against his wife."

The resentment against his wife, Genevieve, and the opportunities that presented themselves to him as headmaster of the school apparently became too much for Bingham to resist. Saether said that Bingham soon "got mixed up with several girls" at Mt. Carmel Academy and left his wife.

Bingham's indiscretions were widely known, but he repented and Houteff finally allowed him to return to Mt. Carmel and—apparently—his previous position as director of the school, which was closed in 1948. The children then attended Waco schools.

The Davidians would not try home-schooling again for another thirty years.

Following the war, Houteff ordered his Sabbath sermons transcribed and compiled into booklets for widespread dissemination. His wife, Florence, who both typed and took shorthand, was in charge of the project despite her youth. Although she liked to go on picnics and play with girls her own age, official duties and Houteff's prodigious writing output kept Florence busy.

Timely Greetings, Texts and Addresses by V. T. Houteff, Minister of the Davidian Seventh-day Adventists was published on August 3, 1946, and issues continued until 1953.

In 1945, Houteff nearly died from a bleeding duodenal ulcer, despite emergency treatment at a Waco hospital. Then, in the early 1950s, his health began to wane. Saether said some of his decline was because he always pushed himself so hard.

"I think he overdid himself, taxed his physical strength," Saether said. "[He wasn't] made out of steel, although you'd think he was. He was on the go all the time. Nothing escaped him. He was watching everything. Everything."

In the late 1940s, Houteff decided to deal with Mt. Carmel's never ending cash-flow problems by subdividing the land and selling it to developers. His failing health and the fear that his lifesaving message was not getting out fast enough may have played a large part in his decision. Houteff believed he could raise $1 million in land sales alone and the commune could go elsewhere, although initially, the plan was to sell only "surplus" or "excess" property at Mt. Carmel—not the heart of the compound.

Waco was by then developing in Mt. Carmel's direction, and the post-war building boom was encroaching on Davidian land. Only towards Lake Waco, where the Davidians had four and a half acres of pasture and gardens irrigated by the lake, were they still away from civilization.

Houteff called the first general meeting since 1948 to make the announcement, and when the first lots were sold, Houteff used the capital from sales to send out men to look up the addresses of SDAs and see whether or not they wanted Davidian literature. By now, the publishing arm was running full tilt, with pamphlets and booklets being sent regularly to a huge mailing list of more than 100,000 SDAs. At its peak, they were printing 48,000 tracts every two weeks.

Houteff wanted to delete the names of people who discarded the mailings and focus the Davidians' remaining resources on those who showed an interest in his teachings. So he decided that Mt. Carmel needed to support "between 20 and 30" field workers with the goal of meeting every SDA family. Houteff called it "The Hunting" because of a reference in Jer. 16:11. The Davidians purchased six new Chevrolets for the "hunters," while others used their own automobiles. Representatives were even sent to Australia, England, India, the West Indies, and Canada.

Saether, of course, was among those chosen to travel. He and another man covered the states of Ohio and Pennsylvania together. But eventually, in late 1953, Houteff called Saether back, telling him they were running short of funds.

The next year, Florence Houteff called Saether aside after the real estate transactions were in full swing and told him that her husband was not well.

"He was not up to par and he didn't hold any meetings any more, either. Others held the meetings. He didn't speak, just once in a while he'd have something to say. The doctrines had been drawn up and published. His work was finished and as far as the work on the outside, he still kept his eye on that, but he was in quite bad shape," Saether said.

Houteff's decline was obvious to everyone at Mt. Carmel and many began looking to Saether for leadership.

"But I didn't want the leadership, especially the way he dealt. It was pretty ironclad and when you're a leader, you're on a pedestal by yourself. You're a lonely person. I didn't want it.

"Mrs. Houteff said that he told her that he wanted her to be the leader. Well, that was all right. But now, take a man that's ready to die and his mind is not really clear... [still] I thought at the time it was the best way out for us. But I've thought since it was a big mistake."

Some of Houteff's final, painful hours were spent in an oxygen tent at Mt. Carmel, where Saether and M. W. Wolfe helped him at Florence's request. Then, on February 5, 1955, they took Houteff to Hillcrest Baptist Hospital in Waco. Houteff's kidneys were gone and his heart was failing.

Two hours before he died, Houteff tried to tell his wife the meaning of the 42 months mentioned in Revelation 11, but died before he could do so. Wolfe, like many Davidians, was dumbfounded by Houteff's death. Some had an unspoken belief that Houteff wouldn't die before the Millennium.

Thousands of people attended Houteff's funeral—according to some, the biggest funeral Waco had ever seen—including the local SDAs. But even before Houteff was cold in the grave, the jockeying for position had begun.

M. J. Bingham was one of those vying for the job, although he was being asked to go to the Caribbean as a missionary. Saether was opposed to Bingham because of his alleged indiscretions.

"Like I said to different ones at council meetings," Saether recalled, "I said, 'If a man has sinned, the Lord will forgive him.' And we've all made mistakes. We've all sinned and come short of the glory of God.

"[But] when a man has gone and committed adultery, a married man, I think he should take a back seat until he dies. He could do all the good he could, but not have any prominent place in the Lord's work.

"Wolfe was another candidate and I was just as opposed to him, maybe even more so. More so because, primarily, Bingham and I always got along all right. He left me alone and I left him alone. He was always courteous to me.

"There was another man that I think was grooming himself to

be the leader. He'd been here for a short while, several months. He had a garden down next to the lake. I don't know whether it ever amounted to anything. I wasn't here at the time. This was 1953.

"His name was Roden—Benjamin Roden."

Roden had first visited Mt. Carmel in 1945 with his wife Lois and his oldest son George, then aged 10. They stayed for a few days, then returned to Odessa, where Benjamin Roden had been disfellowshipped from the Seventh-day Adventist Church. (At one point, the Rodens barricaded themselves in their church to keep from being evicted.) They returned to Mt. Carmel in 1953 and for a brief time ran an organic garden in the irrigated fields near Lake Waco.

While factions supporting Roden, E. T. Wilson, and Bingham were fighting among themselves, the powerful Hermanson family was quietly arranging for Houteff's successor. Saether claimed that Mrs. Hermanson pulled a *coup d'état* to see that her daughter Florence assumed the leadership role. Even before Houteff's funeral, Saether was visited by Oliver Hermanson, who told him that Houteff had directed Florence to be vice president and manager, and to elect Oliver to the council to assist her. Saether thought that having a woman in charge might relieve the infighting, and it did.

At the next meeting of the council, Florence presented the council members with a written declaration that Houteff had told her to lead the organization. When Wolfe asked how the council could know this was really true, Florence asked how Wolfe would know he was a member of the council. Although her tone was pleasant, the rejoinder was, nonetheless, sharp. Saether and Florence, who had served as the council's secretary for much of Houteff's tenure in Waco, were the only two who really knew who had been appointed to the council at any given time. Mrs. Houteff's question stilled Wolfe immediately: Florence had learned that knowledge withheld is far more powerful than knowledge imparted.

In the days following her husband's death, Florence's actions didn't sit well with other Davidians, including Sidney Smith.

"At first, [Mrs. Houteff] did real good," Smith said, "but her brother [Oliver] was not a converted man and he slowly but surely turned her away. And, of course, she put him on the council right away. And that contaminated the council."

Foregoing the usual period of mourning, Mrs. Houteff

apparently threw herself into negotiating the subdivision of Mt. Carmel.

A few weeks after Houteff's death, the Davidians sold 26 lots of the estimated 600-lot, 200-acre, $900,000 land development. Several of the surviving original 12 had already purchased homes in what was being called Lake Shore Hills.

Once the land sales were safely underway, Florence turned her attention to the other pressing issue in her life, an interpretation of Revelation Chapter 11.

All publishing ground to a halt while Florence studied the difficult language of Revelation 11, the chapter that had been on Houteff's mind in his last days. Then, in early March, Florence found Saether in the office one Friday afternoon as they were closing for the Sabbath preparations, and tried to persuade him to her idea of Revelation 11.

Revelation 11 is one of the main hidden prophetic passages in the entire Bible. In it, the Seventh Angel's trumpet announces the triumph of Christ's Kingdom following the temporary triumph of evil. The chapter opens with St. John the Revelator reporting a vision he has been given after eating a little book given to him by an angel. In it, two "witnesses" are given the secret measurement of the inner Temple, but are told not to measure the outer court because it belongs to the Gentiles.

Verse three says, "And I will give power unto my two witnesses, and they shall prophesy a thousand two hundred and three score days, clothed in sackcloth."

While the bulk of the prophetic verses follow, Mrs. Houteff chose to make her prophesy based on verse 3. She selected November 9, 1955, as the day that Davidians received the "light" on the prophetic period of 1,260 days. Assuming those 1,260 days were a literal three and a half years from November 9, 1955, that gave her the date of April 22, 1959, when all prophecy would be fulfilled.

While Saether agreed with her that the prophetic days had not taken place in the Dark Ages, in the days of papal supremacy as the Church and Houteff had taught, he didn't think Florence had any proof of the fact that those days were about to occur:

"I was courteous with her, I wasn't rough. I should have made fun of it, but I didn't. She was in earnest. I thought she'd lost her mind."

Florence talked to Saether all afternoon, pleading with him to agree with her. Then she went to each member of the council individually and talked with them about it. After that, Saether didn't hear any more about Mrs. Houteff's "discovery" and went back to trying to pick up the pieces after Houteff's death.

On October 10, 1955, Benjamin and Lois Roden returned from Odessa with their children and a new convert, a Davidian ministerial student named Perry Jones. It is difficult to single out any one event as the goofiest in the history of this completely goofy church, but what followed is certainly a contender. Benjamin Roden demanded control of the compound, claiming to have received a message while working under a car in Odessa that he was the anointed "Branch," the new leader of the Davidians. When the Davidian elders refused, the Rodens insisted that everyone stop work and pray with them.

Benjamin was quite a large man, and his wife was a strong woman. Together they harangued the Davidians, most of whom could not make heads or tails of what they were saying. The Rodens then crashed the council meeting, where Lois had a lot to say, and said it disdainfully, which puzzled them. It took the Davidians a while to realize that Benjamin Roden was claiming to be "the Branch" who had summoned all the people to Waco.

As darkness began to fall, Roden's followers filed out to their cars, which were parked so that their rearview mirrors would not reflect the fire they thought the Lord would visit on the Davidians for rejecting Roden's message. Saether thought it was all foolishness, until he realized they were using incantation designed to terrorize the Davidians and make them think that fire would destroy them unless they turned the compound over to Roden.

Before Roden's followers left, they drove their automobiles and pickup trucks around Mt. Carmel several times, citing Joshua's encirclement of Jericho before it fell:

"There were some accusations of vandalism or arson at that time. [The Rodens] seemed to be a bit rougher than the people that were here, [who] were very gentle, very soft-spoken people and very nice, except that when they started talking about religious matters, they would get a kind of faraway look in their eyes," Waco attorney David Kultgen said.

The presence of so many people violently opposed to her rule naturally made Florence Houteff somewhat uneasy, so she asked Saether to guard the main office that night. About 2:30 a.m. the phone rang. Saether answered it, and a voice asked, "Is this Mt. Carmel?"

"I said, 'Yes it is, Perry. I'm here alone, the rest are all asleep.' "

Jones was calling to see if Mt. Carmel had been reduced to

cinders yet, as the Rodens had prophesied. (Before joining the Rodens, Perry Jones had worked in the publishing department at Mt. Carmel and in the office that Saether was guarding.)

"They actually thought the fire was going to come down," Saether said, "they were going to go so far away from it they couldn't see the glow of it even.

"I said, 'How far did you get?' Those poor kids [traveling with the Rodens] hadn't had anything to eat. I suppose they didn't give them anything. Nobody was to eat until this thing took place. You know, fanaticism is the worst thing there is."

Apparently miffed over the lack of carnage at Mt. Carmel, Roden and his followers returned to Odessa.

On November 6, 1955, a fragment of what is purported to be executive council minutes has this surprising entry: "You (Mrs. Houteff) have been honest in not claiming to be prophet or even appointed by God to be the president of the council. Therefore, the people feel there may be someone appointed of God to fill this place, to say the least."

The copy of the minutes was provided by the Rodens and is, quite properly, somewhat suspect. But if true, the exchange confirms that Mrs. Houteff was fighting a constant battle within her own organization.

In the meantime, Saether and some of the other Davidians were surprised to see a new issue of *The Symbolic Code* arrive on November 9, announcing that they had entered the final days. After eight months of silence on the issue, Florence had finally published her interpretation of Revelation 11. In retrospect, Saether said his path should have been clear at this point. He just didn't follow it. Perhaps twenty years of Houteff's autocratic leadership had left him without the will or the power to oppose the chosen successor.

Florence's startling message flew in the face of mainstream Adventist thought. Still, Mrs. Houteff went on the attack, much as her late husband had done 25 years earlier. First, she addressed an open letter to the Executive Committee of the General Conference of Seventh-day Adventists:[12]

"If the message and work of *The Shepherd's Rod* is God's Truth as we believe it to be, the 1,260 days of Revelation 11, as *The Symbolic Codes* have explained, will end sometime this Spring. Then will follow the war that will kill the Two Witnesses. Those whom the Witnesses tormented will gloat over this. But after three and a half days, the Two Witnesses will be exalted. At the same time will come the earthquake (shaking) in which will be slain all the hypocrites in God's part of Christendom—the Adventist church...

"Mt. Carmel hereby serves notice that she now leaves the prophecy of Revelation 11 as *The Code* has explained it, as the test by which the Lord will demonstrate whom He is leading."

Bold words for a little colony with only about 90 adherents— about a third of whom were children—in Waco at the time.

Bold words for *anybody.*

The three and a half years that followed Mrs. Houteff's announcement were a blur to George Saether, as he gamely followed her preparations for the End Times despite his misgivings.

But the years weren't without incident.

On October 25, 1956, the Day of Days, the Rodens returned. This time, they sent word ahead of them, and, like the King of Babylon in the book of Jeremiah, organized a holy sit-down strike on the Mt. Carmel grounds!

Saether and the council members vowed to stop the Rodens and talked among themselves about barring them from Mt. Carmel. While waiting outside, Saether saw Perry Jones' mother-in-law, Nelda, with another woman who had come from California. Nelda, who had been well received in earlier years, had become belligerent. Saether reacted quickly to prevent the women from participating in the sit-down strike. Then the two women marched to Building 8, where Saether's wife was working in the office.

"One was the spokesman and she knocked on the door: 'Behold I stand at the door and knock. So you open the door.' No answer. 'Behold your house is left unto you desolate.' You see, that was incantation. It's from the devil.

"I went back to the office later on and the wind was out of their sails. They were allowed to come in the office, two or three at a time. Roden was in there. He wanted to buy some charts and Hermanson asked him, 'Are you prepared to pay your bill here?'"

(When Roden had volunteered to come and start an organic garden at the compound, he had run up a bill for about $700 in rent, food, and other living expenses.)

Roden left without buying the charts—or paying his bill.

But the Rodens—who believed Benjamin Roden was both "the Branch" often predicted in Scripture, and the son of man predicted in Revelation 14—were not able to take control of Mt. Carmel. They often stayed in Waco, occasionally returning to Odessa, slowly growing in power and influence.

Meanwhile, the sale of Mt. Carmel continued at a rapid rate. By the fall of 1957, the group had sold all but 10 acres[13] on what was by then called Mt. Carmel Drive. Mrs. Houteff had had her agents fanning across rural McLennan County, looking for another temporary home. Flush with cash from the sale of the land, the Davidians in December 1957 purchased 941 acres about nine miles east of Waco, just a mile from the tiny farming community of Elk. The rolling farmland, which Mrs. Houteff called "New Mt. Carmel," cost only $85,000. Saether once again found himself at odds with Mrs. Houteff and disagreed with the decision to move. He was not the only one. The Rodens, the Binghams, and others on the outside opposed it.

But when he saw that arguing with the Hermanson contingent was useless, Saether accepted his orders and got to work. The group immediately started to make itself self-sufficient once again— until the appointed date with destiny. They built a new headquarters, church, office building, eighteen homes, farm buildings, a dairy building, feed barn, hay barn, large implement shed and garage, and a machine shop.

With a new printing press, Mrs. Houteff continued to expound on the apocalyptic message of Revelation 11. Response among Davidians and SDAs alike was decidedly mixed. But nothing could deter Florence from presiding over what she called "The Year of the Kingdom."

Mrs. Houteff next "...issued a call to its adherents in North America to assemble this week at their world headquarters in Mt. Carmel Center, Waco, Texas. ...the purpose of this gathering is to pray solemnly and earnestly for ultimate world peace and for the fulfillment of definite promises of God that will bring it about...

"Davidian Seventh-day Adventists are convinced that finite men of themselves are incapable of solving the world's problems. They declare that the world's only hope for ultimate peace is in the establishment of the Kingdom God promised in Daniel 2:34, 35, 44, 45, and many other scriptures.

"This group expects it to be set up soon in the Holy Land according to Ezekiel chapters 34 and 36 and Isaiah chapters 4 and 11, with many other scriptures. Afterward, they say, nations will join it as predicted in Micah 4:1, 2 and Isaiah 2:2–4.

"Testifying to their conviction that the fullness of time has come, many Davidian Adventists are severing all earthly ties, if necessary, in preparation for this Kingdom of Peace, as a symbol of the time when the Great Exodus spoken of in Isaiah 11:11–17 and Jeremiah 16:14, 15 shall commence.

"They believe this exodus will commence shortly after the predicted war of Zechariah 14 breaks out in the Middle East."

The prospect of war in the Middle East didn't deter the Rodens from flying to Israel in June 1958. Once there, the Roden colony encountered problems with Israeli labor unions. Mrs. Roden, who had sailed to Israel later with a new one-ton Chevy truck, nearly didn't make it out of New York Harbor after "an Arab boat rammed the Israeli ship and nearly sunk [sic] it."[14]

As the date began to close in—and it fell, coincidentally or not, on the Jewish Passover for 1959—even the local newspaper began to take note of the strange doings at Mt. Carmel.

On April 14, 1959, the *Waco Tribune-Herald* headlined a front-page article by an unnamed reporter. It said that Davidians believed that "the fullness of time has come" and that Davidians from across the globe would be traveling to Waco.

Not surprisingly, George Saether was selected as the Davidian spokesman. Saether told the *Tribune-Herald* that the war to begin on April 22 did not herald the end of the world, but would precede Christ's reappearance on earth to set up His earthly kingdom:

"We do not know how soon after the 22nd war will follow—it may even begin before then—or how long it will last. But after that Christ will come."

Saether predicted that "hundreds of Davidians" would make the trip to Waco and that some would live in tents on the New Mt. Carmel grounds, while others would stay in area hotels and private homes. Mrs. Houteff had advised followers to sell all their property that could not be transported to Waco, but Saether said Davidian leadership was not asking that any money raised be given to the church. The Mt. Carmel Davidians did ease the financial burden of some of the more distant followers by paying their transportation costs to Waco.

Non-stop saber-rattling in the Middle East seemed to justify Davidian prophesy, although Israel and its Arab neighbors had lived in an uneasy peace since the war of 1956, when Egypt had nationalized the Suez Canal.

Mrs. Houteff expected members to begin arriving Thursday and scheduled a series of meetings on Saturday, meetings which would continue daily until the 22nd. Just as she had envisioned, a steady stream of people began arriving in Waco, and could be seen driving up to the compound in trailers, cars, and trucks—vehicles that ranged from old-model Fords to late-model Cadillacs.

Although Davidian officials had originally said that all meetings would be open to the general public, a *Tribune-Herald* article announced that they would be closed in preparation for the Second Coming.

Saether served as spokesman for the Davidians, issuing news releases containing the full text of the three talks given at the Saturday meetings. These consisted mostly of Davidian history and an account of the controversy between the Davidians and the mainstream Seventh-day Adventist Church.

Saether also said the Davidians were expecting three events to occur in the days ahead:

1. The beginning of war in the Middle East within a few weeks after April 22.

2. The 'purification' of the church through the coming of the Lord 'to render His anger with fury and His rebuke with flames of fire.'

3. The establishment of God's Kingdom in Jerusalem followed by a period of peace and tranquillity.

(However, Saether explained that the Davidians were not expecting the second coming of Christ at that time. "The Lord will come," he said, "but we may not even be able to see Him." Pretty good hedge: for all we know, the Easter Bunny may be here, too.)

The Davidians were meeting in a huge, blue and tan circus tent on "a lush green hill" at Mt. Carmel. The floor was covered with sawdust and wood shavings. The pews were unpainted benches capable of holding about 1,200 people. By Saturday, Davidian officials said that "more than 500 persons from almost every state in the nation and Canada" had arrived in Waco.

Dudley Goff was listed as one of the principle speakers. (Goff had apparently come to a position of influence at Mt. Carmel in the late 1950s.) Other speakers included G. Walton and M. W. Wolfe. Saether said that meetings would once again be open to the public—and newspaper photographers—the following Monday. Tuesday was to be the final full day of scheduled meetings for Davidians as they continued to hear prophesy on what to expect in the hours ahead. In addition to signs previously mentioned, Davidians were also told to expect the "purification of the remainder of the world's population."

In a later article, the newspaper reported that children attended all meetings with their parents and were "surprisingly well-behaved..."

The following day, another update ran on the front page of the *Tribune-Herald* under a large photograph of four women who were preparing the three-times-daily meals for the mass of people congregating at Mt. Carmel.

A host of new arrivals was interviewed for the article:

"We were living in Narco, CA, when we received the notice to assemble in Waco," Tommy Thompson, a lean, weather-beaten man in his 60s recalled. "I owned a trenching machine business.

"After we received the notice, we sold the business, our home and furniture. We packed the rest of our belongings—our bedding and cooking utensils—in the car and a rented trailer and brought them with us."

Thompson and his wife lived in a tent on the Mt. Carmel grounds and reported no particular problems—other than the ever-present mud.

"George Walton brought his wife, son and 30 to 35 other members to the center when he came from California. And they, like the Thompsons are living in a tent at the center.

"'We burned all our bridges behind us,' Walton said. 'We came prepared to meet whatever comes our way.'" Excepting, perhaps, nothing.

Walton was an employee of the Board of Education at Los Angeles and the leader of Davidians in the city.

A number of people from a Davidian-sponsored old folks' home in Salem, North Carolina, made the long trek, including residents in their 70s and 80s.

"Mr. and Mrs. William Glenn of Bend, OR, are luckier than most.

"They have two daughters living at the center. They invested part of their money in a house trailer before they came to the center.

"'We came in a caravan,' they said. 'There were five cars in all when we started out, but we didn't all arrive at the same time. Some drove straight on through, but we stopped every night.'

"Mr. and Mrs. C. C. Lyons of Portland, OR, were Bible workers and they said they 'were prepared for the call.'

"'The Lord was with us,' Lyons said. 'We sold our home—signed the final papers and all—and moved out in the two-week period between the time we received the call and the time we were supposed to arrive.'

Among those with the furthest to travel was Richard Strutz of Saskatchewan, Canada. Strutz, who had left his junior hockey team, was originally joined by his parents, but his father was forced to fly back to Canada to make final arrangements to sell the family's 640-acre wheat farm."

A later article quoted dairy worker James Bowie, 50, of Skowhegan, Maine, who said there wouldn't be time to find jobs in the Waco area because the establishing of the Kingdom of God was coming soon:

"It was a hard decision to leave everything behind in Maine and come down, but there was really never a question in my mind about answering the church's call.

"I know how hard it was for me to give up everything and come down here, so I really marvel how people with children can leave their homes. I know one woman who has 10 children down here with her."

"I have turned my life over to the Davidian movement. My wife divorced me because of my devotion to my religion, so I have no family. I live in my panel truck. It will do until the kingdom is established, then I won't need it any more."

Perhaps he is living in it still.

But all was not well in Mrs. Houteff's Waco empire.

The executive council was receiving regular messages from an anonymous source in Springfield, Missouri, claiming to represent a large number of unhappy Davidians. The letters, signed by "The Branch," claimed that Mrs. Houteff had illegally usurped the position of leadership within the council, and ordered her to resign in favor of Ben Roden and the Branch.

An undated copy of three articles from the *Waco News-Tribune* also tell of a rival group predicting that April 22, 1959, was not only the wrong day, but that Mrs. Houteff was the wrong leader. The claims were made by Benjamin L. Roden, shown in a large photograph with William Worrow of Miami, Florida, and Perry D. Jones, of Los Angeles, California, looking at what appears to be a Bible.

Roden's followers apparently believed that Roden was the modern counterpart to Joshua, the Biblical prophet. Roden claimed to have spent the previous 10 months in Israel, laying the groundwork for the influx of the 144,000 Adventists he expected to stream to Palestine to establish the Lord's earthly kingdom.

Follower Worrow said that Davidians believed that Houteff, Florence's dead husband, was "the antitype of the Biblical prophet Elijah," and that, unlike Houteff, the modern-day Joshua would never die. He also said that the Davidians' beliefs had changed after Houteff's death. While they had previously believed that instructions could come to them only through a living prophet, the absence of one after Houteff's death had made them change their belief in this. That would certainly do it.

"Besides, they don't have any provision for the modern-day

Joshua who will lead the people to the Kingdom," he said.

That prophet, of course, was Roden.

Roden blithely predicted that the April 22, 1959, date was in error and said that the prophesied events would not occur until at least the summer of 1960.

John Chizmadia of Benton, Arkansas, a former SDA who was concerned about the Davidians' very souls, was at Mt. Carmel:

"I urged them to start using the true name for the Father and the Holy Spirit," Chizmadia told the Waco newspaper. "But they wouldn't listen to me. Most of them seem to be under some sort of spell. I'm going back home now. I feel sorry for them, 'cause they are going to be hurt when the events they expect don't take place."

Chizmadia said that Davidians were not allowed to read any "religious" literature save their own. Some might argue that was more than enough.

Finally, Wednesday, April 22 dawned cold with frost in low-lying areas. Some had expected the blessed event to occur just after midnight and had stayed up on the wind-swept hills. Others had expected the Kingdom to be instituted with the dawn. Still others had been told that a sign might come at the final morning meeting.

At the morning meeting, an estimated 600 Davidians were officially told for the first time that V. T. Houteff "was in truth the latter-day prophet Elijah who is to return just before the Day of the Lord."

The report that Houteff might be resurrected startled some and soothed others.

But by 12 noon, no visible signs of the new world order had come.

While Goff delivered yet another sermon on Revelation, the Davidian council met in a separate session. Davidians were urged to "wait and pray."

They waited as the hours of Wednesday, April 22, 1959, ticked slowly, quietly away.

In the few seconds before midnight, some were waiting still, still watching, still praying.

Still hoping.

[1.] All who came were poor. Four of the 12 had the use of only one hand— a strangely off-kilter percentage that even Houteff couldn't tie to a promising Biblical passage. One of the 12 was an ordained minister.

2. 5 et al. Mary Elizabeth Power, M.A. Thesis, "A Study of the Seventh-day Adventist Community, Mount Carmel Center, Waco, Texas," 1940. Baylor University.

3. One of his first duties was to build a cemetery at what is now the intersection of Bishop Drive and Valley Mills Drive in Waco. The elderly Mrs. Charboneau died in late 1936 and was the first person buried there.

4. In a later newspaper article, writer Chris Whitcraft described the process: "The group labored with hand stump pullets, axes, mattocks and unquestioning faith to clear the almost impenetrable growth of brush which covered Waco's highest hills.

Later, they raised the money to buy their first bulldozer, then replaced it with a larger one.

Long and slow was the work. The center had to build its own water cistern—a dam, filter, pumphouse and storage tank. But even throughout the drought, the new Mt. Carmel was never without water."

5. Glen Webster Green, Sidney Albert Smith, and Bonnie Louise Smith, "Oral Memoirs," Baylor University Institute for Oral History. Interview conducted by David Stricklin and Dr. Bill Pitts.

The best-trained laborers earned 14.5 cents per hour, with a maximum of $7.92 earned per week. Of that money, 79 cents was always given back to Mt. Carmel's "First Tithe" fund.

6. Children were divided by age groups and required to work. Children aged four to eight were expected to work 26 hours per week for which they were paid the princely sum of 3.5 cents per hour. Since school fees (which included room, board, and laundry) were $3.23 per week, children ended each week $2.32 in the red—and each family was expected to pay the difference.

Children aged 8–13 earned 7.5 cents per hour and paid slightly more in school costs. Teenagers earned 9 cents per hour, and all young people over the age of 18 earned apprentice wages of 9 to 13 cents per hour—and worked a full 40-hour week.

All young people were also expected to tithe from their meager earnings.

7. Mary Elizabeth Power, interview, May 6, 1993. Waco, Texas.

8. From then on, October 25 was observed as a special feast day to commemorate the reconciliation, with no work being done at Mt. Carmel. "So every year after that we would have the history of the year before," Green said. "And so the office would write up the history of the good and the bad and the things that went on, all of the interesting things. We'd have that reading and then we'd have quite a program and then we'd have a big dinner, kind of a picnic dinner out. That was always a big day."

9. *The Encyclopedia of American Religions, 4th Edition.* The encyclopedia says that the "more relaxed view of non-combatancy service" held by the Seventh-day Adventist Church, along with internal pressures from the Adventist Church, "forced the Shepherd's Rod adherents to [then] formally incorporate as the General Association of Davidian Seventh-day Adventists" the following year.

10. Another favorite Davidian activity was singing. Davidians rewrote a number of favorite Protestant hymns, removing most references to Jesus, and substituting their own theology:

"Sweet Shepherd's Rod" (originally "Sweet Bye and Bye"):

1. Unto the prophet of Israel; There came the Word of Emanuel [sic]; 'Go and take the book and eat the roll; As sweetness for the soul.'

(Chorus) Oh sweet is the roll; inspired by the sweet spirit of God; Oh how sweet to the soul; Is the message of the Shepherd's Rod.

2. It's the message of the Shepherd's Rod; Inspired by the sweet Spirit of God; The kingdom message we love to hear; Is the Voice of God so sweet and clear.

3. For the Shepherd's Rod unrolled the scroll; It's the truth found in the golden bowl; And to everyone that eats this roll; It becomes sweeter unto the soul. Others included "Send the Rod" (originally "Send the Light, the Blessed Gospel Light") and "Praise Ye Our God" (originally "Jesus Loves Even Me.").

[11.]"Behold, I will send for many fishers, saith the Lord, and they shall fish them; and after will I send for many hunters, and they shall hunt them from every mountain, and from every hill, and out of the holes of the rocks."

[12.]In a special edition of *The Symbolic Code* (Vol. 14, No. 6).

[13.]The core buildings, some of which were only built to last a year or so, became the home of Vanguard High School, a private college preparatory school, in September 1973.

[14.]From "The Demise of the Antitypical Lucifer in the Branch Kingdom," newsletter, Texas Collection, Baylor University.

SOURCES

Mary Elizabeth Power, interview, May 6, 1993. Waco, Texas.

George W. Saether, "Oral Memoirs," Baylor University Institute for Oral History. Most interviews conducted by Dr. Dan McGee.

Dr. Dan McGee, interview, April 3, 1993. Waco, Texas.

Glen Webster Green, Sidney Albert Smith, and Bonnie Louise Smith, "Oral Memoirs," Baylor University Institute for Oral History. Interview conducted by David Stricklin and Dr. Bill Pitts.

The History and Teachings of The Shepherd's Rod.

The Symbolic Code, Vol. IV, October-December 1938.

The Symbolic Code, Vol. VI, June-January 1940.

The Symbolic Code, Vol. IVX, November 1955.

The Demise of the Antitypical Lucifer in the Branch Kingdom, newsletter, Texas Collection, Baylor University.

Shepherd's Rod mimeographed songbook, Texas Collection, Baylor University, Waco, Texas.

Encyclopedia of American Religions, 4th Edition.

David Kultgen interview, May 17, 1993, Waco, Texas.

Waco News-Tribune, undated articles, from the Texas Collection, Baylor University, Waco, Texas.

Waco Tribune-Herald, undated articles, from the Texas Collection, Baylor University, Waco, Texas.

Waco Times-Herald, undated articles, from the Texas Collection, Baylor University, Waco, Texas.

Waco Times-Herald, February 6, 1955, pp. 1,2.

Waco Tribune-Herald, February 27, 1955, pp. 1,11.

Waco Tribune-Herald, April 14, 1959, pp. 1,5.

Waco Tribune-Herald, April 19, 1959, pp. 1,2.

Waco Tribune-Herald, April 20, 1959, pp. 1.

Waco Tribune-Herald, April 21, 1959, pp. 1,2.

Waco Tribune-Herald, April 22, 1959, pp. 1,4.

Waco News-Tribune, April 23, 1959, pp. 1,4.

Waco News-Tribune, May 2, 1959, pp. 8, 18-A.

Waco Tribune-Herald, May 3, 1959, p. 1.

Waco News-Tribune, May 4, 1959, p. 3.

Waco News-Tribune, May 9, 1959, pp. 1, 3.

Waco Times-Herald, April 22, 1959, p. 1, 4.

Chapter 4

The following morning, everyone was still there.

Newspapers reported peace in the Middle East. No confederation of churches had miraculously arisen and allied to combat communism. The resurrection of the righteous dead hadn't happened. Houteff still slumbered in his grave back in the cemetery in "old" Mt. Carmel.

Saether's worst fears had been realized.

Nobody benefited, save the Rodens, who continued to attend the meetings and—once outside the main tent—to spread their message to anyone who would listen.

Mrs. Houteff and the council's first response was to again close all Davidian meetings to the public and the press from April 22 to May 3, but the group continued to meet three times a day in the giant tent. The meetings doubtless had as much to do with spin control as prayer.

The council's first public response to the situation was to buy an advertisement in the newspaper, announcing that a meeting would be held on Sunday, May 3, at 3 p.m., "because of the increasing, tremendous public interest in Davidians' belief in the setting up of God's kingdom in Palestine."

On May 3, 1959, Ray Bell of the *Waco Tribune-Herald* offered the observation that the "status of the Davidian group is, at present, anybody's guess.

"However, some members of the group have indicated there is a 'feeling of desperation, of panic' among the group despite an outward appearance of calmness and that only about two-thirds of the original number are still present and still attending meetings."

Saether, ever the PR man, told Bell that he was "too busy" to estimate the number of people still at Mt. Carmel, though that number was obviously dwindling.

By May 3, the Rodens had grown so bold as to hold meetings of their own, declaring the Davidians to be sincere but in error.

Roden said that members of "The Branch"—as they now styled themselves—differed from the Davidians in that they believed the church must have a living prophet—Roden. The fact that none of the events Mrs. Houteff had foretold had come about "proved" the Branch theology. The Davidians, he said, had waited for a sign on April 22—but didn't know it when it finally appeared before them!

"...my appearance here—the morning of April 22—actually could be considered a sign. I had been in Jerusalem only a short time before—I flew back—and as far as the people knew I was still in the Holy Land," he told Bell.

(Ben Roden later admitted to Saether that he had written the letters signed "The Branch," and sent them to a follower in Missouri, who had then mailed them to Mrs. Houteff. The letters[1] uniformly attacked Mrs. Houteff's leadership.)

Roden's single-minded intent from the beginning was to prove invalid Mrs. Houteff's claim to being the head of the Davidians. Roden's argument—Mrs. Houteff's admittedly cavalier attitude toward her "anointing" by her late husband—would return to haunt the original Davidians on more than one occasion in the years to come.

At the next public Davidian meeting, the group rather optimistically announced plans to expand their world headquarters to make room for the thousands of people they expected to flock to the center. Dudley Goff urged the crowd of about 450 not to be fearful as they began the task of evangelizing the world to Christ. If those chosen few Davidians were successful, untold thousands would soon begin streaming into Waco.

At one meeting during the first week of May, Davidians distributed an intriguing questionnaire to the remaining faithful. The questionnaire asked the financial standing of each respondent, their trade or profession, and asked Davidians to answer "yes" or "no" to four questions about their degree of agreement with Mt. Carmel's program and the council, and their ability and willingness to pay their own expenses and work for nothing.

The *Waco News-Tribune* reported on May 9 that the council had approved plans to build "10 large barracks-type buildings." But the photograph on the front page of the newspaper was not of the Davidians, but of the Rodens.

The announcement of the ambitious building program at Mt. Carmel was obviously an outward show of the confidence the council had in Mrs. Houteff's prophetic abilities. Privately, however, influential Davidians were apparently warring among themselves again. Opinions differed on what Florence should do. Some felt that if she'd just admitted to a mistake and told everyone to start reexamining or reexplaining things, as they had done in 1844, all of the Davidians would have gone along with it.

But she didn't, and people started leaving.

Nobody stopped them.

The national SDA organization, which had long viewed the Davidians as a dangerous nuisance, responded to the events in Waco with barely concealed satisfaction. The account of the days following April 22 reports that the Adventist organization had representatives in Waco in connection with Mrs. Houteff's announcement:

"As the weeks passed and the people encamped there reflected upon this sad experience, it became quite obvious that they must do something soon. Some of them told us that they were penniless. Many had sold their homes, their businesses, and their property before coming to Waco, for they expected that their next move would be to the Promised Land where the Davidic kingdom was supposed to be set up soon. One after another they began to leave Waco, embarrassed with disappointment, to find work and to start life over again."

On June 20, 1959, well-known Adventist Elder V. A. Olson preached at an SDA church in Waco. The following day, two unnamed Davidians—still disdainfully called "Shepherd's Rod" by Adventists—approached Olson and requested that he meet with Mrs. Houteff and the executive council.

After the meeting, Olson and Adventist minister Elder R. L. Winders of Waco, agreed to speak each evening and on Sabbath afternoon at the Davidians' new tabernacle. The meetings were primarily held for Davidians to question the two Adventists, presumably about Revelation 11 and the events of the previous months. Interest in the meetings grew until both the Texas Conference and the General Conference sent special elders to field the flood of questions.

"Some adherents of the Shepherd's Rod decided to return to the Seventh-day Adventist Church. Others indicated they were seriously thinking of taking the same step," the official Adventist reports said.

Following the July 7 meeting, Mrs. Houteff publicly read a resolution from the Davidians thanking the Adventist ministers for their participation and requesting that the General Conference appoint a special committee of ministers to meet with an equal number of Davidians to "freely discuss our differences" out of a "desire to comply with the Spirit of Prophecy instruction regarding these matters."

The General Conference quickly agreed with Mrs. Houteff's request. The meetings were to be held beginning July 27 and would consist of 19 sessions of two hours each, to end August 7.

The Davidians spent most of the first 10 sessions presenting their teachings in the areas where they differed from mainstream SDA thought, including the prophecy of Revelation 11 and the reasons for the "time-setting" date of April 22, 1959. The next six sessions consisted of the Adventist responses to each Davidian teaching, "pointing out any error found in them, and setting forth the correct view when this was necessary."

Unlike the original meetings with Houteff in California, the Adventists indicated that these meetings were "conducted in a reverent and respectful manner as is becoming to Christians, and without heated argument or unkind remarks from either side."[3] Both sides used the Bible and the writings of Ellen G. White to support their various arguments.

But as the 17th session began, the meetings took a decidedly different turn. Instead of rebutting the SDA arguments, the Davidians presented a motion that "their system of Bible interpretation be discussed without any reference to or use of the writings of Mrs. White."

Confused, the Adventists adjourned the meeting and considered the Davidian request. Then, at the next session, Adventist leaders quoted heavily from the writings of Houteff, who used White's writings as freely as he used the Bible. The Davidians then concluded that Houteff's writings were not "one hundred percent" supported by either the Bible or Mrs. White's writings. Sensing their opportunity to go for the kill, the Adventist leaders pulled out their heaviest ammunition:

"It was pointed out to the representatives of the Shepherd's Rod that the validity of their method of interpretation of the prophecies of the Bible had been put to a decisive test by them in the spring of 1959, and that the results of that demonstration speak for themselves. God and time had proven that their interpretation of the prophecies was not correct."

The meeting was adjourned as the Davidians considered their response.

When the two groups met again the next day, the Davidians reiterated their desire to eliminate the writings of Mrs. White from the discussions. This, not surprisingly, brought the sessions to a complete halt.

After the August 7, 1959, meeting, the Davidians returned to Mt. Carmel, where further dissension occurred, and some of those who had gone to the meeting in Washington left the group.

On August 17, 1959, Vernon Howell was born.

Little is written or known about the Davidians in the two years that followed.

The self-styled Branch Davidians—as they now preferred to be called—remained busy, however. An April 1968 pamphlet claimed that Branch colonists had moved into the Holy Land in mid-1958, where they were apparently well accepted.

As for the Davidians, a single-page photocopy of the minutes of the executive council meeting of March 13, 1961, survives. At the close of the meeting "the question arose: What is the duty of the Association towards the people in their various needs? With all the facilities at hand, is there a purpose in it? What can be done? There is a large surplus in the Second Tithe Fund. Experiences of others in helping the poor, the orphans, and others was [sic] related showing the wonderful ways in which God has helped His people when they have a deep desire to help.

"All were urged to be thinking what could be done with the Second Tithe to help in this work and what kind of enterprise could be successfully launched that would be really helpful in ministering to the necessities of the people."

For whatever cause, Mrs. Houteff apparently underwent some kind of change after this. That change would astound those who followed her late husband's creed, though it may have been the first reasonable thing she had ever done. In December 1962 and again in January 1963, open newsletters from Mt. Carmel told followers that careful examination of Houteff's teachings of Ezekiel 4 and 9 had revealed a message that was in variance with the Bible.

At a meeting held in March 1962, the council members, including Mrs. Houteff, formally presented their fellow Davidians with their resignations, accompanied by a message that, Mrs. Houteff claimed, was the result of careful Bible study. It said that they had discovered that some key teachings based on concepts Houteff, Mrs. Houteff, or Ellen White had elaborated were not supported by the Bible, and that they were no longer sure that *The Shepherd's Rod* was infallible. Because of these considerations, they felt bound to resign. In other words, they might be wrong.

On March 11, 1962, the remaining Davidians, as they had done from the beginning, dutifully followed their leaders and voted to dissolve the General Association of Davidian Seventh-day Adventists.

Mount Carmel Center was formally closed.

Some of its leaders quietly left town.

Its assets were left in the hands of real estate attorney Tom Street, who was appointed as the legal trustee. Street had been the Davidians' lawyer for the preceding 25 years and was charged with liquidating the assets.

The last official notice sent to the faithful told them to discontinue sending tithes or contributions to the office at Mt. Carmel Center. It also outlined monthly lifetime payments— "unless said trust fund and the increase thereof be sooner exhausted"—ranging from $29 to $125 dollars to five Davidians and one family.[2]

The May 17, 1962, issue of *Review and Herald* concluded with this cautionary message:

"We warn our people everywhere that desperate efforts are being made by certain persons who have been a part of the Shepherd's Rod organization, to reorganize it. Several splinter groups from the Shepherd's Rod party are operating under new names and with additional teachings of error. All are bent on luring Seventh-day Adventists into their ranks. Moreover, several small groups having had no connection with the Shepherd's Rod, but whose doctrines are equally delusive and dangerous, likewise have the same goal. Therefore, let all our brethren beware."

Many of the Davidians simply left. Among those remaining behind after the stunning change of events was George Saether, who stayed on as a caretaker at old Mt. Carmel, becoming something of a Bible scholar in his later years, poring over the Book of Revelation.

Still other Davidians, particularly those outside of Waco, remained faithful to Houteff's original message. A group in California coalesced around M. J. Bingham, who had fought what he called Mrs. Houteff's "doctrinal and prophetic speculations." Apparently Bingham's small but vocal group had been instrumental in forcing Florence to come to her decision to discontinue as leader.

Although Bingham's organization opposed the placing of Davidian assets in court-appointed receivership, the group decided to continue the association anyway, reorganizing in Los Angeles in 1961, under the name "Davidian Seventh-day Adventist Association."[3]

As for Mrs. Houteff herself, at some point following her final message, she returned to California, where she became a secretary.

The Davidian Cemetery property was sold, and the caskets were moved to nearby Rosemound Cemetery.

More than 20 years after the events of 1959, Saether told Dr. Dan McGee that he believed those who opposed him in the organization had had a curse placed on them. He explained that a number of Davidians subsequently died tragic deaths: two executive-council members died shortly thereafter of cancer, another died in a traffic accident in Tyler, another (Merritt Wolfe[4]— "one of the ringleaders") fell from a building and died just a few months before McGee's interviews. A member of the Hermanson family was admitted to a mental institution, two of M. J. Bingham's daughters died young, and another young girl died in one of the Davidian ponds. Still others, according to Saether, met similar fates.

Despite the disbanding of the organization, the Davidians still owned their land near Elk and had about $200,000 in banks, mostly from the sale of property.

And then, in 1962, Roden came.

The Rodens claimed they were the only spiritual heirs of Houteff's message—and that they rightfully owned new Mt. Carmel. The remaining Davidians were apparently too dispirited and fragmented at this point to seriously oppose them. After all, none of the old Davidians attached any religious significance to the Elk property, and the memories of their debacle were too painful, too fresh.

But then the Rodens made a move on the Davidian bank reserves.

The Davidians had turned new Mt. Carmel over to Tom Street, who was supposed to sell it and divide the proceeds among the Second Tithe believers. Street did his best, but when Roden and his group moved into the place, the sheriff's deputies were met by four men with guns. Even though a judge had ordered them to remove Roden from the land, they were not ready to tackle the gun-toting Branch Davidians.

At one point, Smith said that exasperated Davidians called *him* in to see if he could mediate the dispute between the Branch Davidians and the remaining original Davidians. Smith said the presiding judge knew him from his tenure at the original Mt. Carmel, and asked him why he was associating with people who were disobeying a court order. Smith explained that he was trying to mediate between the two groups. The judge had a poor opinion of Roden, and didn't think Smith would have much luck in his efforts.

But once the hearing began, Smith saw that the judge's pessimistic tone was justified.

"Sister Roden... kept interrupting and yacking an awful lot, and I finally, not very politely... told her to plain shut up," Smith said. "And her son (George) says, 'You can't tell my mother this.' But Ben says, 'Hush, hush.' Told him to hush and be quiet. I think I'm the first one that ever told her that. Nobody dared to."

Thus began a bewildering array of lawsuits, counterlawsuits, and eviction hearings.

Meanwhile, the once prosperous Davidian farm near Elk dwindled to 77 acres.

On March 10, 1965, Ben Roden issued an open letter urging all believers to come to the first Passover at New Mt. Carmel, and stating that "the Lord has seen fit to overrule and place the option to purchase New Mt. Carmel in our hands."

Roden also requested that all Second Tithes be assigned to the Branch for the purchase of the property. Additionally, selected homes on the property were offered for sale, at prices ranging from $5,000 to $7,500.

But not everything went smoothly with the sale of the property to the Rodens. A letter from Ben and Lois Roden to Street—who by now must have dearly wished he'd never heard of the Davidians—indicates that a clear title to the property was still in question and, for whatever reason, the Rodens did not have access to the administration building. The Rodens were also unable to meet the six monthly payments of $5,000, so they requested deferral of the monthly payments and interest until a clear title was available.

Roden said he wanted the property to establish a rest home for the sick and elderly, and claimed to be planning a project to train volunteers to work abroad. But the October 1965 civil suit in Judge Bill Logue's 19th District Court put the Roden's proposed purchase of Mt. Carmel on hold once again. Logue and a 12-person jury heard five days of testimony in the case. Thirty spectators, most of them elderly Davidians—including the Saethers and Sophia Hermanson—packed the courtroom each day.

Also present was Mrs. Victor T. Houteff, whose remarriage had given her the name of Mrs. Carl Eakin, and who had returned from California as part of the reorganized original Davidians. The upstart Davidians, the General Association of Davidian Seventh Day Adventists Inc., were suing Mrs. Eakin's organization to have the 1962 council decision declared illegal—with the remaining 77 acres placed in receivership.

Mrs. Eakin's group countersued to have the council actions

upheld and keep Street as its trustee. Two other parties in the flurry of suits included yet another action filed by seven other former Davidians from Denver, Colorado, who were also seeking to have the property placed in a receivership.

The final witness on Thursday was, naturally, George Saether, who told the court that he had a letter showing that council members had actually been planning to form a new church before the Davidian sect was dissolved.

The following day, Mrs. Eakin admitted that the Davidian book of rules, *The Leviticus*, contained no clear-cut answer to the problem of succession and authority.

Testimony continued November 8 and 9 when witnesses included Ben and Lois Roden. At one point in the testimony, Roden said that the Lord had spoken to him while he was working under a 1936 Chrysler and said, "Brother Ben, you go to Waco and lead my people." At this point, attorney David Kultgen leaned over to Carl Anderson and said, "Carl, do you think I ought to object to it as being hearsay?"

On November 11, the jury returned its findings, which were generally favorable to the Davidians who hoped to forestall the liquidation of the final 77 acres. In March 1966, Logue entered a judgment calling for the liquidation of the assets and naming Street receiver. Seventeen of those at New Mt. Carmel—mostly Branch Davidians—appealed Logue's decision, which was upheld in June of 1968.

On June 19, 1968, the sheriff was ordered to evict Benjamin L. Roden, Lois I. Roden, and George Roden. When this eviction didn't happen, the Branch Davidians—including a number of Australians who had arrived in 1967—were again ordered to leave. Sheriff's deputies served papers to 14 of the 17, notifying them to appear once again in the 19th District Court on July 1, 1968, to show cause why they were still living at Mt. Carmel.

The following day, the 17 residents of Mt. Carmel—which still included Mr. and Mrs. Perry Jones and their growing family—filed a countersuit, claiming that they were the "joint owners" of the property and asking the court to issue an order restraining Street from evicting them from the property.

Among the Branch Davidians was a young Australian named Clive Doyle, who was the subject of an article by George Roden which claimed that as early as 1967 Doyle had been seeking to overthrow the Rodens at Mt. Carmel. Roden lamented that Doyle's soul would be forever lost "unless by some great miracle he can accept the appointment by Brother Roden of George Roden as the King of Israel to bear the dual civil and religious crown." In other words, Doyle had some major accepting to do.

Doyle's alleged subversive behavior caused George to pray the following prayer each night: "Lord, rain fire and brimstone down on Mt. Carmel Center on the beast and the False Prophet, but do not burn down the ad building to get rid of the Lucifer there if it be thy will."

A few years later, the Lord—or someone—did indeed burn down the administration building. It was, perhaps, a foreshadowing of events that would occur in the future.

[1.] These were later published as *Seven Letters to Florence Houteff and the Executive Council of the D.S.D.A. Association.*

[2.] J. R. Custer received $1,434.50. Glen Green was awarded $3,700. Saether received $7,137.60, and his wife Romana received $4,497.20. Sophia Hermanson (Florence's mother) was awarded $8,734.20. T. O. Hermanson received $7,121.20. Custer later received an additional check for $1,800 on March 5, 1962. While Mrs. Eakin (formerly Florence Houteff) received two checks, one for $5,000 and another for $12,588.80, the Branch Davidians maintained she actually took ten times that amount.

(Green said that whatever Mrs. Eakin received, she'd earned it. She'd gone there in 1935, when she was about 17, and had worked for three years for nothing before she actually started being paid.)

One of the members of the executive council, J. R. Custer, had apparently left his post on March 19, 1961, to take a position in Austin, telling the council, "...I want you to know that my present conviction is to stand for the present program that Mt. Carmel is offering, and I shall endeavor to support it in every way that I can. I have been offered an opportunity elsewhere. I feel that God is leading in that I take advantage of it. It will lead me into a field of experience where I think I can be of more value to Mt. Carmel than by staying here..."

[3.] In the following year, they moved their headquarters to Riverside, California, where they stayed until May 1970, when they moved to rural Missouri. The "new" Davidians remain closely aligned with Houteff's original vision of an agrarian society. The denomination basically follows all Seventh-day Adventist teachings and is currently headed by Jemmy E. Bingham. The group sponsors the Davidic-Levitical Institute and the Bashan School of Prophetic Theology, both in Exeter, Missouri.

Yet another group, also called the General Association of Davidian Seventh-day Adventists, has been located in Salem, South Carolina, since 1970. This group is headed by Vice-president Don Adair—since Houteff is considered the last president—who joined the Davidians in 1951.

Still another group, mostly from New York, joined with some of the South Carolina Davidians and purchased an old Presbyterian church across Mt. Carmel Drive from the original center of the compound in Waco. This group began reprinting many of Houteff's writings, including *The Symbolic Code* and *Timely Greetings* almost immediately.

[4.] Also spelled "Wolffe."

Chapter 5

Eventually, the Rodens managed to gain control of Mt. Carmel—and keep it.

The Branch Davidians believed that a vision Ben Roden had at Pentecost, 1970, marked the beginning of the "theocracy" under the laws of God on this earth—meaning that the laws of men were now invalidated. They also took this to mean that Roden was now the anointed "Antitypical David" referred to in Ezekiel 34–37.

Roden himself reinforced that notion regularly in his writings and sermons:

"Since Immanuel means Christ, 'God with us,' and The *Branch* is Christ, and since Christ is a type; therefore, The Branch message is the antitype of Christ's message.

"Now since Christ was a Davidian (Matthew 22:42) and The Branch believers are Davidians, they are therefore the antitypical Immanuels.

..."Says the prophet: 'Saviours (Branches) shall come upon the mount Zion to judge the mount of Esau.' (Obadiah 21)

"'I *am* the true vine, and my Father is the husbandman. Every branch in me that beareth not fruit he taketh away: and every branch that beareth fruit, he purgeth it, that it may bring forth more fruit. Now ye are *clean* through the *Word* which I have spoken unto you.' (John 15:1-3)

"Since all are Branches, be a real Branch by accepting the message of His new name—*Branch*, and be cleansed."

Roden's first task was to ensure that the path of succession that had bedeviled—and, in part, destroyed—the Davidians didn't equally impact the Branch. Consequently, one of his first official duties was to compose The Branch Supplement to *The Leviticus*. The *Supplement*, written in 1972, claims that while the prophecy started by V. T. Houteff ended with his death, the "harvest" had now begun and "The Branch in the time of harvest was seen by Ben L. Roden in September 1955, in fulfillment of Micah 6:9."

Roden, the divinely appointed theocratic king of the community, was now in charge of every facet of life at Mt. Carmel. And whoever succeeded Roden as president chairman of the executive council—assuming the end of the world didn't come first—must have both the Spirit of Prophecy *and* be the one "the Lord Himself names."

Then, "the chairman of the Executive Council, at the command of Heaven by the Lord Himself, transfers the office of the president to the One (Jesus the Branch) that God so names, as was the case in David and Solomon's time."

What could be easier?

Meanwhile, with the help of Perry Jones, the Branch Davidians were trying to rebuild the rich ceremonial life the Davidians had experienced at "old" Mt. Carmel. The main Branch Davidian holy day was the Jewish holiday of Passover.

The Branch Davidians, particularly Jones, consistently invited Dr. Dan McGee to join them on their feast days in the 1970s and early '80s.

"Perry invited me out there for special worship services, especially the annual Feast of Purim," McGee said. "that was a big celebration for them, bigger than Easter or Christmas in their religious calendar. They would dress the children up in Old Testament bathrobes and do the story of Esther—the Feast of Purim celebration, in which attempts to destroy God's people are overcome by God's power and God's people are victorious.

"I didn't realize it... but looking back on it now, it was a pretty militaristic happening—and in sharp contrast with the pacifist Davidian tradition. They didn't have weapons or anything, but they told a story, and the story of Esther is a pretty militaristic story of God's conquering the enemies of His people."

McGee said he'd arrive in the afternoon before the nightly pageants. All would eat together in the communal dining hall, and George Roden, a scary-looking character, was always moping around in the background.

"They never allowed me to talk with Ben Roden alone. Lois was always with him. It was very clear that she was the quick-witted one. He never gave me any answers to anything directly. She'd be the one to ask questions, penetrating questions, probing questions.

"My general impression of them both was that they were kind of paranoid. It was also clear to me that she was the power behind the throne.

A well-known Waco attorney had a slightly different assessment of the Rodens:

"Ben Roden's appearance, mannerisms—he could have been a professional man, president of a corporation. He was a fine-looking man, very impressive, very straight-forward, a nice-looking man. I never did see him when he wasn't dressed in a business suit, just like he was going to a business function. He was courteous, extremely courteous—very intelligent, I thought.

"Lois Roden was a strong woman. I always sort of visualized her as a pioneer woman. She had strong hands and she had a strong, firm conviction about things.

"They were a team. Any time they were in my office, he would take the lead on things. They never came without George. I always kind of admired that. We've all got friends that maybe had a child that had a special problem and they recognized that and they wouldn't scold him. He just never said anything when they came. He was always kind of obese, but he would just sit there and he'd quote a little Scripture. I had no idea what was wrong with him. He twitched. He had a little twitch: he'd blink his eyes and twist a little."

Ben Roden's surviving written record—if he indeed wrote most of it—is fairly similar to the writings of Houteff. But Roden had two preoccupations: the establishment of the Davidic kingdom in Israel, with himself as the ruler; and a virulent strain of anti-Catholicism.

His voluminous apocalyptic writings feature page after page of fractions of verses analyzed and translated using the same virtually unfathomable logic used by Houteff. Roden's works return over and over again to a certain underlying thesis:

"Since Inspiration says that the *Branch* is to build the temple, logic tells us that it is not the Stem—Jesse (SDA). It is not the message that was to gather the 144,000 that builds the temple, nor the Rod message (DSDA) that tells us about the Davidian kingdom and seals the 144,000, but rather, it is the Branch that marks and delivers the saints, the 144,000.

"Furthermore, Inspiration declares through the servant of the Lord: 'Who is to bring this Revival and Reformation, this great change? the *Branch*...' Joshua is well instructed that the burden and the ingenuity for building this spiritual temple belongs to Him whose name is the *Branch*. He is to grow up out of His place. To Him be the glory. He alone is to be exalted. He is to build the temple of the Lord."

To anyone with half a lick of sense, this sounds incredibly self-serving, especially since there is no way to check the references or sources of "Inspiration."

Roden's anti-Catholic bent is even more troubling, especially for a group which prided itself on accepting all creeds and nationalities. But there is precedent for it in both the writings of Ellen White and Victor Houteff.

One of Roden's more overt pamphlets was titled *We're Fed Up! Catholics Crucifying Nixon!* from 1974. The inside headline reads, "Foul Waters, The Pope's Watergate and Kennedy's Chappaquiddick."

Among Roden's claims:

"Watergate is a Catholic plot used by the Pope to cover up Kennedy's Chappaquiddick, impeach Nixon or bring him under papal control, and prepare the way for Kennedy's election to the Presidency...

"We contend that [Nixon] needs to fire the rest of the Catholics in his administration...

"We, the Branch Davidian Seventh-day Adventist Association, are the only ones who know what is at the bottom of Watergate and it is our responsibility to expose the crimes of the Vatican and Catholics in America..."

And that's one of the tamer little booklets!

When they weren't publishing their pamphlets, the Rodens continued to travel to Israel to continue their work and encourage their supporters—as finances permitted. Sometimes their supporters needed *lots* of encouragement. As early as August 1960, Ben Roden had written a letter because "there is some misunderstanding as to why Sister Benjamin Roden is in Israel... There are murmurings in our ranks that say this movement to Israel by the Adventists is just an affair fostered and controlled by one family."

Roden then recommended that no printing or reprinting of Branch studies be done in Israel without Lois Roden's supervision. He also appointed George Roden as the "overall leader at Gan Yavne."

Their earliest surviving tracts single-mindedly urged all Seventh-day Adventists, former Davidians, and new Branch Davidians to move to Israel as quickly as possible:

"If you want to be a pillar in the temple of the Lord; if you want to help proclaim the law from Zion; quickly lend your ear and open your heart to The Branch that he may 'build' (save) you..."

The continued Branch Davidian presence in Israel wasn't all milk and honey—particularly for the Israelis. An undated report from the Department of Absorption of New Immigrants of the Jewish Agency reveals a number of difficulties. At one point, the

committee called for a meeting with the Adventist families and
Lois and George Roden:

"These families have settled well, except the Roden family,
with whose adjusting a number of difficulties have arisen in
connection with their use of appliances, use of their land, etc.

"The relations are very bad... the Adventist families, with the
Rodens, who are considered leaders, do not follow the
organizational order and disobey the collective discipline essential
for the daily life of the village."

The report claims that the Adventists, under the direction of
the Rodens, refused to work with the Israeli unions, avoided
associations in the nearby village, and refused to join the medical
associations. Other difficulties involving language, citizenship, and
their relationship with other Adventists were also noted. The
Israelis concluded that assigning the Adventists to Amirim was a
mistake which would probably continue to cause friction.

According to George, all was not bliss back in Mount Carmel,
either. He writes[1] about the divisions caused by the Australian
contingent, most of whom had apparently come to the United
States looking for spouses. When one of the young men developed
a "special fondness" for Lois Roden, the male Rodens had his visa
revoked.

At some point, Lois Roden went to Israel for three years.
Apparently, that was too long for the lusty Ben Roden:

"One time before my mother came back to America, my father
was in the same room as my sister Jane," George wrote. "And
Janey was dressed in a beautiful dress, black, I think, like my
mother used to dress in. That was too much for my father and he
took out after my sister. But my sister left out of the room and
nothing ever happened. But my mother always held that against
my father and my sister, not knowing that it was really her fault
because she would not come home [no matter] how many times
that my father called her to come back.

"I told all at Mt. Carmel Center that if my wife had been away
from me that long, that I would rape every woman in the house."

It was hardly the kind of public statement people expected
from a man campaigning to be the next President of the United
States. (George claimed to have been planning his first bid for the
Oval Office since November 1974. The Branch community
indulged this fantasy, paying for numerous brochures and
pamphlets and his long campaign trips. Perry Jones even served
as his campaign secretary.)

George's rambling, populist writing and speaking style earned him no votes, access to no statewide ballots, and virtually no media coverage. He was not even admitted to the Democratic National Convention.

The next major event at Mt. Carmel came from Lois Roden, who had a vision in 1977. As she later told Mark Bonokoski of *The Toronto Sun*, the vision arose unbidden at 2 a.m. while she was studying Rev. 18:1.

"Roden looked out her bedroom window and saw, as she describes, a 'vision of a shining, silver angel flying by.

"'Nothing was said. But I knew right there the angel represented the Holy Spirit Mother.

"'It was feminine in form,' she explained. 'Until that moment, I had always thought the Holy Spirit was masculine.'"

Mrs. Roden's message became *The Living Waters Branch*. Among its many tenets was a belief that, in the Second Coming, the Messiah would reappear in female form. Mrs. Roden told interviewers she would spend seven years teaching this truth to the religious leadership of the world before she was allowed to take it to the laity. She threw herself into an intensive study of the scriptures and other source materials, including the original Greek and Aramaic. She began publishing her studies in a series of pamphlets called *The Holy Spirit, She*. Within a year, Mrs. Roden was ordained to the ministry by the Branch Davidians—but not by the Seventh-day Adventist denomination.

Perry Jones told the *Dallas Times Herald* in 1980 that Lois' message wasn't universally popular, even at Mt. Carmel:

"'It was a hard time,'" said Jones. 'She knew her husband was sitting there and she didn't know whether he was accepting it. But she had to speak the message... I thought it was blasphemy. I couldn't sleep at night."

Mrs. Roden told one newspaper, "It is just as reasonable to say our mother who art in heaven as it is to say our father who art in heaven. It's just a matter of terminology. [God] is both a female and a male image.

"My work is to bring forth the femininity of God in the Bible."

Nearly half the Branch Davidians left when Lois began preaching about the femininity of the Holy Spirit.

Mt. Carmel didn't look particularly idyllic in 1978. Some of the buildings needed paint and junked cars were scattered about.

Nevertheless, there was a waiting list to live at the center, and there were plans to redo the barracks—some of which looked ready to fall down—for future occupants, who were expected to be numerous.

Pictures of Lois Roden, several residents working in a field, a feeble-looking Benjamin Roden, then 76, shoveling oats, and a very dapper Perry Jones, dressed in a white suit with white shoes, and sitting in a rocking chair, were featured in the Waco newspaper.

Roden, now visibly weakening, was "greatly comforted" in the last year of his life by "a most precious message about the Holy Spirit" that was given to Lois. He tried to carry this truth to the elders of the Seventh-day Adventist Church in Washington, D.C. The strenuous trip may have been too much for him. He died four days after the Rodens returned to Waco.

After Ben's death, Lois Roden immediately declared 40 days of mourning, and just as immediately found prophetic "coincidences" about it:

"Elder Roden went to his rest between the two Sabbaths, the seventh-day Sabbath and the Sabbath of the last day of the Feast of Tabernacles. Likewise, Jesus died between the Passover Sabbath and the seventh-day Sabbath."

Nearly as significant was the fact that the Millerites had believed that October 22, 1844, was to have been judgment day, and that later, White had said that the cleansing of the heavenlies actually occurred on that day.

The Branch Davidians then declared that the Seventh Seal mentioned in the book of Revelation had been opened on October 22, 1978, at the death of Ben Roden.

(Later Branch Davidians, of course, would hold other interpretations of the opening of the Seven Seals.)

Lois Roden then threw herself into her new role as leader of the Branch Davidians. But she wasn't particularly interested in anointing George as the temple builder, nor did she have a desire to involve herself in the day-to-day operations of Mt. Carmel. She had been given her own prophecy and had her own agenda.

In the October 27, 1980, issue of the *Dallas Times Herald*, staff writer Mary Barrineau reported that Mrs. Roden and a small band of true believers quickly hit the road with her radical new message:

"They dogged the Pope every step of the way during his visit to America last year, this religious band led by a 64-year-old grandmother, handing out literature to all who would take it.

"They hit the Washington for Jesus rally in April, too, where Christians surrounded them on street corners, chanting 'Devil, devil, devil.'"

Barrineau quoted an unnamed SDA leader who said Mrs. Roden's concepts weren't particularly popular in his denomination, either. "Women preaching is like a dog walking on two legs. It's interesting, but it's not right."

At the 53rd Seventh-day Adventist World Conference in Dallas in April 1980, Branch Davidians tried to pass out literature to attendees. But an Adventist spokesman said that he had informed Mrs. Roden that if Branch Davidians tried to enter the convention center, security would be contacted:

Still other groups physically threatened Mrs. Roden and Jones.

On the other hand, Mrs. Roden claimed to have had a receptive audience among Jewish rabbis when she returned to the Holy Land in 1980. By April 11, 1981, she told the *Waco Tribune-Herald* that her "followers are in the thousands. We hear from Africa and India where whole denominations and conferences of churches are interested in aligning with the Branch."

In addition to the ubiquitous Jones, Mrs. Roden's most enthusiastic supporters were Canadian Gladys Ottman and the Australian Clive Doyle. When she decided to publish a magazine to support her message, she tabbed Doyle to serve as editor. Ottman, meanwhile, became her traveling companion as she spread the word across the United States and Canada.

Interestingly enough, Canadian newspapers were particularly intrigued by Mrs. Roden's message and she found a reporter willing to listen to her in nearly every town.

Mrs. Roden named her magazine *SHEkinah*, a Hebrew word meaning the presence of God in the world. From the first issue, it contained Mrs. Roden's writings, occasional editorials from Doyle, and reprints of both interviews with Mrs. Roden in the mainstream press and related articles on the significance of gender in religion.

In October 1982, Mrs. Roden left once again for Israel, but this time with an unusual request—to have her husband Ben's body buried on the Mount of Olives. Surprisingly, the Israelis granted the request.

Mrs. Roden returned to Waco in November and immediately continued her travels. An article in the December 4, 1982, *Oshawa This Week* publication shows "Living Waters Branch Bishop Lois Roden" with Gladys Ottman—characterized in the publication as a laid-off stenographer—in Oshawa. Sometime in the previous weeks, Roden had apparently been promoted to the rank of bishop.

Roden continued her barnstorming tour of Canada and in January 1983 told one newspaper that she'd heard that the Pope had made some "negative" comments about the feminine Holy Spirit.

Roden's reply? "God has news for the Pope."

Back at Mt. Carmel, trouble was brewing once again. George Roden was not used to being left behind—and had said so from the beginning. He believed he'd been groomed since infancy to become the great leader of the Branch Davidians.

He claimed he, not his mother, was to take over the leadership at Mt. Carmel after his father's death.

"I never took the leadership of the work of the Lord until the death of my Father and I did not do that until I understood what my Father told me one month before he died, that I was the Man Whose Name is the *Branch* and that it was my responsibility to rebuild the temple in Jerusalem just like Solomon was to do so at the death of his father."

But Lois had the support of most of the remaining Branch Davidians and continued her travel and writing while George remained in Waco and brooded.

As early as 1979, George had called for an election to choose the leader of Mt. Carmel. Lois and George had both lobbied hard for the position. Once again, the election results ended up in court, where Judge Bill Logue ruled for Lois Roden and enjoined George from interfering with the operation of Mt. Carmel. George immediately protested the election process *and* the judge's decision. In time, George's protests got ugly.

The Branch Davidian tax problems also got ugly. The Axtell Independent School District had traditionally never taxed Mt. Carmel, even though the compound was in their tax district. But during this time, a new appraiser reevaluated the land and decided that it was indeed taxable.

The Rodens hired lawyers, claiming it wasn't the amount of money they were protesting, but the degree of control that taxation gave the district over them.

The case ended up—once again—in Judge Bill Logue's court. George insisted on testifying with the other Branch Davidians over his lawyers' objections and launched into a wild, rambling tirade. Afterwards, Lois Roden privately asked the lawyers to see if the judge would hold her son in contempt of court. Before his trial could be held, Lois withdrew the charge, however. A few days later, Logue ruled that only certain buildings and about two acres of the property were tax-exempt.

The Branch Davidians appealed the ruling, but before the appeal process actually began, George filed a $100 million suit against his lawyer, Logue, and his own mother.

Eventually, Lois was forced to ask for a restraining order to keep George completely out of Mt. Carmel. George then fought the restraining order in court and asked the court to rule on the legitimacy of his mother's succession. George lost again.

"I moved out of Mt. Carmel Center in [August] 1979 after the court declared my mother President because of the votes she obtained by a fraudulent election of the Branch people and members of the Branch Davidian Seventh-day Adventist Association by only allowing the Branches to hear only her and not what I had to say," George later wrote. "This, and those, her so-called friends, did because they had control of the name list and the tithes and the printing presses."

Those against George were Perry Jones, Clive Doyle and his mother Edna Doyle, Catherine (Kay) Matteson, Bob and Janet Kendrick, and Raymond and Tilly Freisen.

"These united in convincing my mother that she should be president because they thoroughly detested me," George later wrote. "I had presented to the jury that I was the vice president to take over after the death of my father and that I was the heir to my father's crown of the House of David as he had shown us through prophecy and all of the Davidian and Branch Davidian literature and doctrines that had proceeded out of the Seventh-day Adventist Church."

George further claimed that on November 9, 1978, *all* Mt. Carmel Branch Davidians met and proclaimed him the new "antitypical Solomon, the Son of David."

"At the evening meeting they, the ones I mentioned above, got to my mother and had convinced her that she was to be the new president and that I should be discarded.

"So at that time began the terrible conflict between me and the so-called faithful workers in the association at the camp."

Seemingly defeated, George moved his double-wide trailer house to Bellmead. But, despite the restraining order, George kept coming back to Mt. Carmel, often allegedly threatening Lois' followers while his mother was on another of her lengthy evangelical trips. He hung around the periphery of the compound, occasionally making menacing forays into the Administration building to see his mother or look for names, addresses, or other papers.

McGee, who continued to visit Mt. Carmel through the late '70s and early '80s, said that there was an obvious tension on the grounds in those days:

"I drove up on one occasion and parked my car at the edge of the compound. Perry Jones was waiting for me and he met me and I went in and did whatever I did and Perry escorted me back to my car. As I stood by the driver's door of my car and opened it, I saw on the driver's seat a handful of pamphlets and maybe a note. Perry saw it too. He reached beyond me and took them off of the seat. He said, 'You don't want these; these are prepared by troublemakers.' There was somebody out there in the late '70s trying to get a message to me that was obviously different than the message Perry wanted me to know.

"There was always kind of a motley crew out there. And from time to time, I would see people I hadn't seen before. I know they had people in and out. They had people coming in and they were trying to proselytize. And obviously they had some divisions within their ranks."

While George was—more or less—exiled to Bellmead, a thin young man named Vernon Howell found his way to the ragged collection of shacks outside of Waco. It was an unlikely destination for the bespectacled 21-year-old with long, flowing dark hair and delusions of grandeur.

"I didn't know what went on there," he said years later. "I was just a bonehead coming in to see what was going on."

Howell's life before Mt. Carmel remains something of a mystery, despite the volumes of articles that have been written about him. He was born out of wedlock to a 15-year-old girl—Bonnie Clark—in August 1959, in Houston. The task of raising him during the first five years of his life fell to his grandmother, Erline Clark. For those five years he was by all accounts just another little boy—sweet, obedient, eager to please his family. But in his fifth year, his mother, newly married to Roy Haldeman, came to claim her son and move him to Dallas. And the sweet little boy was suddenly furious: "You are not my mother!" he screamed.

As he followed the family and bounced from school to school in Dallas, Tyler, and Chandler, Texas, Howell did nothing to distinguish himself. He didn't play football, involve himself in student politics, or do anything else that might have caused him to stand out or create expectations of future promise.

Some years, he wasn't even in the yearbooks.

Part of his backwardness may have been his dyslexia, a learning disability diagnosed when it became apparent he was not scholastically on a par with his age group.

Though several years in a Dallas program for the learning disabled later taught him to compensate, the other kids would always make fun of his disability. "Retard" was the word kids called him on the playground.

(He spoke in later years of an attempted rape by three other boys when he was seven.)

Howell developed twin fascinations in junior high school: the electric guitar and the Bible. Bonnie Haldeman said that Vernon had "memorized much of the New Testament before his 13th birthday."

Dropping out of Garland High School after the 10th grade, Howell stayed with friends and took various odd jobs—including carpentry—before ending up in Tyler, where his mother had relocated some years earlier. In time, he joined Bonnie's SDA church. He was a cocky, smart-mouthed teenager with an extensive knowledge of the Bible, and quickly became something of a pariah among the church members.

At one point, Howell told the pastor of the church that God had told him to marry his underage daughter. The pastor refused to allow this, but Howell continued to hound the family for years.

Finally, in 1981, the church voted to disfellowship Howell after a series of disruptive services where Howell was "ranting and raving."

And somehow after that, perhaps somewhat naturally, given the number of kindred spirits, Howell found his way to Waco.

With membership dwindling, Howell was welcomed with open arms, particularly by Perry Jones and Mrs. Roden. His carpentry skills were especially useful, since most of the buildings hastily constructed in 1959 were already falling apart. George, despite being officially removed from the property, was glad to have another recruit and claimed to have taken a shine to the young man as well.

But Howell's presence soon escalated tensions—again—between George Roden and almost everybody else.

At one point, George wrote that his mother's followers had him locked out of the printing shop in the Administration building:

"They had the print shop under the control of Clive Doyle

and I just went and took a nail bar and a crowbar and took the doors and the facing and the frame of the doors off the Administration building so I could come and go in the print shop as I pleased. They therefore, in the night, moved the printing presses down to Bellmead, in[to] a rented house."

George continued to prowl around the complex and eventually drove Howell out of Mt. Carmel and into a rented house in Waco with several of his friends.

At some point in 1983, Lois anointed Vernon as the next prophet, bypassing George completely. She also sent out a call to all Branch Davidians to return to Mt. Carmel to hear Howell's prophetic message. It seemed as if she was suddenly losing interest in spreading the concept of the feminine Holy Spirit. Lois' announcement enraged George.

Howell said Lois began tutoring him privately, but only because "she found I was more pliable than the others."

About this time, a young woman at Baylor University, the Reverend Marsha C. Martie, became interested in Mt. Carmel. Martie wanted to write her Master's thesis on Lois Roden's theology. Her goal was to interview Lois, but in the early days of the project, she was allowed to interview only Perry Jones.

"The first time I went out there, it was kind of a big event— they weren't letting people in then," Martie said. "I went into a big commons area. They showed me a couple of bungalow houses and a number of children. It was beginning to get dark, but when I went back out, I found that my car had been gone through. Perry said I had to leave because you never know what George [was] going to do. Perry rode to the gate with me to make sure I got out safely.

"When we got to the gate house, George came out on a three-wheeler and had a shotgun across his arms. He pulled up beside the driver's side of the car and pulled his gun on me. He wanted to know who I was. I told him, but he wouldn't believe me. He decided I was a newspaper reporter [and] that I was going to print their side of the story and not his. He was very concerned that I hear his side of the story. With the gun at my head, he told me his side of the story. I didn't hear a whole lot of that, to tell you the truth."

Despite her adventure with George Roden, Martie continued to press Jones—unsuccessfully—for a meeting with Lois Roden.

"Perry was excited that things were moving forward," Martie

said. "That something really was happening for their community. And that it was God and Vernon at the helm. When I came along, Lois had just announced Vernon would take George's place [and] George had become violent.

"Vernon had just been installed and for a long time [Perry] did not take me to see Vernon. There was no other contact than Perry. But he began to talk more about what Vernon was saying as we went along. I don't think he understood it, but he was excited about the possibility and the new prophet and that something good was going to happen."

Howell at last permitted Martie to interview him at their small rented house on Herring Avenue in Waco where he spent most of his time avoiding George. Martie eventually interviewed him several times, and found him arrogant rather than charismatic. The interviews were frustrating.

"We didn't talk, *he* did," she said. "He went on and on about Revelation. I noticed nothing connected in anybody's mind but his. To him, all Scripture [was] prophecy for his picking and determining what it meant. He alone knew. There was something horribly wrong if you didn't agree. There was no following him; he was all over the place [but] he clearly had stepped fully into the position of being a prophet."

During Martie's interviews, the Branch Davidians found themselves embroiled in still more legal action. George had begun proceedings to have himself reinstated as head of the group and to have the assets, including the land, turned over to him. Also during this time, the state again started dunning the Branch Davidians for back taxes.

In the midst of the turmoil, the administration building was destroyed by fire. Howell and others claimed that George Roden started the fire, and Jones later said that God started it. Years later, George produced "proof" in the form of a written confession, allegedly by Clive Doyle, that Doyle had started the fire.

On January 18, 1984, Howell married Perry Jones' fair-haired daughter, Rachel, who was just 14. This happened only a few weeks after Rachel had said she "couldn't stand" Vernon. Perry Jones officiated. Four years later, according to Perry's wife, Mary Jones, Howell began having sex with Rachel's 12-year-old sister Michele. Howell would later have three daughters by Michele, in addition to two children by Rachel.

Rachel knew of Vernon's other wives—and that he fathered their children "to save the world." But even though other "wives" and affairs would come and go, Rachel remained. Rachel was the only member of Howell's flock who dared speak back to him, who could cut him off in a conversation, who wouldn't sit in rapt attention every time he spoke.

George Roden claimed[2] that Howell and Rachel went to the Holy Land in 1985 so that she could have their first baby—if it were a boy—in Bethlehem. Then he would be the Messiah mentioned in Micah 5. But the Howells returned before the baby was born because, Roden claimed, they were evicted from their apartment in Jerusalem.

George knew about Rachel, but what he didn't know was that Howell was turning his not inconsiderable charm on George's mother, Lois. According to Marc Breault (pronounced "Bro"), a former Branch Davidian who later provided much of the information used in the various federal indictments against Howell, Howell openly bragged of his seduction of the 67-year-old Lois Roden.

Howell told Breault that the relationship was to fulfill the prophecy of Isa. 8:3[3], but others in the compound believed that the relationship was strictly Howell's way of strengthening his hold over the Branch Davidians, much as he had married Rachel Jones to cement his relationship with Perry Jones.

George Roden said that his sister Jane in California was the first to suspect that Howell was involved with their mother. When Jane would call Mt. Carmel around midnight, Howell would answer the phone, even though the lone compound telephone was by Lois Roden's bed. When this happened often enough, Jane decided to return to Waco.

George was in San Diego, California, at the time, continuing his latest campaign for the presidency. He returned to Mt. Carmel in time to hear Howell's morning message on that fateful day:

"Vernon was giving the lectures on new stuff he was hatching up and I would not go along with it, but listened anyway to see what he had," George wrote. "It seemed that all the group there was taking it in, hook, line, and sinker.

"Then that night, my mother told my sister that she just had to tell someone that Vernon and she were living together—and my sister told her that she knew already. So she told me. I confronted Vernon Howell with the proposition that he would have to marry Mother, to not allow a reproach to be on the association and the family. He said that because she told him that, she and me and my sister and all the Roden family would have to die in the slaughter of Ezek. 9:1-5.

"So there began the death decree against me and the Roden family and my mother by Vernon Wayne Howell on the night of January 13, 1984."

Howell denied Roden's allegations about Lois Roden:

"Twice a day George was coming to Bible studies and wearing his .357 Magnum gun. When I came back from Israel, he had a gun and his sister had a gun. George wanted to be a Messiah. What we assumed to be a mental defect was actually much more radical on his part."

Among those who met Howell during this period was Baylor University professor Alan Robb. One of Robb's English students wanted to do a research paper on the Branch Davidians, so Robb escorted her to Mt. Carmel Center to interview two Davidian women. Once at the compound, Howell introduced himself to Robb, who found him pleasant and articulate:

"He was not the least bit scary in any way. He was a very, very impressive character, very sure of himself, very knowledgeable in a knee-jerk way about the Scriptures. He had the capacity for making you feel like you were the center of the universe when he talked to you, that you were the only thing that counted, that you were very important to him and to whatever he was pitching …I had no trouble understanding how he was able to control or attract people."

Howell worked hard to convert Robb during the course of their 30-minute conversation.

"It was a very interesting pitch," Robb said. "It wasn't so much based on knowledge of the Scriptures as it was on absolute sureness of mission and absolute certainty of being right about it.

"He was the kind of personality that would indeed attract people. I've been around this sort of thing all my life and I understand how it works very well, and he had a great talent for it… He had a real capacity for reading people fairly rapidly."

A letter from Vernon Howell to George Roden on Living Waters Foundation letterhead sheds light on this facet of Howell's character. The letter is dated January 28, 1984. Despite the bad blood between the two men, Howell opens his letter, "How are you doing? I know that you are going through some very hard times. I also know why. *I miss Mt. Carmel so much.*"

Howell then launches into an impassioned point-by-point explanation of Revelation 14. It is the first-known written example of his developing theology:

"Revelation 14 brings to view the 144,000 standing on Mt. Sion with the Lamb. *They* are learning the *(as it were)* new song. They have one seal in their foreheads *(Father's name)*. This designates that they have received the seal of the Sabbath. But notice George, they only have the Sabbath seal. *Where* is the seal of New Jerusalem, or Christ's new name? The truth is, they do not have them. That's right George, these 144,000 are saved and yet they do not have all the seals. This can only mean that your teaching closing probation for the Adventists must be wrong. If the 144,000 can be saved with just one seal *(Sabbath)*, then don't you think others can too? The Sabbath seal was brought by Sister White, the Kingdom seal by Victor Houteff, and the New Name seal by Ben Roden. So, as you should be able to plainly see, the 144,000 do not have to have Bro. Houteff's or Bro. Roden's messages to be saved. This is presented to you, *George*, so you can consider your ways. You need also to put away your guns. There is no one at Mt. Carmel that wants to hurt you, and besides if *God* is for you, who can be against you?

"*Now look!* As the 144,000 stand on Mt. Sion, they learn all the other truths that they need. Revelation Chapter 15 brings to view the harpers of Revelation Chapter 14. These harpers are the wave sheaf. They are the ones who get the victory first. They teach the 144,000 the song of Moses *(Rod-Kingdom)* and the song of the Lamb *(Christ's new name—Inspiration)*. Isn't this wonderful, George? I could go into greater detail, but for now it is better not to.

"You also know that the angel of Revelation 14:17 is what I claim to be. I teach, in the name of the Lord, that this *angel* takes the title David. The reason is that David was the seventh son of Jesse. Revelation Chapter 10 tells us that when the seventh angel shall begin to sound, the mystery of *God* should be finished. One of these mysteries is that ever since 1955, the Lord has been gathering the Wave Sheaf. All of Revelation Chapter 14 is for the gathering of the Wave Sheaf first. Then the rest of the work is finished in power.

"Let me make this last point. Verse 7 of Revelation 10 says, 'But in the days of the voice of the seventh angel, when he shall begin to sound...' The word voice shows that the angels speaks to the people before he sounds his trumpet. That is why I teach, George, that this message hasn't really started yet. *God* is giving the Branches every possible way to be saved. This is the probationary year for the Branches. Oh George! I hope that these points will do you some good. May God help you to see. I could give ten times more proof than what this letter contains, but would that do you any good? Please consider the fate of Saul.

"With love,

V. T. H.

V. W. H."

Obviously unmoved by Howell's plea, George Roden and his few followers continued their systematic pogrom of Howell's followers at Mt. Carmel. In June 1985, George, who was now in control of the mailing lists, called for another election. This time, he won, changed the name of Mt. Carmel to Rodenville, and began to make a sweep of all remaining dissidents:

"Rodenville is now clear of the vile V. W. H. group, except for one man and his wife, and they are moving, they say tomorrow, the 17th of March, 1985," Roden wrote in *The Red Heifer*. "We gave them a paper to sign that they would recognize the management of Rodenville and help bear their share of the burden financially here, and they all said *no*, they would not sign the paper, we want to move. So they all have moved, except one, and it was their own choice and not a forced move by us.

"The vile Vernon and his gang want to try to use Sr. Roden to get back into Mt. Carmel Center, Rodenville; man that is the reason they are trying to help her retain her Presidency even after the people have voted to have me take care of the property and preserve it for their benefit.

"Sr. Roden said that she and I would have to put them off the property before Passover because V. W. H. was sending their people secretly on the property with Perry Jones', Raymond Friesen's, Bob Kendrick's and Kay Matteson's help to take over the property illegally and by violence. That is the reason we keep our arms ready because they say that they are going to use the most drastic measures to take over the property.

"May God the *Branch* guide you in your life and works."

The departing families claimed that Roden stood over them with an Uzi, but George denied ever brandishing a weapon:

"There was no chasing them away at gunpoint, but I did carry my gun at all times because of the death threats of Vernon Howell against me and my family and to keep the peace in the camp, for I had said there was not going to be raping going on in this camp any longer and they got the message."

Taking over the compound was one of the highlights of George Roden's life. He lost no time in setting up a system of rules and regulations for Rodenville—most of which were designed to consolidate his rule.

The "Resident Occupancy Agreement at Rodenville Branch Center" contains some revealing listings. Besides the usual rules governing Sabbath-keeping, pork-eating, speed limits, and the mandatory $20-per-month water, sewage, and trash-service fee, one rule barred Vernon Howell and Charles Pace from the property.

But Howell wasn't without a backup plan. First he moved his group of about 40 followers to the small Central Texas town of Mexia for a month. While there, they scoured Central and East Texas for a possible camp and, through Branch Davidian connections, found a secluded clearing in the piney woods near Palestine. Howell reportedly was pleased with both the biblical connections of the name and the relative inaccessibility of the land. The entrance to what Perry Jones called their "temporary base" was an unmarked path off a red-dirt county road.

Two *Waco Tribune-Herald* reporters, Alan Nelson and Sandra Gines, traveled to the wooded setting, and said the little compound of ramshackle plywood boxes, a tar-paper shack, and several rusted buses looked like a '60s hippie retreat. There were five-by-seven plywood boxes with small wood-burning stoves. Toilet facilities consisted of individual plastic buckets. Jones admitted that the winters had not been pleasant: "Our heads are warm, but our feet are cold."

About 20 children, aged 3 through 16, were wandering through the rugged campsite. School, usually held in a bus without wheels, was taught by Sherri Jewell. The grounds were littered with junked vehicles, couches arranged around burned out campfires, weight-lifting equipment, scattered toys, and cooking utensils.

And as before, Howell's followers continued to observe Davidian rules regarding vegetarianism, Sabbath-keeping—and hour after hour of intensive Bible study, always led by Howell.

But while the Palestine campground appeared harmless and just a little off-kilter to outsiders, others would later report an entirely different scenario, one that would have profound implications in the years to come.

It was in the camp near Palestine that, for the first time, Vernon Howell had complete, unchallenged control of his little band of followers. Marc Breault, the computer whiz/keyboard player from California, was among those who joined Howell in East Texas. But he saw a darker side of the intense young man. Breault told of eight-month-old babies beaten by Howell until their bottoms bled, for crying during Bible studies. He told of Howell openly bragging of sleeping with uncomprehending preteen girls and adding the wives and daughters of his followers to his harem. In fact, Breault independently confirmed many of the claims originally made against Howell by George Roden some years earlier.

Howell dominated every facet of life in Palestine, according to Breault and another of Howell's "wives," Robyn Bunds. With no accountability to anyone but himself, Howell's rule became harsher, his teachings more radical, his tactics more confrontational. In time, he began to cast his eye covetously back towards Mt. Carmel Center. While George Roden had won for the moment, Howell believed he had only to be patient and wait for the opportune moment to make his triumphant return.

As was true for much of George Roden's life, his triumph turned to disaster. Buoyed by his successful eviction of Howell, he continued to appeal various cases through the Texas judicial system. By 1985, he'd become such a nuisance at the McLennan County Courthouse that many lawyers refused to work for him.

Then, on March 28, 1985, Lois Roden filed in the 19th Judicial District Court of McLennan County to hold George Roden in contempt of court for violating the terms of the permanent injunction filed against him in June 1979.

Serving as his own attorney, George filed a lengthy response to the motion, claiming that *he* was the real president of the association, quoting scripture, Victor Houteff, Ellen White, and his father, accusing his lawyer of misleading him, Howell "and his crew of thugs" of abusing Lois Roden, and his mother of systematically starving his family while spending "$100,000 on registered quarter horses." Roden also alleged that Howell had raped his mother, burned down the Administration building and the peach orchard, and brainwashed his mother into saying that she wanted George off the property when, in reality, she wanted him to stay on the property and defend her from the sex fiend, Vernon Howell.

Interestingly, Roden made several new accusations that were later echoed and supported by a host of Howell's accusers:

"This V. W. Howell is a cult leader who uses hypnotism, mind-altering drugs and sex as a means to seduce people. He restricts their intake of food and all of them have lost weight, especially my mother. Although the efforts of my sister and I have been untiring, she has improved somewhat, but is still under his satanic spell. The Lord and I was [sic] responsible for kicking him off the property and maintaining order here to preserve the property. He says that he owns all the members' property, including their wives and daughters and that he can have them anytime he wishes and no one can say a word about it.

"He always has a so-called prophecy from the Bible when he wants to seduce a woman and that is the way he defiled my mother and says that the scriptures are responsible, that is, God is responsible.

"He boasts of his knowledge of chemicals and of his life in the drug culture... that he would ruin the Roden name and I still believe he was sent here by the General Conference of Seventh-day Adventists goons to destroy Mt. Carmel completely.

"His tactics are to keep the people under his control by keeping them up all hours of the night and deprive [sic] them of their sleep (even the old people) and then the food to scarceness and drilling them hour upon hour."

Court records show that between May 24, 1985, and September 5, 1985, alone, Roden was involved in an incredible 43 legal documents that were filed, exchanged, served, dismissed, and amended. During that time, George, serving as his own attorney, filed against virtually everybody. Roden's briefs are filled with specific citations and lengthy legal opinions, in addition to his own florid, often grammatically incorrect charges and claims. They are also filled with venomous profanity and threats against everybody from Catholics to lawyers to Communists.

In one appeal that included more than 80 typewritten pages, Roden's spleen spilled over from Howell onto Judge Walter Smith. In the appeal, Roden accused Howell of having three wives—two of whom were aged 14, and one of whom was pregnant—before he impugned Smith.

Perhaps George was right in another of his accusations. Perhaps Vernon Howell and Charles Pace did kill Lois Roden. Perhaps she was simply worn out from a lifetime of working long hours without pay, of spreading two unpopular messages, of living in often Spartan, sometimes primitive, conditions. Perhaps, as George Roden's second wife, Amo, says, Lois had been diagnosed with terminal breast cancer. Or perhaps it was the chaos and lawsuits of the previous few years. Whatever the cause or causes, Lois Roden died on November 10, 1986.

Lois was given a small obituary with sketchy personal information. The most interesting section was the second sentence: "Services will be held in Jerusalem, Israel."

Apparently, that's exactly what happened—and with unseemly speed. The late Mrs. Roden was whisked away, apparently without anyone seeing the deceased or her medical record.

The loss of his mother was too much for Roden. His next series of appeals and countersuits became increasingly frenzied and abusive, culminating with the now legendary—among Texas legal circles, at least—No. C 6692, dated September 19, 1987. In it, Roden requested a petition hearing before the Supreme Court of Texas regarding his ongoing tax dispute with the Axtell Independent School District and the McLennan County Independent School and Appraisal District.

Roden's two-page direct appeal starts off innocently enough, digresses into a discussion of the Texaco/Pennzoil case, touches on Mt. Carmel's tax problems, then gets nasty in a hurry. It is filled with expletives and dire predictions of God's judgments being visited on the Supreme Court.

It then ends with, "Thank God we still remain by his grace."

Not surprisingly, Roden's motion did not sit well with the Texas Supreme Court. "Freedom of speech is something that needs to be protected, and I'm all for freedom of speech," Justice William Kilgarlin told the Associated Press. "However, there is a provision for unauthorized practice of law.

"As to the language in the motion... the remedy of contempt is always available."

Roden had still other problems. By May 1987, 35 people were living in the Branch Davidian community, concentrating on growing organic fruits and vegetables, studying the Bible, and living in harmony with nature. However, they had neglected to pay their taxes since 1968, and owed McLennan County $40,175.85 and the Axtell Independent School District another $22,484.99—a total of $62,660.84.

If the back taxes were not paid, McLennan County sheriffs would sell the property on the courthouse steps in January 1988. By late 1987, Roden had almost no money, few followers, mounting debts, and an angry Texas Supreme Court justice on his trail. His world, his plans of leading the 144,000 to rebuild the temple in Jerusalem, his very life, were crashing around his ears.

There must be some way to regain his wayward flock in Palestine, some way to prove that he—not "Vermin" Howell—was the true Branch.

He needed something so potent, something so powerful, that it would break Howell's mind control over his former followers and send them rushing back to Waco.

He needed a resurrection.

[1.] *The Demise of Antitypical Lucifer in the Branch Kingdom.*
[2.] In an article titled "The Red Heifer."
[3.] "And I went unto the prophetess, and she conceived, and bare a son. Then said the Lord to me, call his name Maher-shalal-hash-baz."

Chapter 6

What happened next is bitterly disputed. What it boils down to is that Roden tried to resurrect Anna Hughes. (Roden denied this, saying he was simply moving all the caskets from the makeshift cemetery to consecrated ground next to the chapel, when his bulldozer broke down and he couldn't finish the job. So he put Anna's casket in the chapel.)

Resurrection or accident, the Palestine Davidians were aware of Hughes' disinterred body. Howell's followers were enraged at Roden's actions. Perry Jones had an infant son buried at the makeshift cemetery.

Roden had given Howell the excuse he needed to retake Mt. Carmel.

Meanwhile, Roden claimed that the remaining families at Rodenville had received "threatening" letters from Howell during the last week of October. Fearing an assault, he told *Tribune-Herald* reporter Drew Parma, he promptly armed himself and his followers.

"'When they sent that letter out, I knew they were coming. They sent an article removing me as trustee; now they've come to finish the job and remove me from the land,' Roden said."

Although the families in Palestine were still living in unheated boxes, Howell bought matching camouflage fatigues for seven of his men and augmented their existing store of weapons with an Israeli semi-automatic machine gun.

Howell's plan was to sneak into the compound in broad daylight, dressed in camouflage and armed to the teeth; waltz past Roden, his followers, and a pack of noisy dogs; open the casket, take photographs of the corpse of the unfortunate Miss Hughes; then calmly stroll out again.

By this point, none of Howell's followers felt secure enough to identify the flaws in their master's plan, and blindly followed orders. So in the early afternoon of Tuesday November 3, 1987, Howell and his men drove up to Rodenville and attempted to carry out the plan.

Only Roden and maintenance man Donald Williams were on the grounds when they arrived. Roden ducked behind a tree; Williams dove behind a nearby automobile.

Within seconds the air was filled with hundreds of rounds of ammunition. Nonetheless, Roden managed to hold the eight intruders at bay. The tree—which was slightly narrower than George's mammoth girth—splintered under dozens of bullets, but held.

The wild gunfire continued for 45 minutes. Nine McLennan County sheriff's units responded to the shooting, accompanied by two Department of Public Safety units. The 11-vehicle convoy arrived with sirens screaming and lights flashing.

When the smoke and dust had cleared, all 10 participants were still standing. Roden's right hand had been wounded slightly, but otherwise not a single bullet had hit its mark on either side. (Roden was treated and released from a Waco hospital.)

Howell and his men waved happily at the oncoming officers and appeared to be genuinely confused when they were promptly disarmed, handcuffed, and whisked to the McLennan County Jail.

Deputies seized 12 guns—including a machine gun and several .357 Magnums and semi-automatic rifles—along with loads and loads of ammunition.

Howell, aged 28, six of his followers from Palestine, and David Michael Jones of Waco were charged with attempted murder. Bond was set at $50,000 each by Justice of the Peace Alan Mayfield.

A dapper older man with slicked-back white hair approached reporters at Mt. Carmel and explained that Roden had illegally forced them off the property at gunpoint. Perry Jones was not charged in the shootout, despite his being at the crime scene. Instead, he patiently tried to rationalize the presence of eight heavily armed men in camouflage. Since the allegedly exhumed body was not found on the property that day, Jones faced an uphill task. Still, he told Parma that the eight men were only armed because of Roden's bad reputation:

"We felt that going onto Mount Carmel unarmed is something you don't do."

Within a week, Branch Davidians living in Palestine and elsewhere had raised bail for Howell and one of his men. Bail on the other six was lowered to $20,000 or $30,000.

In the days following the shooting, members of the Palestine Davidians somehow found the money to pay the back taxes owed on Mt. Carmel Center. They also asked Judge Logue to enforce the various restraining orders he had issued against Roden over the years.

Roden reveled in the media attention. He roared to all who would listen that the eight were connected with the Palestine Liberation Organization and that the CIA and the FBI had told him to wear a bulletproof vest for protection. Roden confidentially told reporter LaMarriol Smith that Howell and his men were sneaking on to Rodenville to help fulfill the prophecy of Ezekiel 9:

"They think it is the holy war they have to wage against everybody."

"They were coming to kill me and they knew I'd kill them," Roden told reporters Nelson and Gines. "What you have with Khomeini against Israel, you got [in] Vernon Howell against me."

A week after the shootout, Amo Bishop Roden, Roden's second wife—since Carmela, his first wife, had never returned from a trip to Israel—sent a letter to Branch Davidians everywhere:

"Obviously life has been exciting here. As George says, 'The wrath of men shall praise God and the remainder shall He restrain.' Amen!

"George sustained three flesh wounds to his right hand and a puncture wound and powder burns to his chest. A bullet fragment in his chest was originally overlooked...

"George says to say that the battle is waxing hotter and we can see it's a real battle, good and bad angels in the form of men of war. We believe that this episode is the beginning of God's deliverance during this great time of Jacob's trouble, which will finally culminate in the completion of the deliverance and the special resurrection of God's saints.

"We have seven families here, we're being bombarded by champions out of hell on every side, but the Lord is still in control. Micah 5 says that the seven shepherds and the eighth principle man, the Messiah, at Rodenville are raised up against the Assyrian when he walks in our borders and treads in our palaces. The scriptures say that the eighth principle man, the Messiah, will maintain the peace and remain in control when this event happens and will be the peace officer."

Roden said that Howell and his men congregated at the foundation of the charred ruins of the Administration building and launched their assault from there:

"When I arrived at Brother and Sister Roden's house armed with a semiautomatic Uzi carbine, I pinned all eight of them down in a 45-minute gun battle in which 200 to 300 rounds of ammunition were fired," Amo said.

Later in the letter, Amo adds a more personal note:

"This threat to our community has washed away our differences and brought us together in our determination that the Branch Center survive. It is your home as well, and frankly, we need both guns and butter to fight the wicked. George is sure of the Lord's influence on your hearts to support the work, even at a great sacrifice as we are all sacrificing here with the grinding of our noses in the dirt with abject poverty.

"I'm sure that our efforts together will conquer all the forces of hell and set up God's kingdom."

If Roden was busy, Howell was busier still, making frequent trips to California to further his connections in the music industry. Howell fancied himself a singer/songwriter/guitarist and was already beginning to spend thousands of dollars on expensive musical and audio equipment.

Perry Jones told Nelson and Gines that he believed that Howell was a major talent.

"Believing that the Kingdom of Heaven is on the horizon, the Branch Davidians are pushing their evangelistic efforts," the two wrote. "They believe music will be the vehicle of enlightenment. They have opened a music studio in Waco to make an album under 'Cyrus Productions,' and they hope to do videos.

"'The whole world's going to hear about it, and it's going to be through music,' Jones said."

While his fellow Branch Davidians continued to shiver by kerosene lamps in uninsulated shacks, Howell threw himself into work in his studio. With a group of Waco musicians, he quickly recorded a song titled "Mad Man in Waco" and released it in both 45 and cassette formats, allegedly in hopes of raising bail for the other six from the proceeds. "Copywright [sic] 1987 Cyrus Productions," the song's lyrics have an eerily prophetic bent. While Howell is actually writing about Roden, the lyrics seem, in retrospect, to have a strange resonance for a later time. About a mad man worshipping Baal, the song is also a plea for the sheriff—as well as the Lord—to help those who are risking their lives for the Lord.

Not surprisingly, few copies were sold in Waco-area record stores and Howell's followers languished in a jail a little while longer. Probably the major significance of the recording was Howell's choice of "Cyrus" as a title, since the Greek word for "Cyrus" is "Koresh."

At the end of November, Roden responded to a letter from three Branch Davidian women living in Redlands, California, who obviously questioned George closely about the events of the previous weeks:

"To begin with, my mother was not deceived, she was raped at gunpoint..."

Roden spends the rest of the letter defending his marriage to Amo with increasingly graphic descriptions of sex acts between God and the Virgin Mary. The "marriage" by George and Amo Paul Bishop Apps was done by "contract" on October 23, 1987, and the contract very clearly left open the possibility of future wives in the Roden household.

In one of Roden's "Rough Winds" teaching lessons published at this time, the language and descriptions are quite literally pornographic as Roden portrays cosmic religious sex acts—all in defense of his taking a second "bride."

In the weeks that followed, two *Tribune-Herald* reporters— Tommy Witherspoon and Mark England—who would play a significant role in the events of 1993, began covering the various Branch Davidian legal proceedings. Witherspoon, a physically imposing former football player well-liked in McLennan County courtrooms, police stations, and law offices; and England, a quiet, introverted, methodical reporter with a passion for facts.

One of 'Spoon's (as he was universally called) first stories was coverage of Waco lawyer Gary Coker's attempt on January 21, 1988, to have all charges against the eight men—all of whom had long since been freed on bond—dismissed by claiming that Roden was mentally unstable. Coker entered as evidence some of Roden's expletive-filled legal briefs—including the famed appeal before the Texas Supreme Court.

Coker further claimed that the charges against his clients were "vague and general."

The Branch Davidians quickly embraced Coker, whose carefree demeanor and easy-going style suited Howell perfectly. Soon Howell and the others were frequent visitors to Coker's downtown Waco office.

McLennan County prosecutor El Hadi T. Shabazz, on the other hand, probably wished he'd never heard of George Roden. Other lawyers privately wondered if Roden would do the state's case more harm than good if allowed to testify.

Roden had still other things to worry about. Back in January 1987, George had contested his brothers' appointment as administrators of his mother's will. Not surprisingly, Roden lost the case and two appeals.

Roden's next blow came on March 21, 1988, when he was served with a contempt citation signed by Judge Logue for violating restraining orders in continuing to live at Mt. Carmel.

Then U.S. District Judge Walter S. Smith, Jr., delivered the crowning blow, sentencing George to six months in jail for continuing to file expletive-filled motions despite orders to cease and desist. Witherspoon reported that Smith ordered Roden jailed after finding him in contempt of court:

"Before the ruling, Roden, a former presidential candidate, launched into a rambling narration in which he quoted the Bible, called Pope John Paul II a communist, said a conspiracy led to Richard Nixon's resignation, called the judicial system an 'American Gestapo' and said Smith deserves a deadly plague for his rulings against Roden in several civil proceedings."

Four federal officials handcuffed Roden and led him away.

Smith's sentencing pushed Howell's trial to April. It also opened the way for the triumphant return of Vernon Wayne Howell to Mt. Carmel.

On March 23, 1988, Alan Nelson reported that's exactly what happened, only the procession from Palestine was not led by Howell, but by the silver-haired patriarch of the Davidians, Perry Jones.

The procession was met at the gate by a defiant Amo Bishop Roden.

"I'm angry," she told Nelson, "These people are trespassing. I don't understand what's going on."

At one point, baited by some of Howell's followers, she reached for a gun in the back of a pickup truck. Roden's friend Don Williams and Nelson grabbed the gun first and Nelson locked it in the cab of the pickup.

(During an earlier interview with George, Roden had stuck a handgun in Nelson's face on several occasions and the reporter was not in the mood for a repeat performance.)

The rest of the Branch Davidians ignored Mrs. Roden, crawled under the barbed wire surrounding the compound, and inspected their former homes. Some had been in Palestine since 1985.

"It's beautiful!" Jones shouted. "It has all worked out by the will of God."

But Nelson wrote that there were few shouts of praise when the Branch Davidians actually entered the tiny homes. Many of the wood-frame homes on the property were completely trashed, the roofs on a number of them had caved in, and all were badly neglected:

"Hogs wouldn't even go in my home," said church member William Kendrick. "But I'm glad to be back. I lived there 21 years. It's home."

As for Anna Hughes, Jones said they found her casket in an open shed on the back side of the property and were making plans to bury it again.

Roden promptly filed a handwritten $15 million damage suit against Sheriff Harwell and the sheriff's department, alleging that *they* were the ones who sent Howell and his men, not the Seventh-day Adventists or the PLO. The suit was written on the back of "Roden for President" campaign stationary and pages from Roden's 1986 tax return.

The attempted murder trial of Howell and his "Mighty Men" was finally set for April 11, 1988. Roden, still sitting in prison, told Witherspoon that he could have killed Howell "at least seven times" during the shootout, but chose not to." And besides, prison wasn't so bad: "After all, Paul did more preaching from prison than he did anywhere else."

Roden said he had no intention of apologizing to Judge Smith:

"I am not interested in apologizing unless the judge is willing to repent."

The same day, Shabazz proclaimed Roden perfectly competent to testify. Vernon Howell, on the other hand, had his doubts:

"There is a thing called right and wrong and the Bible is the guideline for right and wrong. But if there is a God in Heaven, and I know there is, George will do what he has to do, and God will do what He has to do. But that is not to say that we are going to be ostriches and stick our heads in the sand, either. We have placed the situation in God's hands."

Howell's lawyer was busy in the final days before the trial. Coker instructed the Branch Davidians not to rebury Anna Hughes because he believed that the casket might be used as evidence in the attempted murder trial.

On the day before the trial, Amo Roden said she visited George, her "husband by contract," in the McLennan County Jail:

"I found him incoherent and was unable to hold a conversation with him. I asked him what was wrong with him and he did not notice my question. I asked him again what was wrong with him and he continued to talk and did not answer my question. I asked him a third time quite forcefully what was wrong with him and this time he answered that the generic medicine given to him to control his Tourette syndrome had given him a headache and that he had been given Tylenol for the headache, but it hadn't worked.

"I did not attempt further communication with him in the remainder of the 15-minute visit because it was too difficult."

If the deck wasn't already stacked against Roden, Tourette syndrome meant he was fighting aces with deuces. Tourette's is a neurological disorder that begins in childhood and can manifest itself with single or multiple tics, ranging from uncontrolled blinking to grimacing and shoulder shrugging. The tics may also worsen with age.

To make matters worse, many Tourette sufferers are also susceptible to a brutal array of vocal tics, including grunting, sniffing, shouting—even barking. But the most insidious aspect of the disease is that about half of all patients develop "coprolalia"—compulsive swearing!

The symptoms of Tourette syndrome wax and wane through a patient's life, but if Roden's medication were altered, or administered erratically—or, possibly, not administered—while in jail, he was simply in no condition to testify in a court of law.

When the trial finally began, Shabazz said that Howell and his men were part of a paramilitary group that went to Rodenville to "assassinate" Roden:

"The evidence will show there were 14 to 18 bullet holes in the tree that were so deep that they could not be dug out. The evidence will show that if you had removed that tree, George Roden would not be here today."

McLennan County Sheriff's Deputy Kenneth Vanek told the jury that he believed the department saved George Roden's life the day he was attacked by eight men carrying high-powered rifles:

But another deputy, Dan Weyenberg, testified to Roden's bad reputation, noting that he often carried guns, although those guns were legal.

For the first time, Howell took the stand. He'd filled the courtroom with his followers, including women, children, and babies. There was a constant stream of traffic in and out of the courtroom. Among the modestly dressed women, one stood out even without makeup—the exotically beautiful Robyn Bunds, whose flashing black eyes and long black hair made her a popular target of newspaper and television photographers in the hallways outside the courtroom.

One incident in particular stuck in the minds of reporters and other observers at the trial. Before the trial even started, Judge Fitts asked if there were any witnesses in the courtroom who needed swearing in. Though a buzz went through the crowd, nobody moved.

Howell's lawyer Coker repeated the question. Again, no one moved.

Finally, Howell got up and stood by Coker:

"'It's all right, you've done nothing wrong,'" he said, raising a hand to the crowd. 'Stand.'"

The witnesses all stood in unison.

Dressed in a natty suit and smiling frequently at the jury with his deep dimples, Howell made a marked contrast to the twitching, blustering Roden. Roden's beer belly and threadbare, outdated clothes, coupled with the physical effects of Tourette syndrome, made him a much less sympathetic figure.

Howell, a superb manipulator of people, was the very voice of reason on the stand:

"We went over on the 2nd and the casket was gone," he told the jury. "That's when the longest night began, contemplating how to find the casket. As far as we knew, it was in the city dump. We went on the property trying to find the casket. We had no intention of shooting anyone. The guns were strictly for self-defense."

The second day of the trial, Sheriff's Department deputy Lt. Elijah Dickerson testified that he believed Howell and his followers had tried to "manipulate" the department into getting Mt. Carmel back for them.

Shabazz entered Howell's munitions—which included 2,996 rounds of ammunition for the five assault rifles—into evidence.

Coker offered a spirited defense:

"The only way George held the land was that he terrified everyone. These people are not violent people. They work, farm, and pray a lot. They may have wanted the sheriff's department to arrest George so they could peacefully retake their land, but it was because they didn't want to confront him."

But the following day, Thursday, April 14, some of Roden's children and friends testified that he was a generous man who gave them free rent and food. England reported that the witnesses testified that they "rarely" ever saw Roden even carry a gun.

On Friday, prosecuting attorneys Shabazz and Denise Wilkerson did what most Waco lawyers expected them to do—they rested their case without calling Roden to testify.

But Howell had his own idea of why the prosecution rested:

"I know why [Roden] wouldn't testify, he had 15–20 years of bad reputation built up before I even came along in 1981. Everyone who has been young and wanted to help, he's run off. How? George communicated. Sign language, you know."

Coker jumped at the opportunity to attack Roden's character. Catherine Mattson, Lois Roden's longtime secretary, testified that she once heard Roden pray to himself at the 1984 World Congress of Branch Davidians in Waco, saying, "In the name of George B. Roden, amen."

Edna Doyle, Clive Doyle's mother, testified that Roden once shot the tires of a bus carrying former residents when they tried to enter Mt. Carmel for a visit in 1984.

Martin, a lawyer from Pennsylvania who was not licensed to practice in Texas, told England that other lawyers had refused to help them evict Roden in the past because they were afraid of being sued:

"When George Roden brings litigation, he sues everything but the doorknobs on the courthouse."

Shabazz tried to rally, asking Jones where a group living at subsistence level in Palestine could come up with $3,000 worth of guns and, most importantly, $62,000 to pay the back taxes on Mt. Carmel. Jones responded that church finances were "up and down" and that an unnamed "Hawaiian couple" had paid the back taxes following the November shootout.

When Roden finally did testify, the Branch Davidians made a show of taking their children out of the courtroom, claiming they didn't want their children to hear Roden's colorful language. On the stand, Roden basically repeated his previous assertions, although he did admit, for the first time, that he had tried three times to resurrect Hughes' body. He also, in an offhand manner, admitted that he was indeed the Messiah.

The trial finally went to the jury after both sides made typically melodramatic appeals. Wilkerson said Howell's plan was to force Roden into a confrontation, then claim they shot him in self-defense:

"They came armed with the same weapons, so none of them would have to take the responsibility for the shots that killed George Roden."

Shabazz characterized Coker's arguments as the "rabid dog defense," making Roden look so bad that the shooting was justified.

As for Coker, his impassioned appeal included references to

the "type" of people living at the self-styled Rodenville, mentioning by name an ex-convict named Donnie Joe Harvey, along with Roy (Boy) Wells, another resident who had been charged with conspiracy to manufacture methamphetamines in connection with an Elm Mott drug raid.

While waiting for the jury to reach its verdict, Howell told England in the hallway that he was disappointed that Shabazz didn't believe him:

"Maybe after the verdict he'll come up and give me a hug."

But Howell had to wait at least one day for the hug. The jury deliberated all day Friday without reaching a verdict, although they told Judge Fitts that they were deadlocked at 9–3. England reported that the jury gave no indication whether the majority were in favor of conviction or acquittal. Fitts then gave the jury the weekend off.

On April 25, jurors found seven of the eight defendants not guilty of attempted murder. Jurors split on Howell, and Fitts declared a mistrial. Roden's lawyers were disappointed, but determined to continue the case against Howell.

Howell quietly told England, "I don't care if I go to prison. I just didn't want these men to go. If I go, I'll convert the prison. The decision is in God's hands. Who knows the minds of men? I'll wait on God."

But the jurors made no secret of their preference for Howell, embracing the Branch Davidians and blasting Roden after the verdict was announced. Jury foreman Randall Toups said that Roden's testimony badly damaged the prosecution's case.

"A lot of jurors commented that they felt frightened of [Roden]," Toups told England. "They didn't feel his testimony was honest. They just didn't have any faith in what he said."

Coker was in a particularly triumphant mood:

"Live testimony beats hardware any day. Hardware doesn't talk very well. An assault rifle can't say, 'I shot to kill.'

"Our witnesses were nice people with no criminal record who don't believe they're Jesus Christ."

Well, that was then.

The days that followed were happy ones for Howell. He embraced Coker as a long-lost brother and couldn't do enough for the silver-haired lawyer. They threw a victory party following the verdict and Coker was the guest of honor—as were several jurors, including Kenneth Thun. The Branch Davidians had also opened a vegetarian restaurant near Baylor University and invited Coker to dine there every day.

Anna Hughes was finally laid to rest—again—on May 4. Howell said a few words, then the casket was placed in a freshly dug grave. Howell told England, who covered the brief ceremony, that both the Branch Davidians and Anna Hughes were back where they belonged:

"There can't be any tears shed. Let's face it: you can't cry twice over someone. When I saw her, she looked like something from a horror movie. Time was, when someone did what George did, he would have been taken out back and drug over bull nettles. Today, I don't know. I can't figure it out. I wasn't raised that way."

A few weeks later, Shabazz and Wilkerson admitted defeat and dropped all charges against Howell as well.

But for George Roden, the nightmare was only beginning. After the trial, he filed another civil suit in May to be declared rightful owner of Mt. Carmel. In June, he filed a $10 million lawsuit against Howell's Branch Davidians, claiming the group was illegally occupying Mt. Carmel and that group members had "besmirched" his name. In September, Judge Byron McClellan sentenced Roden to yet another 90 days in jail after finding him in contempt of court for violating the 1979 court order forbidding him to live at Mt. Carmel. Roden would not be released until December 22.

The case itself was not heard until January 27, 1989, when it lasted only a few minutes. The judge granted a defense motion for summary judgment in the case and ordered the destitute Roden to pay court costs.

Roden's friends and family also began to feel the heat. In a motion to the United States District Court, Western District of Texas, Amo Roden said that in March 1989, Connie Tye Harvey was sent to prison for two years for forgery. A month later, Donnie Joel Harvey was convicted of illegal possession of a firearm. About the same time, another friend, Thomas Drake, lost his house in a small claims court. In all three cases, according to Mrs. Roden, important documents and information were suppressed by Waco courts.

With his friends in jail, his family property barred to him, and penniless, Roden continued gamely to fight back the only way he knew how—through the very courts he believed had betrayed him.

In February 1989, 54th State District Judge George Allen rejected Roden's bid to represent Connie Tye Harvey. After his brief court appearance, Roden told Witherspoon that he planned to appeal. Again.

But Roden's various suits and motions were being dismissed faster than he could file—and the costs were mounting up. Finally, he left Waco and returned to his native Odessa, leaving behind Amo and their daughter Zella.

On Tuesday, October 18, 1989, Odessa police charged Roden with the murder of an unnamed 56-year-old man.

Roden claimed the man had been sent to kill him.

Months later, Roden was sentenced to an indeterminate stay in the Vernon State Hospital in Vernon, Texas. He'd been found innocent of the man's murder by reason of insanity.

On May 15, 1990, Vernon Wayne Howell asked a court in Pomona, California, to legally change his name to David Koresh.

On August 28, 1990, the court granted Koresh's request.

Chapter 7

Where Roden dominated Mt. Carmel with the sheer force of his aggressive, overbearing personality, Koresh had others do most of the dirty work for him. He assembled what came to be called his "Mighty Men."[1]

The Men were needed because life at the compound was anything but placid. Numerous former Branch Davidians have reported on the petty disputes that bedeviled the cultists, particularly when Koresh was not around. More than one Davidian was banished from the compound for some transgression.

The core of the Mighty Men was assembled in the mid-1980s, at Diamond Head Seventh-day Adventist Church in Honolulu, Hawaii, and consisted of Marc Breault, Paul Fatta, and Steve Schneider. These three became fast friends—Schneider was the best man at the wedding of Breault and Elizabeth Baranyai. Eventually, 14 of Koresh's Honolulu followers were disfellowshipped by the SDAs. Most followed him from California to Palestine to Waco.

Other Mighty Men included articulate, passionate, British native Livingston Fagan, whom Schneider recruited while they both studied at Newboldt College in England, and a wealthy California design engineer named Donald Bunds. (Koresh had earlier visited Donald and Jeannine and their daughter, Robyn, in the Highland Park section of Los Angeles. His persuasive ways soon converted both Donald and Jeannine, a nurse. Robyn was a much harder sell. But the Bunds eventually fell under Koresh's spell to such a degree that in 1990 they didn't bat an eyelid when he told them to buy him a rock-faced house in Pomona for $100,000.)

But of all the Mighty Men who would come and go, there was no one like Marc Breault. Though he doesn't enter the story until 1986, Breault is no less a pivotal character than Houteff, Roden, or Koresh himself.

Breault had been stocking groceries in a Southern California grocery store near the SDA Loma Linda University when he was first contacted by a recruiter for Koresh. Breault was wearing a Dallas Cowboys T-shirt when a small, wiry man walked up to him and asked him if he was from Texas. Breault wasn't, but the man used the icebreaker to continue to chat.

He almost instinctively began hitting the young man's "hot buttons." Breault was nearly blind, with about five percent of normal vision. He had been born a Roman Catholic, but after attending an SDA church camp, had converted to Adventism—and with such passion that, by the time of the encounter, Breault was studying for the Adventist ministry.

The thin man was Perry Jones, in California looking for converts for Koresh (then still called Vernon Howell).

That chance meeting turned out to be among the worst things that ever happened to Marc Breault. But it was to be fatal for both Jones and Koresh.

Jones quickly took Breault to meet his "inspired" son-in-law, David Koresh. Within days, the introspective Breault was playing keyboards in Koresh's band and hanging out regularly with the California Branchers. In time, Breault followed them all to Palestine.

But unlike virtually every other Branch Davidian, Breault wasn't completely, utterly, irrevocably swept up in the Koresh mystique. He held something back.

This meant that, when at Passover services in Palestine he heard some things that didn't ring just quite right, he was still able to register a vague uneasiness. It wasn't much, but it was more than most of the other Branch Davidians could muster.

That day, Koresh reported to the rest of the group that God had instructed him to have sex with a 14-year-old girl in the cult—and a squeaky, underdeveloped, and simple one at that. God told David that the progeny of this union was to be named Shoshonna. Shoshonna would then marry David's son Cyrus, and together they'd rule the kingdom of God on earth.

Koresh continued to spellbind his crowd with another whopper of a revelation: Yes, he'd slept with 67-year-old prophetess Lois Roden, but only because of Isa. 8:3.[2]

Howell said that the elderly Roden had indeed conceived this miracle baby—but since she'd persisted in giving tithe money to her *grown* kids, God had ordained the miscarriage of the child.

Privately, he'd angrily told the Rodens it was because Lois had informed her children of their affair. The Passover announcement was a little extra spin control on Koresh's part.

Like the rest, Breault simply accepted the news. He figured any man willing to calmly state as fact a couple of stories as wild as those two must indeed have some powerful conviction. And apparently Breault had never heard the Hitlerian wisdom that the bigger the lie the more people believe it.

But to his credit, a seed of doubt remained. Perhaps it was

only as large as a mustard seed—but it was a seed nonetheless. And it survived two more years of serious religious brainwashing.

Whenever Breault would begin to lose himself in Koresh's arcane messages, David himself would inadvertently bring Breault back to reality with one of his twin obsessions: guns and girls. Particularly the young girls. Girl after girl after girl became Koresh's "Teddy Bears." It just didn't jibe with Breault's upbringing. And the most rigorous internal rationalizing still could not make any sense out of it. It was simply wrong.

As early as April of 1986, Koresh admitted in front of the entire group that he'd had sexual relations with 13-year-old Karen Doyle, and added that it was only "according to Bible prophecy." Koresh had informed the young girl of God's will. Recalled Breault: "Karen responded by saying that she would do whatever God told her to do."

Koresh's reason for bringing this up before the entire group was to praise those who do the will of God, to shine favorably upon them. Karen was the good example of faithful obedience.

And Koresh, who loved to enhance his lunatic excess with Biblical window-dressing, compared himself to King David—the one in the Old Testament, not the tabloids—who had in his old age taken up the practice of bedding down with young women to stay warm. (The practice, in Hebrew called "abishag," didn't mean the same thing to Koresh, and he started it much earlier!)

Breault was trying hard to suspend judgment concerning David Koresh for reasons that had trapped many a Branch Davidian over the previous 50 years: "If somebody says they're a prophet, and you believe it, then it's hard to go against it. Because the Bible is full of stories of what happened to people if they go against a prophet."

But Breault became more and more curious concerning Koresh's nocturnal activities.

In the summer of 1987, Koresh and Breault had been visiting the group's San Bernardino property. Perry Jones, still Koresh's chief lieutenant, called from Texas and urged Breault to summon Koresh to the phone immediately. So Breault went to Koresh's room: no David.

"I went outside to look for him. Since Perry had informed me the matter was urgent, I called out for Vernon."

There were three small shacks along the side of the San Bernardino house. Karen Doyle was staying in one, and Michele Jones, then 12, was in another. When Breault called out, Michele

Jones answered him: "Are you looking for Vernon? Hold on and I'll get him."

Out came Koresh, shirtless, to take the call.

It was 5:30 a.m.

Once again, Breault's little seedbed of doubt was replenished.

Some time before this incident, Koresh had conducted Bible studies from the Song of Solomon saying that he was entitled to 140 wives. The verse Howell used in order to justify this rather inordinate and taxing number of mates is further proof of his total disregard for the context of the scriptures. The verse in question is from the Song of Solomon, which was a paean to love—one on one:

> Thy teeth are as a flock of sheep which go up from the washing, whereof every one beareth twins, and there is not one barren among them.
>
> As a piece of a pomegranate are thy temples within thy locks.
>
> There are threescore queens, and fourscore concubines, and virgins without number.
>
> My dove, my undefiled is but one; she is the only one of her mother. She is the choice one of her that bare her. The daughters saw her, and blessed her; yea, the queens and the concubines, and they praised her.

What did Koresh read into this? Virgins without number! That's the ticket! Even to Breault—perhaps only to Breault—it seemed that David's brain had by now deteriorated into little more than a device for obtaining sex with the sanction of the Bible.

But Koresh broke it down even further for the group, telling them it meant only "60 proper wives and 80 concubines."

From January to May of 1988, Breault lived in Waco in a house on 19th Street, where Koresh and his band kept their musical instruments and mixing board. During his time there, David continued to add notches to his guitar—and names to Breault's growing mental list.

"During this time, I personally witnessed Dana Okimoto, Robyn Bunds, Sherri Jewell, and Rachel Howell spend the night in Howell's room on various occasions."

Marc's doubts continued to grow, although he still kept them to himself.

With his system of enforcers in place and hordes of anxious concubines in every port, Koresh felt secure enough to leave for longer and longer periods of time. Little is known of his trips in the late 1980s and early 1990s, but he's known to have traveled to California frequently, to Hawaii, Israel, and certainly Australia.

Shortly after the births of Sky Borne by Dana Okimoto on September 10, 1988, and Wisdom (later Shaun) Bunds by Robyn Bunds on November 14, 1988, Koresh visited Bruce and Lisa Gent in Melbourne, Australia. Bruce and Lisa had been David Koresh fans as early as 1986, and had even visited the compound in Palestine. They were already well under his spell when Koresh visited their home. They were glad to see him. But Koresh was more glad to see their daughter, Nicole, 19, when she came home from college.

In previous encounters with Koresh, Nicole had sized him up accurately—as a narcissistic, self-obsessed peacock. But on this trip, Koresh proceeded to seduce her, pulling out his tool, the Bible, and using it with his usual mind-numbing technique. He buried her under great big piles of fragmented Scripture, chasing her around with it in a non-stop marathon of prevarication and versification.

Her brains addled after four long days, she finally "saw the light" and agreed to go to Mt. Carmel to study under Koresh. One night before she left for Texas, she came into her parents' bedroom. She told them that David wanted her to be his little cuddle-muffin for the night. Well under his influence, trapped within the belief system Koresh had inculcated in them, they figured that if David wanted their daughter, it was divine intention. He had blessed their little family unit. How can you say no to the Lamb of God?

And she was his Teddy Bear, and for a time, back in Texas, even had the good fortune to become one of Koresh's favorite wives—though only one of several. Koresh even sent her back to Australia one year later, just long enough to give the lucky Gent family a second blessing. His divine seed had taken root. As with many Davidian babies, no father was listed on the birth certificate of Nicole's baby.

In the spring of 1988, Breault confided to Koresh that he was saddened about breaking up with a girlfriend. Koresh took Breault off to one side and told him: "I'm having girl troubles of my own. It isn't easy having all these women. Guess which one's my favorite?"

"Rachel Howell?"

"Nope."

"Sherri Jewell?"

"Nope. Michele Jones. Can you believe it, Marc? She's been with me since she was 12 years old!"

Michele was the younger sister of Koresh's legal wife, Rachel.

Later, Koresh gave a blow-by-blow account during Bible study of his original rape—physical, not just statutory—of Michele. Koresh made a big joke of it, relating how the girl had thought she was getting into his bed so she could "get warm." Koresh had immediately started pulling off her panties. Michele tried to get him to stop and even resisted him physically. But he wouldn't stop; wouldn't stop because, he explained to her, he was doing what God had *told* him to do.

The other Branch Davidians merely nodded. Breault felt physically ill.

Not long after the Bible study, Breault went to use the phone at the nearby home of Michele Jones' father and mother, Perry and Mary Bell Jones. And there was Michele's baby, Serenity Sea, only a month or two old. Mary Bell Jones was looking after it. She told Breault specifically that Vernon had told her to hide the baby in case any outsider or fringe member came by. He didn't want anyone to know he had been sleeping with Michele, who was then 14 years old.

But Breault's education wasn't over yet.

For all of Koresh's boasting and blustering about bedding 12- and 13-year-old girls, Breault was still somehow daily convincing himself—or trying to—that it wasn't really happening. But Koresh had an ever-growing, insatiable appetite for young girls, the last victim of which—Aisha Gyarfas—Breault knew was 13 years old.

In March of 1989, Koresh told him that the Gyarfas family was coming to visit from Australia, and casually asked Breault if he thought Koresh should pay for Aisha Gyarfas' way over, since he wanted Aisha as one of his wives.

"I objected strenuously to his intentions," Breault recalled, and remarkably, Koresh acquiesced, agreeing to drop his amorous intentions toward the girl. Breault, however, felt that this was out of character. So he began spying on Koresh.

"I was seriously considering leaving the cult in the summer of 1989 because of what David was doing to young girls. But I wanted to make sure. I saw Aisha Gyarfas enter Vernon's room on a number of evenings. She entered alone. The next morning, she would emerge."

For absolute confirmation of his suspicions, however, he stayed all night in the office downstairs, which was the only way out of Howell's quarters, on the pretext that he had some work he needed to do.

"My PC was in the office, and I did write a few unimportant

letters. In reality, I was playing a Star Trek simulation game. The next morning, Aisha emerged from Koresh's room and was somewhat surprised to find me in the office so 'early' in the morning."

Somehow, Koresh managed to find time to put into his other recruiting efforts—and they were paying off as well. Sometime during the summer of 1989, Michael and Kathryn Schroeder and their small family sold their belongings, left Zephyrhilla, Florida, and moved to Mt. Carmel. Koresh considered Kathryn a particularly valuable addition since she had a military background and was considered an excellent marksman. Some Branch Davidians allegedly called her "Sarge" behind her back.

Later that same summer, on a trip to Pomona, California, Koresh called all of the Branch Davidians together. Old-timers sensed that something significant was in the air. Among those in attendance was a recently married and increasingly troubled Marc Breault.

Koresh began another of his 13-hour Bible studies, stopped, and smiled beatifically into space. It was as if everything fell into place for the first time.

First, he announced that he was the Lamb of God. He'd done that before. But he was really, *really* the Lamb of God this time. Then he explained what he would later call the "New Light." ("Blue Light Special" might have been a better appellation, because it was a pretty good deal—for David, anyway!)

He eagerly explained what his Lamb of God designation now entitled him to in terms of sexual privileges—and loss of privileges for everyone else.

As Breault put it: "As the Lamb of God, he (and only he) was entitled to have all women and girls sexually. Only he had the right to procreate. Koresh said that he would give some married couples time to adjust to this new 'revelation,' as he called it. At one point during this study, Koresh saw that the married couples were very upset. Koresh commanded everyone to look at Sherri Jewell.

"Sherri was actually quite taken by the study, and Koresh pointed this out," says Breault. "He said Sherri liked this doctrine because she'd been practicing it for years and now it was the married couples' turn to sacrifice." And Breault reiterates: "In fact, Sherri Jewell was *quite* enjoying this study."

Koresh then, on the spot, "annulled" all marriages, and said that he alone would thenceforth service all Branch Davidian women, because only he, as the Lamb, had been meant to procreate.

Koresh then commanded that the "New Light" he had been given be kept a secret from outsiders.

But his finest hour may have been when he attempted to convince the suddenly consortless and quite shocked and dispirited men—many of whom had nothing left but their wives anyway, thanks to Koresh—that he was doing them a big favor by taking away their last treasure.

Marriage, Koresh told them, was really just fancified adultery. Legalized violence.

He told the men they need not worry; their perfect mates already resided with them, within their own bodies. When they got to Heaven, they would each be awarded perfect mates, mates that would spring from their own ribs.

Most of them bought it, since, after all, it came from the Lamb of God.

Livingston Fagan later burbled that garbled "theory" from his jail cell.

"You don't *understand*. You don't understand at all. We as Branch Davidians aren't *interested* in sex. Sex is so *assaultive*, so aggressive. David has shouldered that burden *for* us."

So, take my wife—*please!*

Koresh was also determined to keep them from slipping into evil, into the temptation to consort with their own wives. So he decreed that the men and women should be completely separated. But, kind and loving leader that he was, he at least explained it to them. It was Show and Tell. During yet another Bible study, Koresh instructed one of the women to stand up, turn around, and raise her skirt. She complied. And Koresh asked all the men who found this display arousing to raise their hands.

Hands shot up, including Breault's.

Koresh explained that this sad state of affairs, this attraction between men and women, was what made it impossible for them to be friends. That's why they couldn't live together. Because men will always want to have sex with women.

So it's for your own good.

But a couple of the Davidians didn't buy it. This separation, this New Light thing, this taking of the wives was the last straw, the one that would lead to mutiny, and thus to the end. One of those almost at the end was Marc Breault, who had been married to his new wife, Elizabeth Baranyai, for just three months.

Koresh must have noticed Marc's tortured face, because following the Bible study, he came over and draped his arm over Breault's shoulder.

Breault later told the *Waco Tribune-Herald* that Koresh ribbed him thusly:

"So, Marc, how does it feel, now that I'm stuck with Elizabeth?"

Breault was already planning to leave—but had no plans beyond that. That little remark cinched his resolve to do something about David Koresh.

The annulment of all of the other Branch Davidian marriages also had a profound impact on Robyn Bunds. Once Koresh's favorite, she'd fallen back into the pack. In fact, Koresh often made a point of publicly demeaning her. The crowning blow came in September 1989, when he ordered her to marry British native Cliff Sellors at a Las Vegas wedding chapel so Sellors could remain in the United States. Sellors was a gifted artist and Koresh had big plans for the humble, soft-spoken Englishman. Robyn knew she was simply a convenient means for Cliff to stay.

One final casualty of the New Light was Livingston Fagan. For the crime of initially disagreeing about Koresh's doctrine of multiple wives, he fell out of both the inner circle and the Mighty Men. He remained a valued recruiter and enthusiastic supporter, but he was no longer one of Koresh's confidants.

But the greatest loss—though Koresh didn't know it at the time—was Breault.

One month after the New Light revelation, Breault planned his escape. He had already surreptitiously applied for an Australian immigration visa. Fortunately, Elizabeth, an Australian national, had already returned to Melbourne. In September, with the help of a sympathetic aunt, Breault followed her. He had to leave everything behind, but he made it.

Months later, David Koresh still haunted Marc Breault's dreams, even in Australia. He'd gone there to forget, to rebuild, to make up for the lost years, to start anew. He started a computer company. He made a new home with his wife.

But there, waiting at the edges of his mind, was guilt.

He'd recruited many of Koresh's victims, had plunged them into the Sordid Savior's pit of sexual degradation and slavery. He felt responsible for them—but he also knew the power of Koresh's hold over them; it had been very difficult for him to leave, and he'd been blessed with a whisper of doubt from the beginning.

But there is justice in this, because Breault had an inspiration, one that might be the only truly God-given one in the whole affair, because this one accomplished actual good.

Breault's inspiration was to steal a page from his leader. Do a Dave. Become a prophet. Or say that you are—which in David Koresh's case was the same thing.

Breault told every Australian Davidian that he could lay hands on about his new, personal revelation: That he himself was a prophet. And so they almost had to listen, to heed his words, as Davidians had done for the past 50 years.

His words were that David Koresh was no Jesus Christ, and Jesus Christ was the Lamb.

Just as Koresh would have done, Breault cited the Scripture. Only Breault's citation was accurate, with the book open, there for doubters to read. Slowly, if necessary.

John 1:29: *The next day John seeth Jesus coming unto him, and saith, Behold the Lamb of God, which taketh away the sin of the world.*

For these Bible believers, it was hard to dispute the words of John, and many began for the first time to truly question whether David Koresh was in fact a false prophet.

Slowly but surely, Breault built a network of dissenters—and when the Lamb of God found out, boy, was he mad!

The man who had once bragged of hearing young girls' hearts beating like hunted prey as he defiled them, now began to sense that soon he himself might become the hunted.

Once word trickled back to Koresh—and, just as importantly, tithes trickled to next to nothing—Koresh responded.

Breault later discovered that Koresh immediately sent word to the remaining faithful among the Australian members that together they were to implement three plans of action:

"One was that Vernon had created a hit list and that I was on top of that list," Breault recalled. "This was because I'd been instrumental in causing Australian members to break away from Howell.

"Howell told them that if I came to visit them at their home, they were to open the door, kick me in the balls, and slam the door in my face.

"And finally, we were told that Howell had sent some of his followers to spy on us, driving by our home at about two in the morning to see if any Australians who were considering breaking away were, in fact, visiting us."

The naturally paranoid Koresh's paranoia could take no more of this... this *heresy* coming out of Australia.

Koresh then sent them a strange audio tape that reveals his ever-increasing confusion of sex with spirituality:

"You have only one seed that can deliver you from death... Remember Mary and God? Yeah? God couldn't make any advances because the world would misjudge."

When that didn't have the immediate reaction he desired, Koresh decided the only way to shore up the shaky Australian branch was to go there himself, and deliver the *new* New Light.

So in early 1990, Koresh traveled to Melbourne to win back former followers with the new "Sinful Messiah" message in person. England and fellow reporter Darlene McCormick say that Koresh stayed at the home of Bruce and Lisa Gent, both of whom were visibly wavering.

For the next several days, Koresh turned his powerful personality on to reconverting the Gents. At first he denied his New Light revelation, but finally he admitted that all wives were indeed called to leave their husbands for him.

Yes, Koresh said, it is written that the married men must find their perfect mates only in heaven; the women were for Koresh's pleasure only.

And then, as he had done with Breault with the "guess I'll be taking care of Elizabeth" line, Koresh rubbed salt into the wound, and took that one step too many over the line. He complained that some women in the cult who should have known better still had the unmitigated gall to go to bed with their own husbands—and he very pointedly raised his arm toward the bedroom of Bruce and Lisa Gent.

Finally, he threw down his wildest card, his trump, his ace in the hole.

According to the Bible, he said, only the Lamb could open the Seven Seals, and John had referred to Jesus as the Lamb of God—right? Therefore was it not true, since Koresh had "proven" to them that he could interpret the Seals, that that made him in fact Jesus Christ?

You could have knocked Lisa Gent over with a feather. Nearly overwhelmed, she fled from their home and checked into a nearby hotel. But she took along the book that had been the means of their undoing, hoping that it could also somehow be their salvation—a Bible.

Away from Koresh's nonstop browbeating, she read the

Scriptures over and over again. Away from the threats and pleading and dizzying cross-references, she re-discovered a very simple story about a simple Man whose greatest weapon was love—not fear. A Man who spoke about a loving God who had a Home big enough to hold all who simply asked for admission.

Is the story true? Each must decide for himself (and, most importantly, for himself alone).

But this much is certainly true. There was no mention—in the words of Jesus—of another Messiah, "sinful" or otherwise; no mention that only a tiny remnant of 144,000 out of earth's teeming billions might enter heaven, no complicated code that required cracking before anyone gained entrance.

And ultimately, not one single word about anybody who changed his name to David Koresh.

Lisa Gent returned home and told Koresh to leave.

You could have knocked Koresh over with that same feather. It might have been at this moment that Koresh saw the handwriting on the wall, the future revealed; or it might have been the moment that the Gents walked purposefully up to him, together, man and wife, and told the Lamb of God himself that he was no longer welcome in their home, and should take a hike. It might have been here that David Koresh got his first true vision, a real-life glimpse of the future.

Koresh should have cut his losses and headed for Texas, but megalomania has its own momentum, like a freight train headed for a cliff. He instead moved in with James Tom and his wife, Michelle, the daughter of Lisa Gent.

He called Steve Schneider in Texas, and through him, arranged a meeting—perhaps "showdown" is the better word—with Breault. And Breault, courageously, considering Koresh's considerable powers of confusion in verbal battle, took him up on it. But he took him up on it only after first notifying his in-laws to call the police if he and Elizabeth didn't get home by 10 p.m.

Once at the Toms', Breault tried calmly to lay out for Koresh the list of facts supporting Breault's contention that David was not a prophet or a Lamb or the Son of God. Koresh predictably fell back on the usual Seven Seals snow job: Oh, yeah? Well, didn't I teach you the Seven Seals? So doesn't that make me Christ?

Koresh also claimed to be the Man on the White Horse, the Lion of Judah mentioned in Revelation. His reasoning: he was a Leo!

But Breault was pretty well-versed in all the places and things that Koresh had claimed to be over the years. He reminded Koresh that he had also purported at times to be the man on the black horse carrying a pair of scales, so didn't that really make him a Libra?

Koresh exploded, calling Breault a Judas and making dire threats.

Not a little sadly, Marc and Elizabeth left and walked home.

Koresh continued his mad tirade, frightening the Toms, prophesying demonic curses on Marc and Elizabeth.

Suddenly, just after 10 p.m., there was a knock on the door. A muffled voice said it was the police. Frightened, Koresh dove out the back door, grabbed a bicycle, and pedaled frantically into the night.

But it wasn't the police. It was John Baranyai. He had somehow missed Marc and Elizabeth in the dark and had come looking for them.

After Koresh returned to the United States, Breault tried to pry other Texas Branch Davidians loose from Koresh's grasp, but without luck.

Meantime, emboldened by what they'd done and seen, the Australian former Branch Davidians began to meet regularly and compare notes. It was like a therapy session. Soon long-hidden memories and dark secrets began to emerge. Among them, the Toms, the Breaults, and others began to paint a picture of a man who raped children and beat children in God's name—and bragged about it. Koresh battered and psychologically terrorized the children, including—and perhaps especially—his own son, Cyrus.

Breault recalled an episode at the Pomona House when Howell had asked Cyrus to call Nicole Gent 'Mommy.' (The child's real mother is Rachel Howell.) Cyrus would not, and, as punishment, Howell forced Cyrus to sleep on the kitchen floor with only a thin blanket for covering.

"On the following day, Howell ordered James Tom to prepare a place in the garage for his son Cyrus to sleep in that night. Howell emphasized to the little child that there were large rats in the garage and they would eat him because he had been naughty.

"The child was absolutely terrified, and began begging to be allowed to stay in the house. Howell then tried to force Cyrus to call Nicole 'Mommy,' but the child would not. James Tom also objected strenuously, but his objections were silenced by Howell."

Shortly thereafter, on another occasion, Howell asked his son Cyrus, "Do you like me?"

The child replied that he did not.

"Vernon was enraged," says Breault, "and beat his son severely. He then asked the child again if he liked him. Once again, he replied that he did not. Vernon continued to beat the child until Cyrus finally said he loved his daddy."

Other horror stories emerged. Koresh maintained a "whipping" room, a door that led to a basement area where children were taken for beatings when "they don't want anyone to hear us."

There was a paddle called "The Helper," specially designed so that it left round, inch-wide welts on their bottoms. Koresh was known to leap unpredictably from the lectern during his rambling Bible studies to paddle the young ones... to stop them from crying or, crazier still, from sleeping.

Michelle Tom, later testifying in a custody case in Michigan, said that her daughter, Tarah Tom, once was sitting in Koresh's lap, and began to cry. Koresh grabbed a wooden spoon and beat the child for 30 minutes, until the child's buttocks bled. Tarah Tom was eight months old at the time.

Koresh had a theory which made this all okay. The theory was that even if a child died from a spanking, it would go to heaven.

Other memories came vomiting out: uncomprehending 11-year-old girls virtually raped, children taught how to commit suicide with real handguns, young girls taught in graphic detail about their upcoming sexual encounters with Koresh.

The little girls continued to haunt Breault. Most of all he remembered Sherri Jewell's little daughter, Kiri. It was to rescue Kiri Jewell and those "Teddy Bears" still to come that the small band of former Branch Davidians spent much of their savings.

The Australians carefully crafted a host of sworn affidavits to present to officials in California and Texas. On September 18, 1990, they hired private detective Geoffrey N. Hossack to alert law enforcement officials in Waco. Hossack brought signed affidavits notarized by the American Consul in Australia. He met with U.S. Assistant Attorney Bill Johnson, then McLennan County District Attorney Paul Gartner, and his aide Ralph Strother; Sgt. Terry Lee, an investigator with the Texas Department of Public Safety; and Lt. Gene Barber of the McLennan County Sheriff's Department.

Hossack was met with a frustrating lack of response, particularly from the DA's office, the group best placed at the time to do something about David Koresh. Much later, Strother told the *Tribune-Herald* that Gartner's office needed either people to come in person, or further evidence, before the DA would be able to act.

Hossack hotly disputed the DA's account: "I also indicated that these people were willing to come over to the United States and appear in any court and give any evidence that was necessary. And they were."

And they did. On behalf of Kiri Jewell.

Meanwhile, Koresh returned to La Verne, California, to lick his wounds and "minister" to his harem. But one of his consorts— Robyn Bunds—had had enough.

In the summer of 1990, she told Koresh she was leaving.

Robyn Bunds had three claims to fame: She'd once defied her parents by fleeing from Koresh to stay with relatives in Massachusetts; she was among the earliest of the Branch Davidian women to sleep with Koresh; and her mother was one of the very first *married* women to sleep with Koresh.

Subsequently, Robyn had followed Koresh through the fight with Roden and back to the Mt. Carmel property from Palestine. And at the age of 19, she'd given birth to his son, Wisdom (whose name was later changed to Shaun).

Perhaps because Robyn hadn't come from a deprived, under-educated background, perhaps because she'd read a little and been a few places, or maybe just perhaps she had stronger self-esteem than most of the Branch Davidians, this business with the New Light revelation was the last straw for her. It took her a full year, until the summer of 1990, to reach certain conclusions. But in that year, what had once passed without comment suddenly became repulsive.

Robyn hadn't even planned how to tell Koresh. But one day he took her off to one side to kiss her and she burst into tears— not the response that King David expected from his harem. When pressed, she told him she was leaving. When he sneered and asked her just where it was she thought she could go, on impulse she threw down the name of a long-gone and, in fact, almost-forgotten boyfriend.

He flew into a rage, and stomped away.

That seemed to be the end of it. The next morning she went as usual to her job as a receptionist.

When she returned to the La Verne house, all of her belongings were missing, and so was her son Shaun. In her absence, Koresh had packed the child off to Texas under the care of a Branch Davidian named Nicolette Sinclair.

Koresh had been planning to "show" Robyn, to prove yet again the "truth" of what he'd been drilling into her and the rest of the Branch Davidians: that they were useless without him, incapable of thinking for themselves—and subject to some serious consequences should they try.

But this time, Robyn refused to be cowed back into dancing in the Koresh line. She did the bravest thing she'd ever done in her life. She went straight to the La Verne police department and told them the whole story, right down to the last sordid detail— multiple wives, underage sex, the whole clammy ball of wax.

The police found this rather interesting. They'd known of the Branch Davidians' presence in their little Los Angeles suburb for quite some time and considered them weird, maybe, but generally harmless.

Bunds led police back over to the house on White Avenue and right up the stairs—past the celibate and emasculated Mighty Men gathering for a meeting downstairs—and to the second floor, where they found Koresh in his element of choice: One man. Twenty women.

Police began to question him, to demand answers from him— him, David Koresh, the Lamb! He confirmed what Robyn had suspected: that Shaun had "gone to Texas."

Police ordered Koresh to return the child within 48 hours or face kidnapping charges.

The world would have been a different place, of course, if they'd gone ahead and arrested him.

But the police and the Davidians as well had noticed something amazing—David's voice was quivering. Because he was no longer in control.

Unveiled for all to see, the Lamb of God had cloven hooves of clay.

This moment, this unbuffered, uncushioned confrontation with true, duly constituted authority, revealed something to his followers. It showed how completely dependent he was for his "authority" upon their own unquestioning acceptance.

Here was David Koresh suddenly confronted with people who did not believe that he was entitled to every woman and barely pubescent young girl in the world; who, in fact, had never believed that there was anyone in the world capable of espousing such a concept; people who probably would have fallen over in helpless laughter had anyone dared to suggest so ludicrous a notion—and who would have clamped him in the deep under the jail or in an asylum once they realized that such an assertion was made in all seriousness.

And Koresh, poised there on the edge of the world's Reality and the Reality he'd created from smoke and mirrors to furnish his own little world, knew it.

Because, all the trappings of religion and rock and roll and personality aside, David Koresh was at heart a child molester. A child molester writ large, true; a child molester who dared to think about little girls on a grand scale, and all the petty sickness that implies. But a child molester nonetheless.

To be successful as a child molester, you must find a simple innocent, a toddler. Whether the toddler qualifies by reason of chronological age or on grounds of intellect does not matter. David Koresh indisputably proved that toddlers come in all ages, all sizes. And in child molestation, it's not the age of the victim but the sick, secret pleasure of Taking Advantage that's the thing.

Find the ones who haven't had to learn to defend themselves from those who would take advantage of them. And then, take advantage of them while telling them you're doing them a favor.

When dealing with the chronologically young, the molester can take his pick. It's a matter of simple, uneducated ignorance.

When dealing with the chronologically mature, Koresh discovered that the thing to look for is the blindly faithful; people to whom he could say just about anything and have them believe him. Christianity is, sad to say, a good place to start looking; Adventism is an even better place to narrow the search.

With the chronologically young, offer them a cookie, with the implication that if they don't take it, why, they might get a spanking.

With the blindly faithful, dangle a bigger cookie: Heaven—to be among the elect. And keep ever-present in their minds the terrors of the alternative.

You make that simple, guileless innocent think that you are her friend, an older and wiser friend, of course. You tell her you're something important, like, a doctor, or the Lamb of God— a friend who knows everything, and will *show* her some things, very interesting things, things that will feel good and keep on feeling good, but only as long as Mommy and Daddy don't find out. Mommy and Daddy mustn't find out.

Mustn't find out that we are secret friends, doing secret things, forbidden things, things that are forbidden, because stupid people might not understand. Because, little girl, there is something wrong with those people. No, those people are Babylonians. Your mommy and daddy, the society that you were raised in, no, little girl, they are not your friends. They pretend to be your friends. But I am *really* your friend, because I show you the secret things.

God has told me, told me to come to *you*, to show you the secret things. God talks to me, little girl, and he tells me that He wants you to know them. GOD, do you understand?

Now, the secret things I've shown you? It was hard on me, to show you those secret things. If you don't follow me, as God intended for you to do, why—I shall take back the cookie!

Or send you to a place where you'll burn and burn and burn and scream and pop and hiss like *thisss*...

Robyn realized—though not all at once—that, unlike most child molesters, who spend years picking and cultivating and misleading their victims, Koresh now had a whole miniature society of them to choose from. A cafeteria of carnal opportunity.

If cleanliness is next to godliness, then the bloated self-absorption of narcissism (the state where no one else really exists) is the next-door neighbor to a sort of living necrophilia, to the state in which people are treated as things, objects to be manipulated.

And for Koresh, it was a wonderful day in the neighborhood.

And the thoughts and intentions that accompanied this narcissistic necrophilia wormed their way in darkness through a mind filled with wet, rotting leaves, hiding behind smiles that disguised rather than revealed, statements that confused rather than informed.

He had managed through the magic of words to invert, subvert, and pervert the concept of God, twisting it into something that pushed down rather than pulled up.

Yes, David Koresh had a secret, and it wasn't the Seven Seals. The secret was that he was a child molester, pure and simple. A vampire of the innocent, the sucker of virgin blood.

David Koresh was a thing of darkness.

David Koresh was a cockroach, albeit a big one, waiting for the lights to go out so he could paddle his feet in our butter and scuttle his claws on our bread. David Koresh was a cockroach that ran over children's faces while they slept, to deposit his filth in their dreams.

Robyn Bunds wasn't to the point where she could see that—

yet. In fact, she didn't even hate David for what he'd done to her childhood. She just wanted out.

After the police left that day, Koresh almost had a psychotic break in the wake of this "terrible betrayal" by Robyn Bunds, the woman who had only wanted her child and her life back. He wandered slowly, stiffly about the La Verne house in a daze, all the stuffings and support knocked out from under him by just one reality check.

A few of the Branch Davidians couldn't help but notice how little it took to shatter the Lamb of God. One of them was Jeannine Bunds, who had been told by Koresh that she would soon be pregnant. Imagine that! A grandmother having one of these beautiful, angelic babies of her own. Being a mother all over again.

Forty-eight hours later, Shaun was flown back to La Verne, and Robyn left forever. And in September of 1991, Jeannine Bunds left also, and not even a little bit pregnant, prophecy notwithstanding. She wasn't even terribly amazed. Like her daughter, she didn't immediately hate Koresh. She just felt a little... used.

Half a world away, Breault could wait no longer. In October 1991, he made discreet inquiries and quickly discovered that Kiri's mother, Sherri Jewell, was as infatuated as ever with Koresh, but her ex-husband, a non-Davidian, had no time for Koresh, and he did have joint custody of Kiri.

Marc Breault finally tracked him down, called him up, and asked him one simple question: Did he know whether or not Kiri wore a pendant, a pendant shaped in the Star of David?

She did. And Breault told Kiri's dad what that meant.

David Jewell, then a disc jockey for WNDU-Radio in South Bend, Indiana, was not amused. So the next time Kiri came to visit, at Christmas 1991, he filed for emergency custody of his daughter.

He had already heard the warning signals, he would later testify.

Sherri Jewell had first told him that she wanted to take Kiri to join Koresh's group in Palestine in 1987—and added that if he opposed the move, why, he'd go to Hell. She told him that in such certain terms, in fact, that for a minute Jewell almost believed it.

The custody hearing, starting on February 25, 1992, (and ending one year to the day before the ATF assault in 1993), was held in the court of Judge Ronald Taylor in St. Joseph, Michigan. It was the first public condemnation of David Koresh.

Breault, his wife, Elizabeth, and Jean Smith all flew in from Australia to testify—but Breault's testimony and sworn affidavit were the most damning of all.

By October of 1987, Sherri Jewell and Breault had become friends.

Jewell, a former high school instructor and aerobics teacher, had joined the group in the mid-1980s, when she met members while on a trip to Hawaii. She'd been involved with the California branch of the group, but had come to Waco to stay because of the pastoral atmosphere.

One day she took Breault aside and told him the good news. She had become one of Koresh's "wives."

"She said she wanted me to know because she felt she could trust me with that knowledge. At the time, Sherri Jewell and Dana Okimoto were sharing the same shack. Sherri said that she and Dana had become very good friends now that they were both in the 'House of David.'"

Shortly after, Dana Okimoto also confided some of the details of her relations with Koresh, confiding that her "first time with David" was on August 31, 1987. Breault says the two were so forthcoming because "Sherri and Dana felt I was going to be one of the group's evangelists, and that I should know what was happening. Howell did not mind my knowing.

"Kiri Jewell would also sleep in the same room as Vernon and his women. I know this because I used to sleep in the living room and I often saw Sherri and Kiri enter Vernon's room to go to sleep for the night."

Breault also documented the secrecy, which was just one more damaging element of child abuse (and perhaps a large part of why McLennan County child welfare workers had not been able to document it).

"I can say for certain that Kiri Jewell knew about Sherri's sexual involvement with Howell. Sherri would often employ Kiri as cover for her when outsiders were involved. Sherri told me that she was drilling Kiri in case she was questioned by outsiders about her [Sherri's] involvement."

One day in 1988, Breault said, Koresh had the little girl in his lap. Sherri Jewell was in the room. Koresh told Kiri that she was his daughter, and asked: "Are you going to behave yourself?"

From that point onward, Sherri Jewell would emphasize to Kiri that she was indeed Howell's daughter. And by early or middle 1989, Breault remembers, Sherri was starting to prepare Kiri to become a member of the 'House of David.'

By this point, Breault had become quite disenchanted, but had no other place to go. But he did try to intervene.

"I often took Kiri aside and explained to her that she was very young and that she should wait before she decided whom she would marry."

Nevertheless, he noticed that Kiri and her friend, Rachel Sylvia, and a girl named Audrie were "intensely interested in marriage and were primed to look forward to it [with Koresh]. Sherri would often teach Kiri Koresh's doctrine and even take pride in the fact that Kiri knew and memorized the Scriptures Howell used to teach his 'wives' his doctrines."

As part of the initiation process, Kiri was dispatched to watch the birth of Dana Okimoto's baby, and then to return to Howell to bring the proud father the news.

Further, at prayer meetings, Breault said in sworn testimony, "In Kiri's presence, Howell would describe Sherri's sexual habits with him, as well as her genitalia."

The two parties in the custody suit—David Jewell and Sherri Jewell—were able to negotiate an arrangement whereby Sherri could continue to have joint custody, but only if she kept Kiri away from David Koresh.

In itself, it was another small, almost hollow, victory for the Anti-Verns.

But even before the suit with the Jewells was settled, Koresh had decided to bunker down at Mt. Carmel. With both Australia and California lost to him, Koresh returned to Waco. He threw himself into preparing the compound for war, a war he'd predicted long before.

Perhaps Koresh's greatest achievement—or failing—was his clear understanding of the smoke and mirror tricks of which he could avail himself once he donned the garments of "prophet." As the blueprint for his adopted personality seemed to be laid out in the Bible, so there also he found the tools of his trade.

Want to make a hit in the prophet game, even if you can't foretell what's in the refrigerator, much less the events of years and centuries hence? First, don't set any dates. Koresh had learned this lesson from the Millerites and original Davidians. Second, simply make sure that all your "prophecies" are self-fulfilling.

It's very easy. Go out, write several thousand dollars' worth of hot checks. Come home. Tell your family, in deep, dark intonations, that "I foresee that men will come demanding money."

Or very visibly and indiscreetly set about buying $200,000 worth of explosives, hand grenades, assault weapons and the means to make them automatic, and balefully warn those who follow you: "Babylon will come for us. We must prepare."

And then tell them, "Told you so."

Prophecy.

He also learned early the power of the phrase, "God said," when directed at God-fearing Christians. (Much of what passes for Christianity is based on faith, not in God, but in men.)

Koresh, in sort, was becoming a sorcerer—a sorcerer of words.

He was able to tap into that most ancient of man's frailties—the willingness to be defined, and the belief that someone saying a thing is so makes it so—that from words, worlds follow.

And, in these lapsed Adventists, he found better than average pickings.

First, they had the recent tradition of Prophecy: Even the most conservative Adventists were open to prophesying in modern times. It was, in fact, what the Church was all about. As Breault said, "You don't want to go against a prophet."

Second, Hell is not so abstract to persons raised in the Adventist tradition. It is a place. It is to be feared. And Koresh would feed these fears with graphic descriptions, and show his audience very loudly how people scream in Hell.

Another trick is to take the credit. If you are on the way to the airport and every light is green, smile knowingly, as if to say, "I did that." And with Koresh now at Mt. Carmel full time, all his tricks came into play on a daily basis. With the rumblings that were reaching his ear—and, more importantly, his followers' ears—Koresh needed them all.

The best way to make sure outside information doesn't reach the faithful, of course, is to create a sealed, fortified, utterly impenetrable fortress. And that's what happened at Mt. Carmel.

A furious building campaign was begun. Guard duty was made mandatory. In early 1990, Star-Tex stopped delivering propane to the compound because employees kept getting met by men with guns.

At first Koresh bought his own guns, but he didn't like the questions in Texas' perfunctory gun registration laws. So in early 1991, Mighty Man Paul Fatta began buying guns in earnest, particularly from Henry McMahon, Jr., a gun dealer based in the Waco suburb of Hewitt.

No longer free to ramble around the world at Branch Davidian expense, Koresh was forced to make his own entertainment in Waco. He bought expensive cars and Harley-Davidsons. He bought more guns and exotic guns, including a .50 caliber Barrett Firearms sniper rifle. And using the guns, he began to play army on a giant scale, using his followers as his foot soldiers.

Not that that was anything new. He'd begun militarizing the compound in May of 1989. But it was the intensity and size of the arms buildup in early 1991 that alarmed the few remaining rational Branch Davidians.

Koresh began systematic video screenings of war movies such as *Platoon, Full Metal Jacket,* and *Hamburger Hill,* which he required the children to attend. Marine training exercises were also shown in great length.

By the time Koresh had established the physical training program, Sherri Jewell, Jaydeen Wendel, and others had fashioned "marching songs" with lyrics concerning Branch Davidian doctrines, among them references to killing "Babylonians." They would lead the women and girls on marches and runs three times a day in temperatures sometimes exceeding 100 degrees.

The men exercised less formally, usually early in the morning, to have energy left for the compound's seemingly endless construction projects. But Koresh gave no one (except himself) any chance to rest .

Then, after the military exercises, after the physical labor, were more Bible studies.

The Bible studies were typical Koreshian rants—baffle 'em with BS and scare 'em with lightning and thunder. Koresh was able to impart the belief that he alone understood every last word of the Bible and what it meant, and that he was trying to impart this wisdom to them, and they were just too miserable and stupid to understand his Divine Wisdom.

And they bought it. The biggest fear among many of the cultists was that they would not ever be able to understand.

(Livingston Fagan is the living inheritor of this tradition. He first calls your every belief into question, and, rather than replace it with "new wisdom," he tells you that he doesn't think you can handle this powerful stuff; that you need to search your heart, think upon that which he hath said, and then get back to him when you feel that you are "sincere").

Koresh's followers, though they didn't understand a fifth of what he was saying (because they weren't supposed to) got addicted to the feeling that they were in the Presence of One Who Bears the Truth, someone much more wise and knowing and powerful than they.

The truth about most of his followers was that they became desperate to understand what it was that Koresh "understood," when the truth of it was that he was just making it up as he went.

When he got tired of playing soldier, he resumed his musical career with a vengeance. He stocked the compound's music room with Marshall stacks, pre-amps and processors, and Charvel guitars. (Among his regular musicians was drummer David Thibodeau.) The impromptu jam sessions were totally dominated by Koresh. He picked the tunes—mostly heavy metal—he directed the band, he sang the songs. If a string broke, he'd hand it to another musician, who'd stop what he was playing, give David his own instrument, and re-string David's guitar.

Frustrated by the lack of talent at the compound, he began making regular forays into Waco to hear local bands like Flashback, Blind Wolfe, and Riff Raff. He even traveled to hear certain bands, or he'd show up several nights in a row at a Waco club like Cuesticks or the Chelsea Street Pub.

While his entourage rarely ate or drank, Koresh was generous with his money on these outings, buying drinks and food for musicians, urging them to come out to Mt. Carmel to jam and drink beer. And after the last set, Koresh would retire to Whataburger to continue his conversation, eating hamburgers as his vegetarian followers watched quietly.

Koresh began to hang out at Waco-area music stores as well, discussing equipment, creating elaborate musical scenarios, occasionally striking up religious conversations with customers, playing lightning-fast riffs and songs ranging from "Sweet Home Alabama" to anything by Alice Cooper or Ted Nugent.

Barry McCann, a drummer with D'Javaheads (and an English graduate student at Baylor) worked at one such music store. McCann was forced to watch Koresh to make sure he didn't scare off paying customers with his proselytizing.

"He was very focused, soft-spoken, but persistent," McCann

recalls, "like any person who really believes what they were doing. But he was very focused in what he was saying. It wasn't to the point of 'If you don't accept what I'm saying, then you're going to be out on your ear.' He wasn't vengeful, he wasn't mean, he wasn't angry ever—just persistent, pleading."

At one music store, Koresh often left equipment on consignment, hanging around for hours on end, talking to customers and salesmen alike. He proved so trustworthy that he was allowed to take new equipment home to try it out. In return, he often loaned his state-of-the-art PA equipment to needy bands.

He would haggle over the price of strings, one dealer said, then drive back to Mt. Carmel in a $30,000, black, '66 Corvette.

At Christmas 1990, Koresh brought English artist Cliff Sellors to Piazza String World in Waco. Sellors hand-painted an incredible Christmas scene across the windows of the music store, complete with realistic reindeer playing electric guitars. He spent day and night on the windows, staying up in the cold long past closing time. It was with Sellors that Koresh concocted the idea of selling airbrushed guitar bodies through a catalogue. McCann said the artwork was unbelievably vivid:

"One had a black body and on the front was sort of a landscape scene with a graveyard scene at the bottom. The central image was a skull attached to a spine that turned into a rose at the bottom. There were also images of guns, and skeletons rising out of the grave with guns."

Another store owner confirms the quality of Sellors' work and was under the impression that Koresh had dictated the imagery. A few of the airbrushed guitars were left at the store on consignment, but none ever sold in Waco and eventually Koresh took them back to Mt. Carmel.

While Koresh continued to blow hard-earned money on toys, life at Mt. Carmel—which Koresh was beginning to call Ranch Apocalypse—got tougher. Promised improvements never took place. The physical squalor of the site, coupled with Koresh's careening mood swings and voracious sexual appetite, caused a few more believers to trickle away. But not many.

That's because Koresh understood another sad truth of human nature: People throw good money after bad. Once they've made an investment, whether of emotion, time, money, or labor (and in the case of the Branch Davidians, all of the above), rather than face the fact they've been made fools of, and cutting their losses and running, they will continue to invest ever greater amounts of time, money, emotions, and so on.

If they just leave, what do they have to show for all those years, all that money, all that loyalty, all that willingness to believe?

At Ranch Apocalypse, as before, Koresh also took literally—and personally—Matt. 10:35:

For I am come to set a man at variance against his father, and the daughter against her mother, and the daughter-in-law against her mother-in -law.

He separated families as a matter of course (standard procedure from Cult Leader 101: make *yourself* the family patriarch). First take the fathers from the mothers. Then the children, who by age 12 were moved to live in dormitories with members of the same sex.

And they were neglected, both educationally and physically.

During all of 1988, for instance, many of the children were not allowed to go to school—and when they were, Koresh made it a practice to interrupt homework with impromptu Bible studies.

There was no running water in the compound, which made it difficult to keep clean. On at least one occasion, there was an outbreak of lice in the compound that lasted for months.

In fact, during his time in the compound, Breault said, the sanitation conditions were "appalling." Koresh had promised both his members and the media that he would put running water on the property. Because there were no real toilet facilities, raw sewage was simply buried in the ground wherever there was room. Mt. Carmel had a well, but it was never restored. Water would be brought into the compound in a large yellow container on a flatbed truck. Drinking, cooking, and bathing water was obtained from this yellow container, which was rarely, if ever, cleaned.

"Thus this container was literally encrusted with algae and Howell eventually forbade anyone from obtaining their own drinking water," Breault claimed. "Compounding the sanitation problem was the fact that one of Howell's followers was a carrier of hepatitis B, a highly contagious condition. When people carried their excrement to be buried, it would sometimes spill out of the bucket and fall unburied to the ground."

Because of these horrific conditions, someone in the compound was almost always sick. During winter, illnesses were complicated by the fact that there was no heating to speak of, and no way to get firewood.

"At one stage," Breault recalled, "Howell forbade any store-bought firewood. In fact, I cannot recall one instance in which firewood was brought in for anyone."

Koresh even exercised autocratic control over the menu—as he did every other aspect of life in Ranch Apocalypse. For instance, during one period Koresh placed all food, except bananas, off-limits. During another period he forbade anyone to eat oranges and grapes at the same meal—but allowed them to eat oranges and *raisins*.

But nothing, not alcohol, not meat, not prepubescent girls, was denied the "Sinful Messiah."

If he wanted to keep his followers, including the babies, up in Bible studies till 1:00 a.m , and then play his guitar at top volume all night, he did. If he wanted to shoot his new machine guns at dawn, he did. If he wanted to play soldier and throw hand grenades on the property day or night, he did. If he wanted increasingly younger girls for his harem, he took them.

But not even Ranch Apocalypse's 77 acres were totally screened from the outside world. In January 1992, the McLennan County Sheriff's Department investigated complaints of automatic arms fire and explosions at Mt. Carmel. And these weren't just the night-sound concerns of widow women with yappy poodles. Some of the reports came from Robert Cervenka, who owns the property on the east side of Mt. Carmel. Cervenka, an Army veteran, told deputies that, judging from what he could hear, the guns might be M-16s and .50 caliber machine guns.

Also in January, Koresh ordered Sellors to divorce Robyn Bunds. Wayne Martin served as the lawyer.

[1] Based on King David's warrior bodyguard from 1 Chronicles 11:10.
[2] And I went unto the prophetess; and she conceived, and bare a son. Then said the LORD to me, Call his name Maher-shalal-hash-baz.

SOURCES

Davy Aguilera sworn affidavit

Marc Breault interview

Marc Breault sworn affidavit

Earl Dunagan sworn affidavit

David Jewell sworn affidavit

Barry McCann interview

Interview (source requested name not be used, copy of name with publisher)

Dallas Morning News, March 10, 1993

Dallas Morning News, March 25, 1993

Dallas Morning News, March 25, 1993

Dallas Morning News, March 26, 1993

Waco Tribune-Herald, February 27, 1993

Waco Tribune-Herald, February 28, 1993

Waco Tribune-Herald, March 1, 1993

Waco Tribune-Herald, March 2, 1993

Waco Tribune-Herald, March 6, 1993

Waco Tribune-Herald, March 8, 1993

Waco Tribune-Herald, March 12, 1993

Waco Tribune-Herald, March 13, 1993

Waco Tribune-Herald, March 15, 1993

Waco Tribune-Herald, March 20, 1993

Waco Tribune-Herald, March 22, 1993

Waco Tribune-Herald, March 28, 1993

Waco Tribune-Herald, April 17, 1993

Waco Tribune-Herald, April 18, 1993

Waco Tribune-Herald, April 21, 1993

Waco Tribune-Herald, April 24, 1993

Waco Tribune-Herald, May 5, 1993

Chapter 8

For a while, Dave had a heaven. How heady it must have been, to be the Son of God, God on Earth in the late '80s and early '90s. With all the fleshly pleasures and nothing forbidden.

The future was bright: Beer and ice cream. Electric guitars, muscle cars, and machine guns. A bumper crop of eager adolescent females to whom he could issue little Star of David necklaces and cheap gold "promise" rings, and a backup contingent of older, lustier jades doubling as procurers.

An entire compound full of slave labor: Need a swimming pool? They'll dig it. Underground shooting range? You got it. Tunnel system? Roger.

And they paid the Son of God for the privilege, turning over their life savings and whatever they could earn on the side. Want my house? Heck, Dave, you're the Son of God, it's *already* yours. Daughter? Wife? A privilege, uh, Sir. (What's the proper honorific for God?) Consider it done.

It must have been fun, that power—being Lord, and master of that private army. More invigorating than the sex, the money, the unquestioned adulation, was the swaggering, rakish, devil-may-care danger of it all.

Keep your Megadeth, your Alice in Chains, your Guns N' Roses. When it comes to bad, you can't touch this.

Those were the good old days—and Billy Walker remembers those days and their atmosphere. Walker is like a lot of the people in this hardscrabble neck of McLennan County—underemployed. He's a part-time meat cutter at a local grocery chain. Later, he'll feel fortune calling him to come help the hucksters sell T-shirts on Holy Hill, where he has been hanging around, off and on, since the siege began.

It is still early March, mid-standoff. From the vantage point on Holy Hill, one can just barely see the choppers circling on the horizon, barely see the compound, still standing. The standoff is less than a week old.

Billy Walker comes over to the barbed-wire fence and squints, both to better see and to better remember.

Billy still visits David Koresh, but now it's in the Kingdom of Memory.

Billy, like Dave, loves two things: Fishing and beer.

Anybody who lets Billy have his fill of one or the other is pretty much his friend for life. David Koresh let Billy go fishing in the ponds and tanks of Ranch Apocalypse. Even gave him a key to the gate. Billy had to bring his own beer.

Two more things about Billy. He's a likable, countrified, gimme-capped old Bubba of a cuss—and nobody could ever mistake him for danger. These are the reasons Koresh allowed him to see so much—tunnels, day-to-day life—in fairly close proximity. He even invited Billy to have dinner with them.

Billy'd started fishing the compound's three tanks in the mid-1980s, back when George Roden was still in control. He just drove up to the gate one day.

Roden, always on the alert for the return of Vernon Howell, came storming out wanting to know what Walker was doing on his land. Billy just grinned his goofy grin and said, "I go fishing a lot and you've got some tanks down here that I shore would like to go a-fishin' in."

George Roden thought about it for a moment and got a little tickled and said that would be fine. Within a month or two, though, tired of letting him in and out, Roden just gave him a key to the gate.

Roden was not a man of too many words with strangers, but he seemed to have taken a liking to Billy, and didn't push the religion thing.

"He asked me what denomination I was, and that's the only thing he ever said about religion. I told him I was a Baptist but my wife was a Catholic. He asked, 'Do you ever intend to change over to Catholic?' I told him no.

"And he asked me what was my problem with the Catholics. I told him I just couldn't believe that the priests and nuns don't have no sex."

George speculated with him a moment on that, saying he figured they kept on at it right up until they took their very final vows and then swore off for good, and then "that was the end of it. He never mentioned any other Bible stuff."

But at about the same time that Billy started fishing there, Vernon Howell started coming back onto the compound.

"Roden told me a lot of times that he was going to have to run him off. He told me he was going to have to leave out from there or kill him, one or the other. This man just come in there and decided he was going to be the ruler. That was it. He announced it to the whole compound. Old man Roden told me a bunch of times that he was eventually going to have to make him leave from out there or kill him, one or the other."

But, as with the usually cantankerous Roden, neither did the egomaniacal Vernon Howell see Walker as a threat.

According to Walker, he met Howell on several occasions while he was out there fishing, before Roden was run off.

"He preached to me every time I went out there. Every time I seen that man, he preached to me. Never for very long, but he told me that he was a disciple of God and he was going to take God's place before the world came to an end.

"It was all just a bunch of *crap*, you know? Even his people told me this God stuff, the ones who were out there. Roden was still in charge, but he didn't stay there too long after Howell come."

Over time, Walker became fascinated with the now-universal question: What do these people see in Vernon Howell?

Billy spits over the barbed-wire fence. "I never did figure it out—other than this: I think those people thought if they did not do what he said they were going to do, then he would kill them and bury them right there. That's just my saying that; nobody told me that. But when I met them they appeared to be actually frightened of this man to the extent that they would not do anything until they got his approval to do it. They would not just go do something on their own."

Billy didn't see the shootout with Roden, but he did listen to it on the scanner.

And after the shootout, with Roden in the state hospital and Koresh in the compound, Billy just kept on fishing—though the fishing arrangements were a little different.

Under Howell, it was tacitly understood that Billy had to sacrifice about 20 minutes of his fishing time so that Koresh could preach to him. "I'd sit there on the porch and listen to him preach. He always had his Bible, and he'd open it up and show me a Scripture and quote it. Sometimes he'd talk about other things, like playing in a band and such, and then he'd say, 'Go on down there and fish, but if you catch anything, come by and show it to me. I don't want any of them, just come by and show me what you caught.'

"And I'd bring 'em by, of course; I always treated him right because I wanted to keep on fishing in there. There is some good fishing in those tanks, man. I caught some black bass in there that weighed seven or eight pounds. And I'd bring them by, and he'd look at them and say, 'Looks like you did pretty good. Come back when you get ready.' He was always nice to me. I never had a bit of a problem with him.

"Now, I did ask him if I could hunt out there, doves when they were in season, and they would *not* let me do that. They never did say nothing about whether it was a religious thing or they just did not want guns out there because it might fire up the law people or something. They just told me that they did not want me hunting out there, period."

The biggest tank is the one right by the compound. Sitting there with his line in the water, Billy Walker had plenty of time to watch Koresh knock down the ramshackle mess of houses that had prevailed under Roden and transform the property into the solid front the compound presented by the time the siege began.

Sometimes Howell would come out and talk longer than usual, even joining Walker for a beer. "On numerous times he told me that he had numerous wives. He would never point them out to me and tell me which ones they was or nothing; he said he had numerous wives, is all he would tell me. Sometimes he would say 'numerous' and sometimes he would say that he had 'more than one' in the compound. But he was doing pretty good over there."

And, over time, when the Davidians realized that Howell wouldn't become angry if they talked to Walker, they begin to interact a bit more freely with him.

One of them was Robyn Bunds.

Said Walker: "I got curious about this kid [Cyrus Koresh] because she told me that he beat that kid, that he beat that kid until it bled on the butt and everything. But of course that kid had clothes on and everything, and he was just a baby when I seen him. And he always had clothes on, shorts and blue jeans and stuff like that.

"...But them kids, they were all just as friendly as they could be to me. They didn't act real scared or nothing—but they would point at David and tell you, 'That's my God.' They were doing it almost from the first time I went out there... I mean they was crude about it, they was out in the open about it.

"But as far as I know, and I've lived here since 1956, them people never bothered no one else that I know of, community-wise. They have always just stuck to themselves. The women, they come into town and worked some; the men mostly just stayed out there and worked on the buildings."

Smiling, amiable Walker became ever more acceptable to the Branch Davidians, to the extent that Koresh gave him a no-doubt-sanitized tour.

He showed him guns, and he showed him the tunnels.

The tunnels were "just an underground deal that leads to all them houses. [They're] made out of cinder blocks. But it is not nothing special. They just dug a trench, lined it with cinder blocks, put a concrete top on it, and covered it with dirt. You can't see it or nothing. But they did all that stuff themselves. It's a fascinating deal.

"I never did see but 10 semi-automatic weapons. I don't know what they were, but they were semi-automatic. They were not automatic. Now, I'm not saying they couldn't be *made* automatic... At that time, they were in their recreation part thing in an open closet in a gun rack thing. No door or nothing. Looked to me like anybody could go up and get one that wanted one. They were open to them to use."

And one evening Billy Walker finished fishing and took the day's catch by the compound to show Koresh. It was about suppertime, and Howell asked him if he'd had dinner, and if he'd like to stay and eat.

Walker thinks that Koresh really didn't want Walker to take him up on the dinner offer, that Koresh was just being the gracious lord of the manor; but Walker was too curious not to jump at the chance.

Meals, like everything else at Ranch Apocalypse, centered around Koresh.

There was a long, low, wooden table stretching the length of the main dining room, with benches on each side, and covered with a plastic tablecloth. The women—never the men—would bring out the dishes and set them on the table.

"And then they would all, well, not *kneel* down, but sort of bow down and say something or other that sounded like it was in a foreign language, but it really wasn't. I guess it was their language, or something. And then they would all sit down and say to me, 'go ahead and help yourself,' and they'd pass all the stuff around. But they mainly had squash and peas, beans and corn, and then they had a salad made out of celery and stuff like that and everything. They did not eat any meat at all. Some of them wanted to but they would not go against him.

"They actually came out and told me, later. I asked them because I was curious about it, why they were not eating meat and they said that 'the only one who can eat meat here is him.'

"And he was sitting right there in front of everybody, eating meat. I mean, he had *roast*... Likewise, I always carried beer out there when I went fishing, and he'd drink a beer with me. And some of them out there wanted to drink beer with me, too, but they wouldn't do it because they were afraid he would beat them or something, I dunno. I think there were some that wanted to, but they would not go against him. They are dead set, they are actually brainwashed on him. He has got them people where they think he's actually God. It has always been that way. I could tell that when I first went out there."

Before the siege, and probably afterwards as well, Koresh's constituents sat on long, low benches that would seat probably 100 people. (There were about 50 on hand the time Walker was there.) And guess who was at the head of the table. Not on any bench, though. "He didn't have a chair. He had a deal like in a Catholic church, where the priest goes up and sits in it. It was something like that."

You mean a throne?

"Yeah. A throne. Eatin' roast beef and drinkin' beer. Them folks didn't talk much during the meal. They just said that little foreign-sounding thing they said, and then everybody ate, and then after they got through, they just got up. The women picked up everything and cleaned it all up."

All the Koreshians were passive, but the women most of all.

"They all wore long clothes, dresses and stuff. I never did see them in nothing else. And they had a silk-like cape thing that they wrapped around themselves... They didn't wear makeup, either. Some of them are very good-looking women."

Again Walker's curiosity emerged. He approached one of them, a pretty woman about 22 or 23 years old, and said, "I ain't trying to nose into your bidness, and I believe in religion and everything, but I need to ask you a question."

She said, "Ask me, and if I can answer, I will."

"How come y'all don't wear makeup or nothing like that?"

She replied: "Well, we *can*—but he tells us when we can and can't do it. He tells us what we can wear and what we can do. If he wants us to put lipstick on, we do—but he's got to tell us that he wants us to do it."

Walker pauses a moment, thinking back, sucking down about half a can of Coors during the lull. "Oh, yeah. There was this one, she was real open to me. She said that 'anytime he comes in here he can pick any of us out that he wants, and tell us that he wants to see us, and we have to go'... Man, he was living like a king over there."

But David Koresh had an Achilles heel—feet of clay. And these were in his boots.

We have walked, in fact, in David Koresh's boots.

Jesse Amen was the visitor who sneaked into the compound on March 16. He was the last to enter the Branch Davidian compound after the siege and the last to leave it before the fire. Jesse was already quite road-worn, even upon his arrival; the eight days he had broken bread and MREs (meals ready to eat) with the Davidians had added little to his sartorial splendor. So the Koreshians outfitted him with better gear for his reemergence and trek back into Babylon. Koresh personally gave him a pair of his boots.

Anyone who long converses with Jesse soon understands that his mind is on larger, stranger concerns than the several thousand dollars he could have easily obtained for such famous footgear, should he have allowed strangers to cast lots for them. Jesse is constantly attuned to the latest intelligence and admonitions from the voice he calls "The Father." And after the fire and shortly after Jesse got out of jail, the Father instructed that he shalt no more wear the Holy Boots.

The Father directed him to give them unto Mariah, one of the watchers on Holy Hill. (See chapter 13.) He gave them to Mariah, a.k.a. Bathsheba, a.k.a. Maid Marian, for safekeeping until such time as their Owner should return to claim them.

And Mariah made a place for them in her shopping-bag luggage ensemble and didst take the boots unto Holy Hill, and display them unto her inner circle.

She allowed some chosen from amongst them to try them on, and we were among those Elect.

It is with some superstitious but understandable trepidation that one puts on any dead man's boots, and especially those of a dead man who some believe is going to be coming back for them.

The thought crosses one's mind, as the boots slide on: What if he wants them back right now? And then, one waits for the "evil" to leave the boots and take possession of one's soul.

And then, finished giggling, one is merely standing up and walking around in them among all the T-shirt vendors selling wares that profane his name, trying to get some feel for the One who wore them—some psychic resonance, some spiritual remembrance of who he was.

Suddenly, the eyes are opened to the essential nature, the

The Symbolic Code, Victor T. Houteff's apocalyptic magazine.

Victor T. Houteff, founder of the Davidian faith, standing on the grounds of "old" Mt. Carmel. *Credit: The Texas Collection, Baylor University, Waco, Texas*

A sampling of Davidian literature since 1930. At one time, the publishing arm of the Davidian organization was printing 48,000 tracts every two weeks.
Credit: Bob Darden

Victor T. Houteff's first book, *The Shepherd's Rod,* the "Bible" of the Davidian sect, written in 1929. Houteff founded the original Waco Mt. Carmel.

Victor Houteff and his wife, Florence. It was Florence who set April 22, 1959, as the day of the Second Coming. *Credit: The Texas Collection, Baylor University, Waco, Texas*

Two unidentified Davidians in front of the dispensary, one of the many buildings built by hand at "old" Mt. Carmel. *Credit: The Texas Collection, Baylor University, Waco, Texas*

In the Domestic Science building, sitting at homemade tables: Fayne and Dorothy Worth, in the foreground, with songwriter Esther Nesbitt (wearing glasses) at the same table with Mr. and Mrs. George Saether. *Credit: The Texas Collection, Baylor University, Waco, Texas*

Davidian founder Victor T. Houteff, flanked by two young friends at "old" Mt. Carmel.
The man on the left may be a young Perry Jones.
Credit: The Texas Collection, Baylor University, Waco, Texas

Davidian young people: Faith, Bat, and Carol Smith in 1948.
Credit: The Texas Collection, Baylor University, Waco, Texas

Right side of dam, pump house, windmill, and storage tank, with feed barn. The original site of the first building at "old" Mt. Carmel is in the background, overlooking what would become Lake Waco. *Credit: The Texas Collection, Baylor University, Waco, Texas*

B-8 office building, eighth building built, 1938–9. Upstairs, to the right, is the apartment of Victor and Florence Houteff. Downstairs and to the right is where Houteff's desk was. The main chapel was upstairs and in the middle.
Credit: The Texas Collection, Baylor University, Waco, Texas

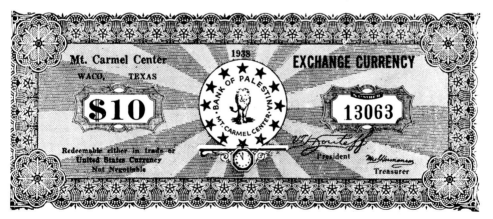

Davidian $10 bill, redeemable in either U.S. currency or trade at the Bank of Palestina, Mt. Carmel, 1938. *Credit: The Texas Collection, Baylor University, Waco, Texas*

Davidian founder Victor T. Houteff's headstone. *Credit: Bob Darden*

Houteff's small grave marker at Rosemound Cemetery in Waco. The Davidians were disinterred following the sale of the "old" Mt. Carmel and moved to Rosemound in 1960. *Credit: Bob Darden*

Branch Davidian logo

Benjamin Roden, "The Branch," and as such, the founder of the Branch Davidians.
Credit: From the collection of Amo Bishop Roden

George Roden, undisputed theocratic king of "Rodenville," following the shootout with Vernon Howell in 1987. After killing a man, Roden was sentenced to an indeterminate stay in Vernon State Hospital in Vernon, Texas.

Credit: "Door" photo by Steve Earley. Inset: Joe Roberts

Vernon Howell/David Koresh publicity photo for his recording of "Mad Man in Waco."
Credit: "Door" magazine

The heated cabin where Vernon Howell lived—while his followers lived in shacks (below) with no heat or running water—during the Branch Davidians' "exile" to Palestine, Texas, in the late 1980s. *Credit: Joe Roberts*

Buses at the compound near Palestine, Texas, where "exiled" Branch Davidians lived and studied under Vernon Howell/David Koresh. *Credit: Joe Roberts*

Branch Davidian compound near Palestine, Texas, April 1993. *Credit: Joe Roberts*

Longtime member Perry Jones shown outside some of the Branch Davidian shacks near Palestine, Texas, in 1987. Jones' daughter Rachel was Vernon Howell's only "legal" wife.
Credit: "Door" photo by Steve Earley

Early spring 1993 photo of "new" Mt. Carmel taken from FBI/DPS checkpoint, about one mile from the compound. *Credit: Joe Roberts*

ATF agents carrying their wounded during the shootout with Vernon Howell/David Koresh and his followers. *Credit: SYGMA, from KWTX-TV, Waco, Texas*

Military and FBI personnel loading wounded officers into helicopters at the staging point/ communications center near "new" Mt. Carmel. *Credit: Joe Roberts*

Aerial view of "new" Mt. Carmel in the days before the April 19 fire. Notice the tracks from the tanks patrolling the compound. *Credit: Brad Bailey*

ATF agents standing in front of a tank during the siege of "new" Mt. Carmel in the spring of 1993. *Credit: SYGMA, by Bob Daemmrich*

"Road signs" at FBI/Texas Department of Public Safety/Texas Ranger command post—a few hundred yards from "new" Mt. Carmel. The pot of lilies is a poignant reminder that the Easter season occurred during the siege. *Credit: Joe Roberts*

Close-up of the Branch Davidian compound, topped by the flag flown by the Koreshians, and with one of the signs they hung out the window. *Credit: SYGMA, by Bob Daemmrich*

Satellite City—the question was, Who's holding whom hostage? *Credit: Brad Bailey*

The Front Line: Photographers stand at closest approach—2.5 miles from "new" Mt. Carmel. *Credit: Brad Bailey*

In the wake of the FBI's crushing of a newsman's car, this sign went up. *Credit: Brad Bailey*

Yard art, Satellite City. Forced by the siege to stay near the compound, many people tried to while away the hours as best they could. *Credit: Brad Bailey*

Atalmadad—"Female disciple" keeping her vigil on Lamb's/Holy/Fools' Hill. *Credit: Brad Bailey*

A fortune teller on Lamb's/Holy/Fools' Hill. *Credit: Brad Bailey*

Merchandisers have a field day on Lamb's/Holy/Fools' Hill. *Credit: Brad Bailey*

Department of Public Safety officer peruses Lamb's/Holy/Fools' Hill offerings. *Credit: Brad Bailey*

Reporters massed for daily press briefings at the Waco Convention Center.
Credit: Bob Darden

FBI Special Agent Bob Ricks talks to David Koresh—through the media.
Credit: Brad Bailey

Koresh's lawyer, Dick DeGuerin, outside the Waco Hilton, detailing his dealings with Koresh. *Credit: Brad Bailey*

Dick DeGuerin accompanies Koresh's mother, Bonnie Haldeman.
Credit: SYGMA, by Bob Daemmrich

"New" Mt. Carmel, at the height of the blaze, April 19, 1993.
(Inset) First plumes of smoke from "new" Mt. Carmel compound.
Credit: Brad Bailey

Chief FBI spokesman Bob Ricks at one of the daily media briefings at the Waco Convention Center. *Credit: Brad Bailey*

A grim-faced Bob Ricks arrives for the final FBI briefing on April 20, the day following the fatal fire at the "new" Mt. Carmel. *Credit: Bob Darden*

After the fire, forensic experts sift through the ashes of "new" Mt. Carmel for bodies and other evidence, under flags flying at half-mast. *Credit: Joe Roberts*

Post-fire aerial shot of the remains of the compound.
Credit: SYGMA, by Steven Reece of the San Antonio Express News

Dr. Dan McGee interviewing George Saether, the source of most of the information regarding the original Davidians. *Credit: Institute of Oral History, Baylor University, Waco, Texas*

veriest core and the penultimate truth of David Koresh:

In addition to everything else he was, David Koresh was also *dumb*.

It was a special kind of dumb; not the kind that comes necessarily from a simple low-IQ lack of mental candlepower. It was the kind of dumb that comes from having all that candlepower, no matter how bright, shining on only one thing, to the exclusion of all else: himself.

David Koresh personified the deepest, darkest, dreariest, and smuggest narcissism-induced stupidity. It was the dumbness of weight lifters who throw away the whole rest of their lives in a quest for better pecs. It was the dumbness of a man who lives in a dump so he can afford an impressive car.

David Koresh was dumb, like a peacock.

This comes through no psychic gift, no sudden bit of spiritual insight; it comes from looking at the boots themselves, and comparing them to the man's record (and tapes and CDs) to see if they jibe.

And they do. These boots were made for talkin'. They gibber and prance and gyrate, tap-dancing out the message: David Koresh was dummmb-duh-dumb-dumb.

We like to imagine our antagonist, the Man in the Dark Tower, as a "malevolent *genius*" or a "mastermind," because this is more televisable, more watchable—than the truth.

The FBI and the ATF also played to this mythic stereotype, for even more obvious reasons. He is a master manipulator, they said. That's why we can't get him out. He is a sociopath who is capable of the direst of deeds. He is a mastermind, a shrewd, calculating adversary who will stop at nothing.

In short, the FBI wanted to say: Who else could have held us at bay for nearly two months?

But this is not how Vernon Howell *was*: It was how he *wanted* to be.

Truth is, David Koresh was just one of the many millions of damaged, disenfranchised, and woefully undereducated folk. And, thanks to his narcissism, he was blinded to all other realities and thus dumber than dirt. So, how dumb was he?

The FBI need not walk a mile in his moccasins to know the truth; they only need to take a look at these boots.

These boots strive hilariously hard to be obviously, leeringly rakish, and were bought and worn by a man who thought such footgear would make him "cool" and furthermore, telegraph his coolness to all who saw them. These two-tone, light-gray and dark-black boots are narrow and sleek at the foot, but at the shank are very floppy, soft, and broad.

Remember the cat in Puss N' Boots? Like that.

Remember the Three Musketeers? Like that.

These boots are a cross between Beatle Boots and what a man would wear if he fancied himself a modern-day pirate.

The shanks of these boots whirl and whisk around the ankles of the wearer, reminding him at every step: I am dangerous, I am rock and roll, I am cutting edge. *Someday, man, I'll be, like, drivin' up in my black Camaro, man, and then I'll be walking out on the stage with my vintage Fender Stratocaster and wearin' these boots, man, and I'll plug into my amp, and WAAAAAAA...*

Party on, Vern.

These boots would be at home on a man who could say: "Now, what better sinner can know a sinner than a godly sinner? Huh?" Or tell FBI negotiators: "Y'all are using psychology on us, but we know more 'bout psychology than you do."

These boots are very heavy-metal, and would be at home on the feet of some young man who is part of a band with some dangerous, pretentious name like Cadaver—or a man with business cards that said, Messiah Productions.

The proof is in the pudding, and by their fruits shall ye know them. David Koresh was just way dumb and bad wrong—dead wrong. So trapped by his narcissistic stupidity that he could not change. So trapped by the notion that his every thought and word was law that he could not reconsider.

So hungry for flattery that he believed his own PR.

So venal and shallow that he actually believed what he saw about himself on the TV.

So vain that he believed what he thought the Bible was telling him about himself; so self-centered that he was not able to divorce this from his own egotistical hungering.

Too dumb to say, hey, wait a minute, maybe I ain't the Son of God, which, think about it, folks, is pretty world-class dumb.

So arrogant he believed himself outside the rules; so haughty he believed in "King's X."

So uneducated that he believed in sorcery, the power of words; in astrology—that the stars not only controlled fortuity, but were furthermore arranged to benefit *him*.

So obtuse that he planned to be a rock superstar, even though both his music and his thinking were terrible.

So goofy that he believed, at least at the outset, that at the end of the siege of his gritty little compound (to him, the center of the universe), he would emerge as the Lamb of God and the King of the World to rule with the help of children begotten of 12-year-olds. Based on some stuff he had read in a book when *he* was 12.

And that most dangerous narcissistic "dumb" of all: So dumb that he presumed that he was smarter than everyone else in the world, when in fact, he was just barely smart enough to get himself into some truly terrible trouble.

David Koresh was so wrong he had to be right, even if it killed him—and it did.

So dumb, so wrong, he's *dead*.

Sin is such a relative thing. Many people on the outside felt called to judge Koresh's activities as "sinful." Others saw that he and his followers were merely stupid.

So what is sin? Usually just stupidity. Does God punish the stupid? Apparently, here on earth at least, it would seem so. Rather relentlessly. The wages of stupidity is death.

Ask MC-DOE-8.

Or just take a look at his boots.

Who was David Koresh—the man inside? What did it feel like to be that consciousness, the one that boiled away from the flesh that became the MC-DOE-8?

David Koresh was Vernon Howell. Who was Vernon Howell?

There are many answers; perhaps the simplest and most telling, however, is that he is a man who changed his name. Why does a man change his name?

Skip purely professional reasons. And skip fugitives, who change names to hide something or to hide themselves from those who are looking for them. Sometimes, people change their names so that they can *become* something—so that they can *be* somebody. They either were not the thing they wanted to be, or they thought of themselves as nothing.

There was, in his early years, at the core of Vernon Wayne Howell, the young man who had not yet become David Koresh, pain and powerlessness, emptiness and insecurity. And perhaps most telling of all, a pervasive impression, among those who knew him, of dullish below-averageness. And he was perceptive enough to know it.

His early life, though less than ideal, in fact was no more grandiosely tragic or cosmically ironic than the early life of, say, Hitler.

And except of course in terms of order of magnitude, the two lives, those of Koresh and Hitler, were not dissimilar, either in early biography or in ultimate outcome—the bunkers, the flames, suicides with their realms in utter ruins.

Just an inauspicious beginning, followed by a long spell of mediocrity, which looked as if it would taper predictably off into minor failure—except, unlike a million other such stories, each suddenly takes a major turn with a "revelation" of great specialness, importance, possibility.

Koresh seems to have emerged from his childhood and early adolescence a soul that was empty at the center—so empty and insubstantial that no identity, no matter how weighty, was ever enough to ground or substantiate him; and adulation, no matter how abject and total, only fed him enough that he always wanted more, to take one more step up the religious "food chain."

Marc Breault was privy to this process. "At first," he said in a sworn affidavit, "Vernon Howell appeared to be a conservative person whose only wish was to reform the Seventh-day Adventist Church. As time progressed, however, Howell became power-hungry and abusive, bent on obtaining and exercising absolute power and authority over the group... by 1989, he had lost all restraint."

Perhaps at the deepest root of the childhood pain and the powerlessness, emptiness, and low self-esteem—the root motivation that urged him to compensate by becoming one who was powerful, one who was esteemed, and one who could inflict pain—was a single word: illegitimate.

Illegitimate. In the society dominated by the "decent" middle class under which Howell grew up, it was a crushing thing to be—and to be called.

Illegitimate. Look up its synonyms and you get a feeling of its woeful weight. Spurious. Invalid. Illicit. Misbegotten. Inauthentic. Ungenuine.

David Koresh's life—his many titles, aspirations, name changes, and adopted identities, from King David to Lamb of God to Jesus H. (for Howell) Christ—can be read as a long, sad search for validity, and for validation. And where he could not find it in Reality, he built it from imagination—an imagination he came to mistake for the voice of God.

Howell's practices in the Davidian compound many years later reflect a strange compensation for this "insult" of illegitimacy and uncertainty of parentage: He insisted that all the children there, regardless of paternity, call him Father. His own "father," he told them, was God. And this entitled him to take the further step of insisting that he was the only one entitled to procreate. And he then set out to father a race of "perfect" children to help him rule the world—children who were, legally as well as socially, even more illegitimate than Howell himself; and many of whose mothers were married to other men.

Through his school years, the young Koresh, by even the more charitable accounts, was remarkable only for being completely unremarkable. A harsher view is that he was just a nobody, a loser.

Then there was an attempted sexual assault by three older boys, when he was seven.

The young Koresh, as both child and young man, was in search of empowerment, of identity, of legitimacy. The thin, frail youth began lifting weights as a means of attaining physical power. But at about age 12, he found his greatest empowerment. It was in a book—the Bible. And through his mother, who led him to Seventh-day Adventism, he discovered some rather liberal and urgent interpretations of prophecy, and the connections that would lead him to Davidian Seventh-day Adventism, and then to Branch Davidianism.

Here was the turnaround.

Just as Hitler would have remained forever a small, sullen man on the fringes of society if he had not encountered racial theory, so likely also would have Vernon Howell, had he not encountered Christianity.

On the subject of Koresh and the Bible, to paraphrase Carly Simon: "Vern's so vain, he probably thinks this book is about him."

The Bible has been a source of inspiration for millions; many believe it holds the only key not merely to a good life, but to a good life after death. Faith in a healthy mind may be truly healthy. But faith in a sick mind is sick—and no less powerful. For the kind of person most likely to be *pathologically* attracted to religion and its hierarchies—needy minds with no clear-cut identity or sense of place in the world who are seeking a quick route to power—faith and Christianity can be as dangerous a recipe for disaster as eugenics was for Hitler's Europe.

Family members in East Texas remember Howell being out in the barn, praying, praying, praying for hours at a time, or on his knees beside the bed all evening, sobbing and having blustery internal dialogues with God.

From those times, David Koresh was already well on his way to becoming the specially chosen, the Lamb of God, the Second Coming—in other words, religiously insane.

And how did he get to be that way? It isn't really all that difficult.

Anybody who goes so far as to claim a "personal relationship" with God, particularly one that involves weeping and wailing and tunic-rending, has already taken a giant step toward claiming a *special* personal relationship with God, and pretty soon a relationship in which God becomes almost like a junior partner.

Leave far wiser heads to debate the issue of whether or not God exists, and let us speculate instead on how man relates to that God when he does believe He exists.

First and foremost, man can only deal with God as a concept—a mental construct. He can read books about Him, books both good and bad. And he can think about Him, thoughts both good and bad.

But there is no external, logical, empirical evidence—other than, very clearly, the existence of the Universe, which is open to other interpretations as to origin and reveals "the hand of God," to the logical mind, at least, only in broad, impersonal strokes in systems (physical, gravitational, meteorological, biological, ecological, social, and neurological) which have clear-cut functions, and rules for functioning.

These rules reveal no recent major meddling or contravention of the rules by a Creator to favor—or even disfavor—any particular individual human creation.

Since the concept of God is based entirely on faith, which can be defined as "the strong willingness to believe, *regardless* of evidence," the concept of God always lands outside the realm of logic—and is thus susceptible to illogic.

And the more "personal" Koresh's relationship with what is, after all, a concept, the more illogical that relationship became, because it had become intermingled and even tainted by an even more illogical system: egocentrism.

We are so constructed that we each see ourselves as not merely part of, but rather the center of the universe. It's apparent, subjective reason for being is simply so that we may see it, be in it, interact with it. As we increase in wisdom, we realize that this is not so, no matter how it seems—or that, even if it is so, we cannot behave as if it were and still expect to get along in this world.

David never got that far. Instead of learning to set this apparent reality aside, he sought further proof that it was so.

Vernon Wayne Howell fell on the Bible like a starving man. By the time he was 13, he was well along the road to completely memorizing it; he was gobbling the words of power.

In his blind hunger, he ignored or distorted its more worthwhile and personally edifying parables and analogies. He instead dived straight to what was, for him, the meat of the matter—the two things he so desperately needed: legitimacy, or a sense of valid place and full acceptance in a scheme of things; and power—the means of making "true" the things that he wanted to have and to be.

It can scarcely be denied by even the most devout that the Bible is chock-full of people making outlandish claims. In addition to the claims of the central character, considered by some to be the most outlandish claim of all, there are:

* Claims by one group to hold divinely-granted dominion over another group, and the right to suppress them.

* Claims that natural events occurred in order to favor their group over others.

* Claims that the seemingly lowly and disenfranchised are chosen because of their lowliness to become great leaders, and the lowlier the beginning, the greater the heights of power— David the shepherd, Jesus born in a manger.

* Claims to be able to foretell the future—followed by subsequent claimants to the futures so prophesied, which, circularly, make the prophesies "true."

And perhaps most important, from the standpoint of manipulation, numerous dire warnings that anybody who argues with the assertion of its heroes is "of Satan" or "the Antichrist."

Mankind was in his childhood when this book was written, and the Swords and Sorceries of it appealed to the child David Koresh. To Howell, at the age where other kids are sending off box tops in the belief they will get a ring that actually decodes, it seemed that all you had to do to get the Power was join this club. Because the inescapable aspect of much of Vernon's later life is, do I want it? Do I want to *be* it? Hey, baby, all I have to do, since I'm a Christian (by his diseased definition), is name it and claim it.

Vernon Howell wanted to be a major player, a big deal. And so he began deciding which Big Deal Major Player he wanted to be. It really wasn't a very hard choice.

Job? Nope. Adam? Uh-uh.

Young Vern particularly liked what he read from Ezekiel.

And I will set up one shepherd over them, and he shall feed

them, even my servant David; he shall feed them, and he shall be their shepherd.

And I the LORD will be their God, and my servant David a prince among them; I the LORD have spoken it.

And David my servant shall be king over them; and they all shall have one shepherd: they shall also walk in my judgments, and observe my statutes, and do them. And my servant David shall be their prince for ever.

And he read from Psalms:

I have found David my servant; with my holy oil have I anointed him: With whom my hand shall be established: mine arm also shall strengthen him.

The enemy shall not exact upon him; nor the son of wickedness afflict him.

And I will beat down his foes before his face, and plague them that hate him...

His seed shall endure for ever, and his throne as the sun before me. It shall be established for ever as the moon, and as a faithful witness in heaven.

And the young boy reclining dreamily with his Bible there in East Texas and the Land of Make-believe began to realize: I'm not really just any old Vernon Howell... Hey! I'm not Vernon Howell at *all*.

What a different result if only he'd been reading *Conan The Barbarian!* Either he'd have gotten over it, or if he hadn't, he would just have smashed up a bar or two with a meat axe before they locked him up with George Roden.

Either way, nobody else would have believed he was Conan.

Because that book is not *supposed* to be true.

Who was David Koresh?

In essence, like all children who never grow up, he was a narcissist. That is why the press—the mighty mirror in front of which David and his Mighty Men might strut and posture and pose and preen—played such a role and every day locked the poor fool deeper and deeper into the inevitability of Dave's Last Resort.

And if a person changes his name to become the thing he thinks a name will make him—to gain characteristics associated with the name—he has descended to the level of sorcery.

It is unfortunate that there is no clear-cut rule for determining when you are talking to God, and when you just think you're talking to God but are really just talking to a part of your head.

It may be that at some point in his life, Vernon Howell may

have had a chat with God. But it is painfully clear that, most of the time, he was talking to himself—and generally, his self was asking himself what it was his own self wanted that day, because he always heard an answer he liked.

There is also some evidence of early absence of—and subsequent deliberate rearrangement of—the "niceties" of human socialization—the rules by which we agree to pretend that we each *aren't* the center of the universe, so that others may live in it with us.

With Vernon, either because of his unsettled early years or perhaps just thanks to the fact that his personal relationship with God kept getting in the way, there was a failure to impart most of the rules for living together by which we abide (and later come to love, for they let us also live).

Odd, that so many of these rules and taboos with which he so readily dispensed came from the heart of his beloved Bible. These rules suppress our darker instincts and baser desires and let our higher lights shine through. Either Vernon didn't have this higher light, or he didn't like the rules. And, moreover, he had the wherewithal to get rid of them in others: with words.

Usually, by using out-of-context snippets from the Bible.

While most people outside the cult decried his behavior, there was, during the siege, also among young males around Waco a fair amount of envy over his sexual arrangements.

It has been often stated that, without benefit of socialization— a hard state of affairs to find in humankind—males are naturally polygamous.

The natural man, Howell surrounded himself with people who devoutly believed in Scripture, so that he could excuse his otherwise intolerable behavior by quoting Scripture: This became his *modus operandum* for obtaining everything he desired.

The Bible, in such hands, becomes pretty much the Pasta Sauce of Guides for Living: "Hey, it's *in* there."

The man who can spout the most Scriptures, in such wide-eyed, gullible circumstances—and particularly the Scripture as he chooses to remember them—wins.

There was little doubt that Koresh could cite Scripture to suit his whim.

Moreover, he was most likely to recruit those without a wide ranging knowledge of the Book, thus allowing him to implant his version of it, which became theirs.

If power corrupts, religious power is of all powers the most easily corrupted and perverted to suit one's whims and desires. Because religious power is by definition absolute—inarguable to its adherents. Even where there is a board of directors or other such body, it usually becomes the rubber-stamp of a charismatic leader and *his* interpretation of Holy Writ.

While the leader in some cases may make noises about it being democratic, the actions of the democratic board are still subordinated to the charismatic leader's interpretation. "Yes," the subtler charismatic leaders say, "except for Koreshians 1:14, which I can only interpret to mean (whatever I want it to mean, which is what you're gonna do)."

In addition, most successful leaders of such groups are able to fully inoculate their followers with the belief that the assumption of these "leadership responsibilities" are an almost unbearable burden, and even elicit their heartfelt sympathy and admiration— when in fact, of course, the leader would not have it otherwise; in some respects, *could* not have it otherwise, as many are failures at everything but manipulation of their followers.

Koresh, however, succeeded beyond the wildest dreams of these lesser cult leaders/manipulators. He had no need of even the thinnest veneer of sham window-dressing. He had a real gift for couching what was good for him in terms that sounded like they were good for anyone who followed him. He could paint his most shameful—or enviable—excesses in terms of selfless sacrifice, of community-minded public service.

Once you are God, your favorable glance becomes reward enough for almost any kind of human behavior. Once you are God, a smile becomes an acceptable *quid pro quo* for almost any kind of humiliation imaginable.

Listen to Livingston Fagan, believed to be the only one of his followers Koresh released specifically to be his spokesman in the outside world. As Fagan confidently, perhaps even a bit superiorly, explained:

"Nobody understands the thing about celibacy and David having all the women. But the truth is, Branch Davidians have come to realize that sex is not a good thing at all. Sex is just a physical assault on another person. But it must be done in order to procreate. David took that burden off of us."

Dave sez: It's a dirty job, but somebody's got to do it.

Dave sez: But what the heck. *I'll* do it.

Dave sez: As often as possible.

Dave sez: Anybody need assaulting *right now*???

This man could sell hot rods and herpes in Heaven and harps and halos in Hell.

The other half of the world, the distaff half, has had some trouble with the sexual profligacy, too. Looking at it with socialized eyes, women find disgusting the Koreshian women's "submission" to Koresh's sexual desires.

But the truest tribute to Koresh's manipulative artistry, his con artistry, was his ability to overturn not only the societally inspired sex roles and taboos in himself, but to so easily and completely overturn them in others as well.

Women whose spirituality led them to Koresh were taught that only by their sexuality could they follow. And once the taboos were rendered moot, like natural women—or like teenagers throbbing for Bon Jovi—they went at it with gusto.

Robyn Bunds and others who have left complain about the arrangements now. But nobody seemed to be complaining back then. Back then, the only complaint came from the ones who weren't "favorites," and thus had less opportunity to "serve under God."

So those who are still looking for a Biblical perspective to put David Koresh into, and one that clearly and comfortably and scripturally designates him as the antichrist, or perhaps Satan, need to perhaps consider this appellation: The Great Seducer.

Chapter 9

Evil.

An ancient word. A hell of a word.

Probably the most dangerous word in the whole history of man, and the most ambiguous. Through its abundant appearances in pulp fiction, cheap melodrama, tabloid journalism, and the rantings of TV preachers, the word has become almost cartoonish.

And that's too bad, because Evil, in the, dark, powerful, monstrous sense, might have been a good word for David Koresh.

Many of his behaviors and aberrations can be explained and apologized away in terms both general and clinical, as being "bad" or "neurotic," but still something less than Evil with a capital E. Even his boots give the connotation "dumb."

His militarism and paranoia was painted by the government in dark and dangerous tones, as though Koresh were planning the Sack of Waco—but that characterization is based as much in the government's justifications for its actions as much as in actual fact.

While he stressed to his followers over and over again that the outside world was evil, such remonstrances were the result of his fear of that world, rather than his desire to correct it at gunpoint. And, while there were some sizable hand-held weapons on hand, the rest of his "military" delivery systems were woefully inadequate or mostly talk.

Koresh *talked* of putting together a radio-controlled plane to deliver "a bomb," but odds are it couldn't have been a very big plane, and it wouldn't have flown very far. There are no indications that one ever got off the ground, despite that period of 51 days when it might actually have been of some use to him.

Koresh *talked* about anti-tank missiles, telling the government he had weapons that could blow up the Bradley personnel carriers. The government had little choice but to take him at his word, and roll in the virtually indestructible M-1 Abrams. But in the final assault on the compound, the government discovered his talk was only the posturing of a frightened man.

The tanks encountered only those hand-held weapons, and the only "explosions" satisfactorily documented so far were those that occurred after the fire—and they were from overheated rifle ammunition and cans of food.

All reasonable and objective indications are that the drills and target practice and other militarizations of his sect were an attempt to prepare defensively. As to the paranoia: Are you paranoid when someone is, in fact, after you?

Some may hold that the rigorous training, miserable conditions, and deliberate physical deprivations he inflicted on his troops were pure cruelty. But they worked.

Thanks to the very rigors of Life With Dave, up to the very last. Koresh was able to trump the government's only major hand, which was to make the compound's occupants mutinously unhappy and divisive by making conditions "uncomfortable."

Since the occupants were already so accustomed to discomfort, conditions during the siege seemed normal to them. Other than cutting off the phones—which occupants rarely used, thanks to Koresh's supplanting himself as their "family"—it was largely life as usual during the siege.

(Most telling in this regard was the attitude of Woodrow Kendrick, following his arrest. According to his wife: "He doesn't *want* out of jail. He's happy in there. He's got everything he needs, and he's looking after his friends. He isn't worried about jail. Lord, no. He's happy where he is.")

Harsh? Yes. Evil? Only if boot camp and Outward Bound are Evil.

But yes: Festering deep in a corner of the heart of darkness hidden inside the mystery that was David Koresh/Vernon Howell/MC-DOE-8, there was Evil.

The word applies in full measure—because of what he did to the children. Not just the ones who died in the fire, but to all of them—both the living and the dead.

There is but one place and one time in the Kingdom of the Imagination in which the mind cannot long remain: the second-floor room. What did they think when Koresh herded them inside? Did he smile as he closed the door? Did he tell them goodbye? That he would see them all in Heaven?

We can mentally take seeing this scene through their eyes perhaps only as far as the smoke starting to come up through the cracks in the floor; perhaps maybe as far as seeing the orange glare of the flames through those cracks, and beginning to feel the heat and the growing terror. Did they claw at the door as the heat increased?

Attempting to travel further than that, the mind's eye is forced to shudder, convulse, and withdraw.

The mind must withdraw from the Evil—in fact, the greatest evil our species can imagine; the one thing which, if ever condoned, will truly mean the end of the world, is the harming of children.

David Koresh harmed children. Consistently. Methodically. Maliciously, capriciously, salaciously, and even rapaciously—and, darkest of all, perhaps, in the name of God.

And before he turned them into ashes, he dragged them through the mud.

The most horrific damage was done to the children he burned alive—but at least that sad story is over.

The subtler but greater damage may be to the ones who escaped the compound, the ones not burned but forever branded. In that sense, David Koresh is indeed still alive. Through them, he reaches through the smoke and flames and into the future to pour his evil there.

Dave was here.

Dave will be here again.

This is another of Dave's hells.

This Hell is for the living, and the future.

This showplace for the end result of Koresh's seemingly unending sexual abuses of young girls is not hard to find. It's about five miles from the compound—and it used to be closer, right on Loop 340 where FM2491 intersects it. It used to be right across from the Mag Bag—a Koreshian outfit which was operated near the intersection—and David Koresh used to go there quite a bit himself.

And in March and April, it was very well-frequented by agents of the ATF, the FBI, and, of course, the cameramen from the media, who, more even than most of us, "like to watch."

It's a place called "Sonny T's," and was a must-see (and for some, a must-see again and again) for every male member of the media or law enforcement agencies who passed through Waco during Koresh's spring siege.

Sonny T's is amazing, from several standpoints—first, from the standpoint that it can even exist, particularly in the shadow of ultra-conservative Baylor University. It's a bring-your-own-bottle, all-nude "gentlemen's entertainment facility."

And if "gentlemen's" is an overstatement of the refinement of the clientele, "all-nude" is an equally charitable understatement of the degree of *déshabille*. This is beyond nude. This is past even "nekkid."

Patrons here pay eight dollars to see what otherwise would

cost them the tuition and years of study necessary to become gynecologists. The lucky patrons are those who come in about half-drunk, whooping and hollering and sticking money in girls' garters—no G-strings here—and then leave, full-drunk, for the next sodden, honky-tonk venue, without ever having to think about this place, or learn about it.

If we want to keep liking to watch, we shouldn't let ourselves think about what we're watching. Because if one thinks too much, one finds himself in the same dilemma as that of a man who catches himself looking a little too long and a little too compulsively at some bit of pornography.

The thrill is gone when he starts to wonder about the naked person, the human life on the other side of the photograph. Would they have done all those humiliating things in front of that camera if they hadn't known that people were going to be buying, and looking? By looking, are we contributing?

Wonder if Dave ever looked that far.

Because David Koresh used to come into Sonny T's of an evening, both to the old place, where rampant play-for-pay forced local authorities to put on enough heat that it just kind of moved on down the road, and to Sonny T's new, supposedly reformed, allegedly no-prostitution venue, just out of Waco's jurisdiction in McLennan County.

Dave would go to the little store next door, which does a land-office business in beer sales because of Sonny T's. There he'd buy himself a six-pack of Budweiser before moseying on over to Sonny T's.

He'd pay his eight bucks at the little window just inside the front door, and they'd buzz him through the second, security door on into the main dancing area—the area with the colored disco lights, and the bump-and-grind, do-you-wanna-do-it music, and the island-shaped stage with naked girls rolling around spread-eagled on it, all smiling and flicking out their tongues and showing off their tattoos.

And Dave would sit there with his six-pack of Budweiser, and he'd watch, molesting them with his eyes and thinking what a *sinful* savior he was being. There aren't many contortions that these girls won't undertake for no more than a rolled-up bill in their garters. But if you're a special kind of guy with money to burn—a guy, in fact, a lot like Dave, there are still some special treats for those of loose morals and wallets.

For $10, one can get a table dance.

For $20, he may be the honored audience of one for a couch dance, wherein the patron sits on the couch while the exuberant "dancer" places one foot on each arm of the sofa, up close and personal, with the patron, surrounded by legginess, locked in the middle.

And $30 gets one the use of a little decorated room behind the cashier's office where a sign warns, "No Touching! One touch and the dance is over!"

It may be that, given the magnanimity of his conjugal arrangements back in the compound, during his trips to Sonny T's David Koresh had no great need for anything more than just coming in and watching.

Or it may be that a man possessed by such an ego would never consider paying for attention of any kind.

Or it may be that he was out recruiting.

By all available accounts, he was able to behave himself.

Sometimes he'd talk to Tiffany (not her real name and, moreover, not even the name she really dances under).

"He never touched me, he never attempted to touch me. He was a real nice man. And I never did a table dance or a couch dance for him. Someone else may have, he may have been in the club when I wasn't here. But I just sat and talked to him.

"It was like, when we'd sit and talk about something, he'd bring up these verses and stuff, but he really didn't tell you the whole verse. He'd just say bits and pieces, you understand what I'm saying. I don't know. He'd tell me a lot that I had the wrong God and all this other mess.

"And I told him, I said, 'Look, I know who my God is.'"

Koresh seems to have known who *his* was, too.

He never came right out and said, "Hi, I'm God," but, Tiffany said "you got the strong impression that he thought he was. Every time we'd talk about something, he'd come out with, like I said, bits and pieces of verses and it always came out of Revelation. I don't know why. In other words, it wasn't like he was quoting from the Bible, it was like he was quoting himself."

Koresh was well-advised to be on his best behavior in here, to keep his other little secrets back in the compound completely to himself. Because people like Koresh create the people who work in places like these—and though the people he puts in them may sometimes resign themselves to it, they don't appreciate it.

No dummy, Koresh must have looked around and noticed that all the girls have something in common. First, they're all in their late teens to late twenties and looking good, but where do they go from here?

Second, he must have noticed that, beyond the mere humiliations implied by the job's gyrations, the girls go further to mortify themselves—to mortify their own flesh.

Almost all have tattoos. And several of them have done worse. One girl has a pierced tongue, a stud in her mouth, which slightly alters her speech. Another has actually pierced her pudenda.

And almost all of them are fighting drug or alcohol habits.

And if Koresh had asked around, he'd have learned they have one more thing in common: someone a lot like him.

To say that every girl that Koresh ever sexually abused will turn out bad—perhaps the better word is unhappy—would be wrong, of course.

But this much is true: Every woman here at Sonny T's was sexually abused as a child.

"All of them. Me too," says Tiffany. "My stepfather."

In fact, almost every hooker on every street corner, every junkie trading sex for drugs, every submissive wife submitting to beatings alternated with forcible sex, every inwardly damaged "office punch," probably has someone in their background a lot like Dave.

Dr. Abby Meyering, PhD, is a psychologist with a private practice specializing in family dynamics and a clinical faculty member at Southwestern Medical School. Dr. Meyering believes that childhood sexual abuse results in intense feelings of betrayal, unworthiness, and a loss of control:

"Girls who are sexually abused become women who have been incredibly betrayed, and the most likely reason is sexual assault in what they thought was the safety of their own home. And if you are going to talk about that as a dynamic, it is a total violation of trust, coupled with the constant requirement from the abuser that secrecy prevail. Without the trust, and with the isolation, it's a feeling of intense responsibility; it feels very dirty, like they [the girls] are causing it—and this is often reinforced when they are *told* that they are causing it. It's a violation of the most basic need that children have—(to be safe. The fact that it happens in secrecy and there are no bodily injuries makes it even more shameful for them."

Many sexually abused female children may go one of two ways as they enter adulthood, becoming either cripplingly aversive to sex or promiscuous to an extreme.

The former is easier to understand than the latter.

Meyering continues:

"A lot of people have theories about the promiscuity—that it's an attempt to have an experience that felt different from the abuse. Or it may be a re-creation of the abuse and an attempt to get control of it. These women do express sexual pleasure; they want to be accepted, and this is how they do it. Most abuse victims tell me that they really just want to be held, but they believe they have to give sex before they receive that.

"You are really talking about women who believe that they cannot control what is going to happen to their own bodies. Their decision to sell them may actually be a means of control; it may be the best that they believe they can do.

"And of course you are also talking about women who sometimes have drug habits, because of that pain. Once the drug kicks in to kill the pain, the desire to overcome the pain in other ways decreases. The likelihood of their believing that anything else could work to ease their pain decreases.

"Add the shame of what they are doing and the shame they feel for what was done to them—and the fact that no one has let them know whatever happened to them as children wasn't their fault—and it intensifies the shame and the pain. It continues to snowball."

Sharon Obregon, director of the Family Place, a Dallas shelter for battered and abused women, agrees.

"It is also our philosophy that sexual abuse as a child is a precursor to prostitution and many other problems. Children who have been sexually molested act out sexually as adults. That's part of their profile; they become very promiscuous.

"That's part of the problem; their sexuality is an issue. And for many, it results in a value system which says that they are only as good as what they are worth physically. Self-worth and low self-esteem has a whole lot to do with it. And for many, it's survival. It's the way they get nurtured. For many, it is quite simply the way they get approval."

Yep. That's our Dave. "Are you being a good girl?" Dave would ask.

In the case of the Branch Davidians, the sexual abuse issue is doubly gnarly.

Because the abuser was the alleged Son of God.

The dancers at Sonny T's all say they enjoy the work. Press them, and they'll admit they enjoy it because it's a payback. They say they enjoy "teasing" their willing victims, but the teasing is a mild form of torture, a means of becoming powerful, regaining control.

Tiffany described the David Koresh she'd met as "a real nice man." And then, as the news of the Waco siege broke, she read about what the papers were saying he'd been doing before the ATF came after him, before the shoot-out, before he holed up in that compound a few miles up the road.

Now what would she like to do with him? "Take some piano wire and hang him up by his [testicles]. And cut them off." Because of the dead ATF officers? "No. Because of what he's done to the children."

You mean, the beatings?

"No. What he did to those little girls."

If there is anything sacred about the human race, it's the children. They are not just the means of continuing the species, but the hope of a better future. They are clean slates upon which we attempt to write the code that means the next generation will be better, more hopeful, less troubled than the last. David Koresh took these clean slates and used filth to inscribe obscenities upon them. He took bright minds and made them dark. He took childish love and perverted it into cheap and dirty sex.

And raping their bodies was, of course, not enough for David Koresh. He also raped their minds—even their souls: He took their natural longings for higher things, a knowledge of their Maker, and gave them a stuttering, Scripture-spouting psychopath in black and gray boots.

The Koreshian kids who survived now write "I Love David," and encircle the phrase with hearts. Psychologists say that these poor kids have learned to confuse love with fear.

They also talk of a whipping room, and recall that David Koresh insisted that they refer to their own parents as "dogs," reserving for himself alone the title of "father."

For the ones he killed and the ones he damaged, there may be some slight consolation: at least they were the means of his undoing.

Chapter 10

The undoing had already started by January 1992. The Jewells' lawsuit was now underway and Koresh didn't like the testimony he was hearing. Nine former Branch Davidians were testifying on David Jewell's behalf. For the first time, there was interest from various media outlets.

At about the same time as the custody hearing, a United Parcel Service employee named Larry Gilbreath was making a delivery to the Mag Bag, just a few miles from the Davidians' compound at Mt. Carmel.

Gilbreath had known for some time that the two were connected because, whenever he would attempt to make a delivery to the Mag Bag, an employee, usually Woodrow Kendrick, would tell him to wait, then phone ahead, and then instruct Gilbreath to carry the packages on up to the Mt. Carmel Center. There he was usually met by Steve Schneider or Perry Jones, who would pay the C.O.D. charges and take delivery of the packages.

Gilbreath never much concerned himself with what he was delivering until February 1992, when he noticed that on several packages there were invoices for firearms parts and accessories, and various chemicals which seemed to him might be explosives.

Once notified, local authorities, while far from panicked—and maybe even far from sufficiently concerned—started keeping a closer eye on the compound. Part of it was the fact that, increasingly, the building plan that Howell was putting into place resembled that of a fort more than a church settlement. The three-story tower topped by the Branch Davidian flag was not especially reassuring.

Then, on February 27, 1992, a Texas Department of Human Services employee asked to visit the compound. Child welfare investigator Joyce Sparks was responding to a complaint from one of the lapsed Branch Davidians that Koresh was sexually abusing young girls.

There is no record of Koresh's response to Sparks' request, but it probably wasn't Scriptural.

When Sparks visited Ranch Apocalypse, she was greeted by Rachel Koresh, who was very reluctant to talk without David Koresh being there, and who told Mrs. Sparks that she couldn't tell her anything because she was under "strict orders from him not to talk unless he was present."

Sparks was finally able to convince Rachel to let her talk to some of the children, one of whom, a boy about six years old, told her that he "couldn't wait to grow up to be a man."

"Why?" she asked.

"So I can grow up and get a long gun just like the other men here."

Alarmed, Sparks asked to return.

On April 6, she talked with Koresh, asking him about the guns. He replied that they were "too few to be of any significance," and offered to show her around the compound. But she pressed him on the guns, asking to see where they were stored. Koresh told her to wait about 30 minutes so he could "get the rest of the residents out of the building so they wouldn't see where the firearms were stored," and said he would then take her for a tour.

But during the tour, each time she asked about the guns, he would brush her off, telling her they were in a safe place where the children could not get to them.

She spotted a trap door at one end of a building and asked about it. Howell allowed her to look down through the door and into what turned out to be a buried school bus. Using a penlight, she could see that at the other end of the bus there was a refrigerator shot full of bullet holes. Koresh told her he used this for target practice, so he would not disturb the neighbors.

Sparks later told ATF investigators that she felt that the entire tour was staged and orchestrated. When she asked to speak to some of the children and other residents, Koresh told her they were "not available."

One wonders why he went to such trouble to hide anything at all, because in the next few breaths he babbled out for Sparks just about everything that he should have been hiding! He told her that he was the Messenger from God, that the world was coming to an end, and when He revealed Himself, the riots in Los Angeles would pale in comparison to what was "going to happen in Texas."

He added that it would be "a military-type operation" and that all the "non-believers would have to suffer."

Unknown to Koresh, following the successful completion of his custody hearing with Kiri, David Jewell had mailed a letter to U.S. Rep. Fred Upton of Michigan on March 17, 1992. In the letter, which both Jewell and Upton later made public, Jewell detailed the numerous allegations against Koresh and included a copy of Breault's signed affidavit. The letter also hinted, because of Koresh's then manic state, of the possibility of a mass suicide.

In early April 1992, the Melbourne (Australia) *Herald-Sun* printed an article quoting relatives of Australian Branch Davidians saying that some of their family members had called from Waco saying they were selling their property—and saying goodbye.

"Hey, I'm not ready to die," Koresh later told *Waco Tribune-Herald* reporter Mark England. "It's all lies. Every year we've gathered here for Passover. Every year.

"Look, the place is being built up. We're spending lots of money. A lot of people are putting time and effort in. When we got this place back from George [Roden], it was terrible. So we've been working three years out in California and other places to raise money to get this place back on its feet.

"I've got the water-well man coming in. I mean, two weeks in a row we're supposed to be committing suicide. I wish they'd get their story straight."

Recalled Breault, "Somehow the Australian press got a hold of it, and it just went wild. And one of the newspapers called the *Waco Tribune-Herald* to ask them about the cult and the suicide plans. And of course the *Tribune-Herald* is saying, 'Whoa, wait a minute, what's going on, *what's* happening?' And that's how they got started on it. They started investigating, digging around, finding this and that; they found me and a few others, and did a very good job of investigating it... "

Actually, the *Tribune-Herald* at first just talked about covering the story. But Witherspoon, Parma, England, and McCormick flat insisted on doing it. But the actual investigation didn't begin until late May or early June 1992.

The entrance of the traditionally conservative and overcautious small-town *Tribune Herald* forever changed the stakes and, in many respects, balanced the scales between the small voices for justice and Koresh's loud posturing.

In fact, the journalistic ball Mark England and Darlene McCormick finally knocked out of the park on February 27, 1993, is still traveling. And it's been all over the world.

Odds are good it will win them a Pulitzer.

That's on the professional side.

On the personal side, like Marc Breault, they sure didn't want to see anyone killed; certainly weren't ready for the morning of February 28, 1993. They were there—but there was no way they could be ready.

But before the *Trib* even made its move, U.S. Rep. Chet Edwards had forwarded Breault's 12-page affidavit to the FBI on April 15, 1992. And when he didn't get the kind of response he thought Breault's torrid testimony deserved, he filed it again in January or February of 1993.

Another unsung hero was making his move about the same time that Larry Gilbreath's growing suspicions were confirmed in May of 1992. At the UPS docks, a package accidentally broke open while he was loading it. Out fell 50 empty hand grenades. Gilbreath delivered the grenade husks—and then went straight to McLennan County Sheriff's Department and Lt. Gene Barber, and told him the whole story.

Barber had been at the original meeting arranged by the Australian Davidians' private detective, Hossack, some months earlier, and, unlike some of the others, was inclined to take the allegations seriously. Consequently, McLennan County officials already had their eyes on Koresh.

Capt. Dan Weyenberg, an accomplished helicopter pilot and Sheriff's Department veteran, flew over the compound taking aerial photographs. The Sheriff's Department personnel did not like what they saw when the pictures were developed and examined— a buried bus near a main structure that was obviously intended for use as a bunker, and the observation tower, which aerial photos revealed included windows on all sides, clearly designed to command a 360-degree field of fire.

Barber notified the Bureau of Alcohol, Tobacco and Firearms. On June 4, 1992, he met with ATF special agent Davy Aguilera and told him what had transpired. He gave him the background on Koresh, the cult, and the earlier violent confrontation with the Roden faction.

The ATF then joined the party. The shadowy Bureau of Alcohol, Tobacco and Firearms is little known to rank and file Americans, save for the members of the National Rifle Association, some of whom consider it Public Enemy No.1, even though it dates back (under different names) to the days of Elliott Ness and the Untouchables. In 1992, it was facing governmental budget constraints and a burgeoning world-wide traffic in the most powerful weapons imaginable. Now it had to deal with a bunch of nuts outside of Waco, Texas.

Still, Aguilera and others began methodically tracking the invoices back to the suppliers. It led to quite an inventory. In 1992 alone, agents learned, Koresh et al had spent in excess of $40,000 on weaponry and explosives!

These included 104 M-16s and 260 magazines; 2,100 drum-type magazines for M-16s, an M-76 grenade launcher, 50 inert grenades, 40–50 pounds of gunpowder, and many other items of military equipment.

More disturbingly, the ATF had learned that Koresh had also acquired from questionable vendors the equipment necessary to convert semi-automatic weapons into machine-guns.

Aguilera's investigation was also turning up the human side of the equation—the abused children, the strange sexual practices—that had disgusted Breault. Aguilera followed the child welfare complaints to yet another sordid saga of sex and guns—that of the Bunds family.

In fact, for Aguilera, what had started out as a weapons investigation was turning into quite an eye-opener.

Aguilera interviewed Robyn Bunds on December 11, 1992. What she told Aguilera about Branch Davidian guns greatly interested the investigator. She said, for instance, that Koresh was always in possession of some kind of firearm, and slept with one under the bed. And she said that after she left the cult in 1990, she returned to the Pomona house, which had been reserved for the exclusive use of Koresh during the late '80s, she found a machine-gun conversion kit under the bed. Cult members Paul Fatta, Jimmy Riddle, and Neal Vaega later showed up to claim the kit.

Robyn then introduced Aguilera to her mother, Jeannine. The Bunds proved to be something of a gold mine for Inspector Aguilera, and Jeannine Bunds, perhaps to expiate any lingering feelings of foolishness, was the most helpful of all in describing transgressions involving both guns and girls.

Jeannine Bunds told Aguilera that she had delivered seven of the 15 children she knew to be fathered by Koresh, and confirmed that some of the mothers were as young as 12.

Particularly helpful to Aguilera's investigation was her description of an AK-47 that Koresh was given to shooting on the grounds of the compound. AK-47s come in two flavors: semi-automatic and thus legal; and automatic and illegal without the proper federal papers, which Aguilera's research revealed Koresh didn't have.

Jeannine confirmed that it was a machine gun. It tore up the ground when he fired it. Which he did. Often.

Aguilera's completed affidavit, which was later made public, would form the basis for the ATF assault.

As the pincers began to close around Ranch Apocalypse, Koresh in June ordered a 1,000-gallon tank for propane. Also in June, according to the *Dallas Morning News*, McLennan County sheriff's deputies received information that machine guns, parts, and grenades were being delivered to the Mag Bag. A few days later, sheriff's deputies investigated reports of more 50-caliber automatic weapons fire and yet another explosion coming from Mt. Carmel. If Koresh was trying to keep a low profile, he wasn't doing a very good job of it.

Later in the summer of 1992, Aguilera's investigation took him right to boastful arms dealer Henry McMahon, Jr. According to the *Tribune-Herald*, McMahon, who no longer lived in Hewitt, said that Koresh had told him even then that the ATF was training for an assault on Mt. Carmel.

Armed with Aguilera's report in the late summer of 1992, the ATF leased a house 300 yards down the road from Ranch Apocalypse, for undercover agents. By now, copies of the various affidavits and accusations were flying everywhere. There is little doubt that Koresh had seen at least some of them. Bob Boyd, director of Children's Protective Services, told the *Tribune-Herald* that, by the fall of '92, he had known of affidavits of child abuse for "some time."

Koresh continued to put on a brave front for his followers, despite the increasing defensive preparations at Ranch Apocalypse. Davidian Wayne Blake is reported to have called his family and, in a profoundly dejected voice, told his loved ones that "The door of the ark is closed."

Shannon Bright, of the band Blind Wolfe, told England that he began "hanging out" with Koresh and some of his followers at Waco's Chelsea Street Pub in October. Despite the buildup, Bright says he and guitarist Eddie Goins were frequent visitors to Mt. Carmel. They told of seeing huge stores of food and water, but were never taken to the gun room. Soon Bright said he was spending all of his spare time at the compound, listening to Koresh's message.

About the same time Bright was discovering Koresh, the *Tribune-Herald* "discovered" Jeannine and Robyn Bunds in Pomona, California. Their testimony and frank interviews would eventually provide a valuable cog in the *Trib's* ambitious "Sinful Messiah" series.

Events then began to occur at a rapid clip:

*Two more explosions were observed at Mt. Carmel the first two weeks of November, including one seen by a passing sheriff's deputy.

*In early December 1992, "Robert Gonzales," an ATF undercover agent posing as a student, moved in with three other "students" at the house just 300 yards from Mt. Carmel. Gonzales reported that Koresh began "courting" him almost immediately.

*On December 15, the ATF contacted Breault for the first time.

*Later in December, a sad Shannon Bright left Mt. Carmel for the last time. When Koresh told him that his girlfriend actually didn't belong to him, Bright knew it was time to move on.

*About the same time, Judy Schneider made her last call from within Mt. Carmel, telling friends "It's too late for you."

*And, in the final days of December, Koresh ordered 10-15 outside surveillance cameras installed.

All of these events led to a sense of urgency among the various agencies and organizations with a stake in Ranch Apocalypse. But there were more to come.

On January 15, 1993, the ATF flew Breault from Australia to Ontario, California, for detailed testimony and to ask him the question that had been on their minds almost from the beginning. Did he think Koresh will fight? Breault believed he would.

By January 1993 the ATF had yet another affidavit. This one claimed that, to that point, the cult had collected nearly 100 fully automatic AR-15 assault rifles, silencers, and grenades—enough firepower for a small army. An army bent on conquest, not self-defense.

Computer buffs trolling through various computer bulletin boards in January might have encountered Koresh, probing for information on stories of government action against people charged with weapons violations. The *Tribune-Herald* reported that he was particularly interested in the outcome of the white supremacist Randy Weaver's bloody story in Idaho.

Other hackers would have been disappointed to discover Wayne Martin's bulletin board—"Seven Seals"—which had provided loosey-goosey information for a variety of people, not just Branch Davidians, was no longer operating by the end of January.

Agent Aguilera, on the other hand, was.

He believed that the agency was closing in on having enough information to declare that the ATF had "probable cause."

On January 25, 1993, he found his probable cause.

The last crucial witness was David Block, a member of the Koresh cult for only two months, from March until June 1992.

Ironically, Block pointed a finger at an important and possibly dangerous mechanical engineer, lathe operator, gunsmith, and designer still inside the compound—Robyn's father, Jeannine's husband, Don Bunds.

Don Bunds is a man upon whom Koresh had done his work very well. Even as he bedded the man's wife and daughter, Koresh was able to see to it that Bunds, above all other things, feared the fires of hell.

Block told Aguilera that he had seen Bunds sitting at a computer using an auto-cad program to design what Bunds told him was a "grease gun" or "Sten gun"—a crude machine gun developed during World War II.

He also told Aguilera that he had heard discussions about shipments of hand grenades and Koresh's intentions to reactivate them, and that he had personally observed a .52 caliber "British Boys" anti-tank rifle.

Aguilera was both excited and disturbed by the news. What *was* Koresh planning with that kind of firepower? He quickly made his report available to his superiors.

On January 31, 1993, the Branch Davidians owed $3,275.88 in back taxes on Mt. Carmel.

A notice was sent to the compound.

There was no immediate response.

Even as the web tightened, Koresh continued to make the rounds in Waco. He was seen in several places during the early days of February. The manager of Chelsea's told the *Tribune-Herald* that Koresh was in the pub during the first week of February, watching bands, having a few beers.

The other principle players in the drama were traveling as well.

Two weeks before the raid:

*Paul Fatta visited another gun show, buying and selling handguns.

*Guitarist Eddie Goins of Blind Wolfe met Robert Gonzales. He later told the *Tribune-Herald* that other cult members knew Gonzales was not what he claimed to be.

*John Segrest, the new McLennan County district attorney, received specific allegations of child abuse at Mt. Carmel. Unlike Gartner, he set the legal wheels in motion to act on the information.

*And on February 18, David Jewell and daughter Kiri traveled to Austin to meet with ATF investigators.

One week before the raid:

*A cultist called his parents and said they'd be reading about Mt. Carmel soon.

*Beth Toben of the DA's office began a preliminary inquiry into allegations of illegal activities at Mt. Carmel and conducted the first interviews.

*ATF agents began practicing for a proposed assault on Mt. Carmel at a specially built mock-up at Fort Hood in Killeen. The exercises were to determine how many seconds would be needed to complete each offensive action at the compound.

*David Koresh was busy wooing a new recruit, the student named Robert Gonzales. Koresh had been courting him for membership for three long months.

Koresh had played his guitar for Gonzales, then read the Bible to him, then plied him with personal questions about his life and his beliefs. After Gonzales had answered the questions, Koresh told him about yet another two-week Bible session that David could give him that would bring him up to speed on the Seven Seals.

Koresh warned him, though, that by becoming a member of the group, Gonzales was going to be disliked by the outside world and particularly by the government, because the government didn't think the Branch Davidians were a "proper" religious group.

Gonzales ignored the warning, and indicated he wanted to join anyway. Truth is, Gonzales almost *ached* to be admitted into the ranks of the Davidians.

Because his name wasn't Gonzales and he wasn't a student.

He was Robert Rodriguez, undercover agent for the ATF.

Most of Koresh's followers were skittish and stand-offish with Gonzales and others except with Koresh himself, who had sufficiently recovered from the La Verne confrontation to have regained his old feelings of omniscience. He happily welcomed the new fly into his parlor, and immediately began to subject him to his bizarre breakneck Bible studies and willy-nilly interpretations. It was unending, morning into evening into night—so long, in fact, that Koresh actually started to make sense to Rodriguez.

Rodriguez later told the *Dallas Morning News* that as time went on, he began to feel that he was slipping unwittingly into La-La-Land. His fellow agents living in the little farmhouse with him were much less exposed to Koresh, and would have to remind him of his real mission—talk him back down out of the crazy Koreshian clouds.

But so much Koresh had been crammed into him that it just had to get out. So to this day, it comes out in his sleep. He has nightmares about David Koresh. To this day, he told the *News*, he still remembers the pretty little girl, the toddler who fell asleep beside him during a Bible study. He remembers wondering, back in February, what was going to happen to the child, what her life would be like. She may have been one who, 51 days later, when she perished in David's Inferno, was wearing the pigtail that Dr. Emily Craig spotted in the rubble.

And he still remembers how he felt when he stepped out the front door of Mt. Carmel Center and into the cold, gray, drizzly daylight on the morning of February 28, 1993. He was trying very hard to look casual, to seem like the same Robert Gonzales who'd been there for Bible studies the day before, and the day before, for three long months.

It wasn't easy. And if they looked very carefully, the Branch Davidians in the room behind him would have noticed the tension in his shoulders and along his spine, at the point where he was expecting, any moment, to get a bullet in the back.

One step, one step more, keep on walking... the bullet never came.

But still Rodriguez knew there was disaster in the offing. And to this day he still wonders: How could so much have gone so wrong?

And stayed so wrong for so long?

Life continued in the compound, as it did in Waco, Washington, D.C., Melbourne, Australia, and around the rest of the world. On February 22 or 23, Perry Jones came to Star-Tex Propane to fill two 5-gallon jugs. He used to come in several times a week to fill Mt. Carmel's host of smaller 5-, 15-, and 25-gallon tanks with propane, but this would be the last time any of the employees would see the dapper little man with the carefully slicked-back hair.

Also on February 22, McCormick and England called Koresh at Mt. Carmel to answer some of the questions their investigation was raising about him. Whoever answered the phone told them that David was working on a car at the Mag Bag, well down the road. And most definitely *away* from the compound.

On February 23, 1993 (according to both the Dallas and Waco newspapers), an FBI memo circulating through agency channels claimed that *no* information had been developed that verified the allegations in the letters they'd received from Rep. Edwards. But some officials later claimed the FBI had made that decision without contacting any of the former Branch Davidians.

On Thursday, February 25, Perry Jones bought a 50-pound bag of popcorn at Chapman's Fruit Market in Waco. In a usual week, Jones would buy $200–300 worth of food using both cash and food stamps.

On Friday, February 26, Paul Fatta left Austin to go to yet another gun show. The *Morning News* reported that he returned on the morning of Sunday, February 28.

On Saturday, February 27, the *Tribune-Herald* unveiled their seven-part series on Koresh, "The Sinful Messiah."

Angered over the provocative nature of the series, the ATF hierarchy scrapped its plans to serve a search warrant at Mt. Carmel on March 1 and decided to go in at 9:55 a.m. on Sunday, February 28.

And finally, more than 60 years after Victor T. Houteff had his first message of the Shepherd's Rod, the players were all in position for the final act of the drama.

Chapter 11

Speed. Security. Surprise. Simplicity. Ample weaponry. Proper preparation. Overwhelming force.

These were the tools that the high-ranking officers of the ATF planned to bring to bear on their Koreshian quarry in the fields of Central Texas just outside Elk on the morning of February 28, 1993.

The problem was that David Koresh seemed to have more of all of it. And the puzzling question is, why did the ATF men believe they had any of the above?

Speed? It was called Operation Trojan Horse. The Trojan horses were three cattle trucks—covered with canvas. And they came lurching up a long, bumpy road, toward a watchtower which commanded a 360-degree view. Towards a compound that not only posted armed guards, but occasionally shot at paper boys. Was David Koresh supposed to be sitting in there saying, *Oh, goody! Wonder who sent me all these cows?*

Simplicity? With three helicopters buzzing overhead—the big *military* kind? And, on the ground, the vehicles of seven waiting newsmen?

But the biggest hole in the simplicity theory is this: If simple is what they wanted, it would have been much simpler to arrest Koresh while he was away from the compound, perhaps at Wal-Mart.

But that wouldn't work, the ATF said, because Howell had become a recluse. Nope, never left the compound. Had to get him there, at Mt. Carmel, because he hadn't been out of there in months.

Hadn't been out of the compound in months.

The media, particularly the *Waco Tribune-Herald*, began to knock holes in that one big enough to drive a cattle truck through. Howell was unbelievably peripatetic, for a recluse. He'd been spotted twice in the past six weeks at the Chelsea Street Pub. Three weeks before the raid, he'd been scarfing bean and cheese nachos at the Richland Mall restaurant, and had, in fact, been stopping by there about once a week from late January to the middle of February. Another store owner said Koresh dropped by three or four times a week.

How did he become such a recluse in the ATF's ever-watchful eyes?

Well, said ATF Deputy Director Dan Hartnett, he'd been under surveillance for several months, but, gosh, they hadn't been watching him *24 hours a day* or anything like *that*.

And then at the same press conference, Dan Conroy, ATF Deputy Associate Director, explained the deductive process which led to the ATF's conclusion concerning his new life as a hermit: Well, he *told* people beginning several months ago that he was not going off the compound any more.

Proper preparation?

The ATF has said that the special operations teams were put through their paces by commando trainers at Fort Hood the week before the raid, with the assault practiced on a full-size model of the compound. But some anonymous officers later said they'd only been brought into the raid the day before, and not informed of its objectives until the morning of the raid.

Security? ATF officials pointed to the fact that most of the raiding party stayed in barracks at Ft. Hood, and drove at dawn to the raid's staging area, the Bellmead Civic Center. But some of the agents, the ones assigned to the raid's command post at Texas State Technical College, stayed in Waco motels. Hotel maids gossiped about the ATF agents in army fatigues all leaving their rooms early in the morning.

Ample weaponry? Sharon Wheeler of the ATF would later tell the press, rather lamely: "The problem we had was that we were outgunned." Undeniably—but not understandably. The very reason the ATF was going in there *in the first place* was that the agency had good, solid, hard-won information that there were at least 100 M-16s and the means to make them automatic, at least 200 hand grenade casings and the gunpowder to have filled all of them, with powder to spare, and at least one M-76 rocket-launcher, and .50 caliber, armor piercing rifles, possibly automatic! And if the ATF couldn't find its own arrest and search warrants to review the Koreshian inventory, they could have read all about it in the *Waco Tribune-Herald*.

Surprise? Those guys couldn't have surprised Gomer Pyle.

The whole operation leaked like the Exxon Valdez, and there is every indication that at least some of the leaks were deliberate, hoping to attract favorable media attention to the troubled agency. The ATF seems to have tried to turn the "leaks" thing into a red herring, but every time they hauled it out, the fishy smell got greater. Ultimately, it would stink all the way to Capitol Hill.

The allegation was that someone in the news media had tipped a cultist concerning the impending raid. And common sense does dictate that one scenario is probably true: That a member of the media, from either KWTX or the *Tribune-Herald*, probably did warn a U.S. mailman, David Jones, that he might want to be careful because there might be trouble with those religious nuts. The warning was probably nothing more ominous than a genuine desire to see that no innocent bystanders were killed; unfortunately, Jones was a Branch Davidian.

The reason the "leaks" herring stinks so high to heaven is that it raises what are perhaps the two most important questions of the entire affair.

First, since so many media people were running around doing all this leaking, how did the media get the information themselves?

Well, uh, *maybe* from the ATF.

The ATF, after squawking about leaks, later acknowledged that ATF spokesperson Sharon Wheeler had in fact contacted at least two news outlets, WFAA-TV (Channel 8) and KXAS-TV (Channel 5) in Dallas to obtain "contact numbers" just in case, she added rather cryptically, there was some kind of ATF action over the weekend.

The ATF offered a caveat—that Ms. Wheeler did not tell what, where, or when whatever it was would happen. And of course that excuse has a distinct hitch: Anybody in Central Texas with four quarters for a newspaper would have known that if you were going to go looking for the ATF on the last weekend in February, Mt. Carmel was a highly promising place to start.

There it was in black and white, two days running, under some of the largest, splashiest headlines the *Tribune-Herald* had ever used, short of assassinations and declarations of war. "The Sinful Messiah, Part One." That was on Saturday. And on Sunday: "The Sinful Messiah, Part Two."

One of the most telling snippets, if you look at it twice, was this paragraph in the *Dallas Morning News*:

"ATF agents have privately criticized the Waco newspaper because it began publishing a lengthy investigative series on Feb. 27, one day before the raid."

Whoa. Let us review and reflect, because something is wrong here. This statement implies *intent* rather than coincidence. It implies that the oh-so-sneaky, oh-so-secure ATF called up the newspaper on Friday and said, "Hey, guys, we're gonna hit Ranch Apocalypse on Sunday, so could ya hold off on that Sinful Messiah thing?"

There are some indications that this might be precisely what happened. The ATF had already been in rather extensive communication with the Waco paper. Bob Lott, *Tribune-Herald* executive editor, explained it all to readers on March 1:

> Federal agents, who had learned of the questions we were asking in preparation for our current series on Mt. Carmel, approached us about a month ago and asked us to hold off...
>
> We waited about a month for other considerations not involved with their request...
>
> The ATF suggested to us in private that they were going to do something but couldn't say what, or really when. How long would the situation remain? After several days of careful consideration, we decided it was time to let the public know of this menace to our community.
>
> We did one thing we don't ordinarily do. As the ATF requested, we let them know Friday, the day before our first story was going to be published Saturday. In our reporting Saturday and Sunday, we avoided even a hint of our knowledge that the ATF might be involved.

If that's the case, then the truth is this: The ATF timed *its activities to* coincide with publication of the newspaper, rather than vice versa. In fact, the ATF later acknowledged, the raid had originally been scheduled for March 1, but had been moved back one day for "logistical reasons."

ATF timed it for the morning of the day after the first "Sinful Messiah" article. Rather late in the morning, in fact, so that even slow readers could have finished the shocking second installment in the Sunday paper. The ATF would be hitting the compound rather conveniently at just about the time the public had started to shout, "Something oughta be done about those pesky Branch Davidians!"

Vernon Howell had also been reading about what a bad and illegal boy he was for two days straight, and they were going to surprise him?

The scarier thing, the second big question raised by all the ATF's moaning and wailing about leaks is: if the ATF team leader, Philip J. Chojnacki, Houston Special Agent in Charge, had so many indications that the all-important "element of surprise" had been lost, why did they go ahead with it?

How did the ATF know about the leaks prior to the raid?

Well, reporters and photographers from the *Waco Tribune-Herald* plus a cameraman and reporter from KWTX-TV standing there, pads in hand, waiting for them to go in and "surprise" Koresh should have been one pretty good clue that maybe somewhere, somehow, the word was out.

A general rule of thumb for anyone who's trying to surprise anyone else, is: if even the *media* knows, it's probably not going to be too much of a surprise to *anyone*. KWTX claims to have divined that the raid was upcoming just by monitoring its police scanners. The *Tribune-Herald* got it from an unidentified tipster. And other Waco residents said they had also listened on police scanners to the ATF agents as they talked to each other on their walkie-talkies.

What's frightening is that the media had been on the scene waiting for the show since nearly 7 a.m.—three hours before the raid.

And for the ATF not to have noticed them—either from the undercover farmhouse or from the air, or from the cabs of the cattle trucks as they drove by—would make one wonder whether the ATF was thinking.

The other thing is, all indications are that the ATF's own undercover agent, Rodriguez, had come out of the compound and told the ATF there was to be no surprising Koresh that day.

An ATF affidavit states that the "tipped" cult member, David Jones, went into the compound a little less than an hour before the shootout. Rodriguez saw Jones' father, Perry Jones, summon Koresh to another room. A few minutes later, Koresh returned, nervously wiped his hands on his pants, and said, "They're coming, they're coming, the ATF and the National Guard. Neither the ATF nor the National Guard will ever get me. They got me once and they will never get me again. They are coming. The time has come."

After that, Rodriguez' greatest concern was initially just getting out of there alive, without saying or doing anything that would reveal he was a police officer. He made some lame excuse about not having had breakfast yet, and came out of the compound about 40 minutes before the raid began.

By the time Rodriguez got back to his three fellow agents in the house across the road, he was in a state of shock, almost hysterical, telling his ATF colleagues the cover was blown.

Yet at the time, ATF officials say they decided to execute the raid because neither the undercover agent nor agents hiding in a nearby house saw any evidence that the cult was preparing for the assault.

That story would change again.

One of the raid supervisors later told the media: "The undercover man is certainly having a hard time dealing with this now, and he certainly reported comments from Koresh that would concern you. But Koresh had said many times before that the ATF was coming and that 'they're not going to get me.'"

And again, the *Houston Chronicle* reported in late March that "Two agents involved in the case said that, at that point, the undercover agent alerted Jim Cavanaugh, an assistant special agent from the Dallas office of ATF, that Koresh knew something was about to happen.

"They said Cavanaugh and the other agents decided to move ahead as quickly as possible, aware that they no longer would surprise the cult, but hoping they could still get there before the Branch Davidians were completely ready for them."

As hindsight would reveal, this was a bad plan. A really bad plan.

And the truth may be that the ATF just didn't want to hear information that would have stopped the raid. The ATF takes some pride in its "cowboy," one-riot, one-agent mystique. They may have just gotten themselves so pumped up that morning that they felt more than able to meet any contingency short of thermonuclear attack.

And perhaps most damaging, the *Waco Tribune-Herald* found a witness who was on hand when the ATF massed at the staging area, the Texas State Technical College—a few miles from the compound—on the morning of February 28.

The witness, who preferred anonymity, said that before the ATF moved out, a federal agent started shouting, "We gotta move. He's been tipped off. He's nervous and he's reading his Bible and he's shaking." The witness added that the officers were "talking and joking around. I don't think they thought it was going to be hard at all."

ATF agents and supervisors at the staging area later confirmed that Charles Sarabyn, tactical coordinator for the operation, was heard making statements to that effect.

And yet the raid still went ahead.

The biggest problem remains surprise, or lack of it.

One very possible reason for the ATF's timing and subsequent continuation of a "surprise attack" they knew to be compromised is painful, even personally embarrassing, for us as American citizens to contemplate.

It may be that the ATF went ahead with the raid not in spite of the leaks, but because of them.

Did the ATF just want the PR? Because budget hearings were coming up in Congress in March. And, for such a low-profile agency, the ATF had been in hot water for quite some time. Many government officials consider the ATF redundant, noting that its jurisdictions overlap those of a goodly number of other federal agencies, notably the FBI. There has been talk of either drastically trimming the agency, or moving it from the Treasury to the Justice Department, or both.

But this time, so the reasoning may have gone, when Congress said, "What exactly is it you do?" if director Stephen Higgins could say, "Why, save little girls from crazy people with guns, like this," well, that couldn't hurt.

Being heroes couldn't hurt.

"Film at 10," showing busloads of scruffy, depraved-looking men being led away in handcuffs, sullen and contrite, and of David Koresh looking shocked, surprised, overpowered, and defeated, hiding his ashamed face from the camera, would make a nice summation of the "mission of the ATF," when Congress asked. So would extensive footage of a cache of hundreds of evil-looking assault weapons. Fade to Waco's safe and peaceful streets...

Pretty little blonde girls, smiling through their tears, being carried out on officers' shoulders past the TV cameras just might make the government think twice about any plans for moving the ATF over to the Justice Department, where they'd have to compete with their longtime rivals, the FBI. Headlines like "Beleaguered Government Agency Saves Day," followed by the ponderous, rumbling fulminations from the pundits about how "instead of finding fault with the government, we might want to consider supporting them. They know how to do their job. We ought to get out of the way and let them do it," would look pretty nice in the clippings file.

We may never hear from the horses' mouths just how important, how commanding, the presence of those cameras and reporters might have been to the final outcome. We will never hear anyone from the ATF say, "Well, I wanted to call it off, but with all those cameras and stuff, that woulda looked kind of bad..."

And it would have. "ATF Chickens Out" is not the kind of headline that a beleaguered agency craves.

Wiser heads almost prevailed, both at the top and among the rank and file. At the top were Ronald K. Noble, assistant Treasury secretary for enforcement, whose command includes the ATF and Higgins. Noble, who on February 28 had been nominated but not yet officially confirmed for his new post, had been a prosecutor in Philadelphia at the time of the ill-fated MOVE bombing, where Philadelphia police opted to end a similar siege with a bomb that left 11 dead and burned three city blocks.

Already preoccupied with the World Trade Center bombing and fearing a repeat of Philadelphia in Waco, Noble counseled against the action, telling his predecessor, John Simpson, that he thought it unwise to sign off on the action. Simpson, who had the final say-so, agreed, and further queried Higgins. Simpson wanted to know (1) if February 28 was the final chance for catching the cult members off guard; (2) if it was going to be a surprise; and (3) if the raid were canceled, what would happen.

Higgins reported back:

1. Yes, last chance. David Koresh *says* he's not going to be going anywhere ever again.

2. Oh yes. Gonna be a big surprise. Planning it for eight months.

3. What'll happen? We're scared they're *all going to kill themselves.*

And so Simpson signed off on it.

Among the rank and file:

As Robert Rodriguez later told Lee Hancock of the *Dallas Morning News*: "I think about it constantly—every day and every night—everything that happened and why. I've come to believe we never stood a chance that day. After learning about all the leaks that we didn't know about, we were doomed from the beginning." But the agent is haunted by his colleagues' deaths and the gnawing guilt for not being able to stop what happened.

He told Hancock that once the tragedy began playing itself out, he predicted a disastrous end, but the FBI, which took over after the ATF, just threw its hands up, and could not grasp his warning.

"What I told them that day, he would never be taken alive. He would never come out. Everything I told them, I predicted to them, they just couldn't understand it."

Perhaps the saddest aspect of all the bungling, however, is that it obscures the genuine bravery of the ATF officers who laid their lives on the line. Four of them lost.

Sometimes, only quiet contrast can capture roaring fury.

Video and audio tapes captured some of the gunfire that day—

but tape never does gunfire justice. Because of the limitations of audio equipment, it sounds hollow, mundane—pop pop pop, like balloons being punctured.

Woodrow Kendrick may indeed be the mad-dog Branch Davidian cop killer that the government has made him out to be—but you sure can't tell it to look at him, or by listening.

When Kendrick, with his elfin features and high-pitched, semi–Elmer Fuddish widdle voice, walked into the courtroom on March 10 and saw all the people sitting there, he broke into a beatific, angelic smile. If Kendrick were a stuffed toy, he would sell very well.

Kendrick, who was not arrested until March 10, was accused of being involved in a second skirmish with ATF officers on the afternoon of the raid. Killed in that skirmish was Michael Schroeder, 29. Slightly injured and then arrested was Davidian Del Roy Nash. But Kendrick denies that he ever saw any ATF officers, and says he certainly never fired on them.

Kendrick was describing his peripatations through the fields of Elk. After seeing the "beautiful helicopters" come thupping over the Mag Bag, Kendrick, Schroeder, and Nash set out to see what was going on.

In the somber, almost prissily formal courtroom atmosphere maintained by U.S. Magistrate Dennis Green, the audience is leaning forward to hear Kendrick softly describe his version of the raid.

Kendrick says he was lying in a cold, wet field a few hundred yards from the compound, wondering what was going on.

"There was a pop," he said.

"And then another one. Pop. Pop."

"And then," Kendrick takes a deep breath, and suddenly there in the hushed, solemn courtroom, the spectators are involuntarily jerking back in their seats, some of them trying not to laugh, because abruptly Kendrick is screaming at the top of his lungs, rattling the rafters with: BANG! BANG! BANG! BANG! BANG! BANGBANGBANG!!

The gunfire actually began before the agents ever got to the compound, by some accounts. Before the trucks ever arrived, an Apache helicopter and two Scout 'copters filled with ranking federal officers flew over the compound—and the Davidians opened fire. Two of the helicopters were hit, and one bullet pierced the cabin to whiz by the head of Philip J. Chojnacki, the man responsible for the operation, and the man in charge of the forces on the ground.

The shots taken at the helicopter should have cleared up any further lingering ATF uncertainty about the 'element of surprise.' Yet anonymous agents later said that the helicopters didn't even notify the ATF on the ground that they had taken fire.

The way ATF director Stephen Higgins described it, an ATF agent walked up to the front door and informed the folks inside that he was a federal agent with a warrant. The man at the door, believed to be Koresh, smiled and shut the door. All the Davidians just started shooting at the government agents through the walls, doors, and windows, and the agents returned fire.

But there is every indication that so much was going on at once that, had the Branch Davidians survived and had a day in court, good lawyers could raise many good questions, particularly about who did what, and when.

It was to have been a lightning raid with the agents hitting the compound and its occupants so fast and so pre-emptively that there would be no time for resistance. The lead agents were to jump off the two cattle trucks and have the front door open in seven seconds; all officers were to have been fully deployed from the cattle trucks in under 15 seconds.

What intelligence there was indicated that Koresh controlled his followers' access to the gun room and so (if surprised) the compound's occupants were expected to be only lightly armed. And the men and women were supposed to be segregated at that time of the day.

A team of male agents was to swiftly round up the men on the first floor while a team that included five women corralled the women and children on the second floor.

A third team was to get to the armory.

The expectation was that if the agents could seize control of the gun room, the worst they'd have to deal with was small arms fire. Within a minute the whole thing would be over. According to the plan.

Waco Tribune-Herald reporter Mark England, there at the scene, reported that the three helicopters were clearly visible to him— and thus, presumably, to any Branch Davidians inside that three-story watchtower—as they circled for several minutes on the horizon.

"As the cattle trucks swung up a long dirt road in front of the compound, the helicopters came in low from the north, a Blackhawk helicopter hovering like an angry wasp over the rambling building. Agents wearing blue jumpsuits and flak jackets leaped out of the cattle trucks, throwing concussion grenades and screaming 'come out!'"

But some agents were taking fire even before they could get off the cattle trucks, and confusion reigned.

So either before, during, or after the point at which the process-server was at the front door, "flash-bangs," or concussion grenades, were going off all over the compound, and six or more agents were climbing steel ladders up a roof adjacent to the room believed to be the Branch Davidian armory.

KWTX cameraman Dan Maloney, hiding behind a bus, had his camera rolling so that the whole world could watch, paralyzed by the horrific drama of the scene there on that roof.

One agent used a crowbar to smash out the window and three agents leaped in. Gunfire had already been coming through the window, and now, while one agent remained on the roof, bullets began to penetrate the roof underneath him and the wall beside him, blowing wood fragments high into the air as they stitched their deadly way toward him. He convulsed as at least one bullet struck him, then was able to hobble to the ladder and slide to the ground, pinned down by gunfire, his comrades still inside.

Six men participated in the assault on the armory, but only three lived to tell about it.

One of them was Bill Buford, an ATF special agent from Little Rock. Buford had seen a lot of strange and dangerous things in his years with the ATF, and, before that, as a Green Beret in Vietnam in the mid-1960s.

He'd been one of the three negotiators who broke the stalemate during the standoff with the heavily armed The Covenant, The Sword and The Arm of the Lord group in 1985. He'd investigated bombers and gunmen of every stripe in Arkansas.

But nothing could get him ready for what he encountered as the ATF came boiling out of those cattle trailers.

It was like a bad dream. It was, in fact, like Vietnam.

Buford and his Little Rock colleague, Robert J. "Robb" Williams, 26, were part of the team assigned to penetrate the armory. With them on the penetration team were New Orleans office agents Conway LeBleu, 30, and Todd McKeehan, 28.

Supporting them in their race for the side of the building were about a dozen other members of the New Orleans office, the smallest team involved in the raid, and the ones who took the heaviest casualties.

As the agents made their dash for the side of the building, the

Branch Davidians waiting for them in windows and on rooftops opened up, spraying them with a hail of fire, including huge, armor-piercing slugs from a fully automatic, .50 caliber machine gun.

Buford and his team members were able to get into the armory—and when the walls erupted around them in bullets and splinters, tried to get out again. While in the armory or on the roof, Buford took several shots in the leg and then was hit in the hip. He crumpled and rolled off the roof, breaking several ribs, and then was struck again as he lay on the ground.

Buford was pinned down for two hours by gunfire, and saw the other agents rolling off the roof.

During those hours, Buford said agent Ken Chisholm covered Buford's body with his own. And Buford saw "Robb" Williams, who was under his command, killed during the firefight.

Williams had been huddled behind an abandoned safe. He fell backwards once, hit in the shoulder, then got back up to keep firing; a second bullet crashed through his helmet, and Williams could tell he was not going to be getting back up. The next day would have been his birthday. Agents, particularly from the New Orleans office, on the side of the compound with the heaviest fire, were dropping like flies; the wounded and bleeding were everywhere, taking cover as best they could.

The problem was that the agents were not allowed to play by the same rules as the Davidians.

To protect children and other noncombatants, the ATF had been ordered not to fire on anyone who was not clearly armed and threatening to shoot, but when those in the compound opened fire, all bets were off. Maloney's footage also shows ATF officers taking cover behind everything thicker than clothes hanging on the line, shooting back for all they were worth. Thousands of rounds were said to have been exchanged.

The agents were backed by 'forward observers' armed with Browning .308 sniper rifles in the underground agents' house across the road from the compound.

Agents in the helicopters had been watching Peter Gent's movements on top of the building. Gent was carrying a gun, but had not been acting in what officers considered a "threatening" manner.

And then he quickly raised his weapon. It was just a face in a gunsight for Peter Gent, atop the water tower.

But Steven David Willis, 32, was cocky, confident, and

deservedly so. He was among the very best of the 40 agents stationed in Houston, which was why he had been chosen for the assignment in Waco. He was a race-car driver. He liked fast boats. He was a take-charge kind of guy, and he had just jumped out of his vehicle and was taking cover, getting ready to take charge when Peter Gent fired.

The bullet went all the way through the vehicle.

Accounts vary of what happened next. The ATF denies that there was firing from the helicopters—though Davidian David Thibodeau later said that gunfire was coming through the roof, and that one Koreshian died in his bed holding a piece of French toast, killed by a bullet that came from the ceiling.

The official version, which individual agents have been sternly instructed not to discuss, was that one of the agents in the house across the road, possibly Rodriguez, got Gent in the cross hairs.

Gent—the son of Bruce and Lisa Gent, the Davidians in Australia who'd finally wrested themselves away from Koresh— was the one that didn't get away. By the next day, his parents would be on their way from Australia, hoping to help the son they didn't yet know was dead.

It was a good, clean kill. Knocked him right off the tower.

Gent fell three stories, but was dead before he came to rest, his body tangled in a tree.

It stayed there several days.

The withering, deafening gunfire of the shootout continued almost uninterrupted for 45 minutes, and sporadically for another 80 minutes. Even as agents lay wounded or dying, the ATF and other officials directed their rage and frustration at members of the press, who were only doing their jobs.

As one of the female ATF agents, during a lull, was talking to Mark England and other reporters, a male agent came rushing up to interrupt the conversation: "Can't you see we've been through it?" the officer howled.

Normally mild-mannered McLennan County Sheriff Jack Harwell had an emotional confrontation with the reporters also, saying their presence and their coverage had contributed to the tragedy.

Meanwhile, Jim Cavanaugh, among those who had made the decision to go ahead with the raid, got on the phone from the "undercover house" to try to begin negotiations with Koresh and the Davidians to at least allow a cease-fire so that the ATF could remove its dead and wounded. He finally hammered out the details, and the gunfire stopped around noon.

The bravest men that day were probably the medics and other ATF agents who went to collect the dead and injured. Koresh's terms for allowing the ATF to remove its injured and dying were that they were to put down their weapons, and approach with their hands up.

The men who walked out from behind cover, unarmed, had every gun in the compound trained on them as they hurried about trying to save their comrades.

Four ATF men were fatally shot: Robert J. Williams, 26, New Orleans, assigned to Little Rock; Conway LeBleu, 30, New Orleans; Steve Willis, 32, Houston Division; and Todd McKeehan, 28, New Orleans field division.

Fifteen more were wounded, and the local ambulance services, even with Careflight helicopters landing, loading, and leaving as fast as they could, were inadequate to handle the wounded. Private vehicles and KWTX's van, itself pierced by bullets, were pressed into service, transporting wounded agents. And Waco's medical facilities were stretched to the limits.

It was bedlam at Hillcrest's six trauma rooms as the hospital began to receive word of the extent of the injuries headed their way. Patrick Burton, an Emergency Medical Technician, said it was mass chaos at the hospital as the weekend staff began summoning every available physician and technician to help handle the load.

When the first ambulance rolled in, Burton said, "the doors just flung open and agents started to pour out from every hole in the ambulance, limping, carrying friends, holding arms, covering shoulders—and they all have their gear on, still have their guns. Some of them are crying, some of them are holding on to friends, carrying their friends into the emergency room. Nurses would try to get them to leave their friends, to go to a waiting area. It was 'No, uh-uh. I'm staying and that's that.'"

Most touching and frightening, in a way, was the handling of one of the dead men.

A friend and paramedic colleague of Burton's had handled the agent while still at the compound, and quickly determined there was nothing more to be done for him, since he had been killed by a massive head wound. He was about to cover the dead man's face when one of his pals, a big bulky man in a bulletproof vest with concussion grenades clipped to his clothing, told the paramedic very calmly and in no uncertain terms: "He's not dead until I tell you he's dead." The paramedic did not argue, and the ashen-faced agent rode in the ambulance to ensure that everything conceivable was done for his friend, no matter how futile the effort.

The same heroic efforts continued at the emergency room. Burton and the others put Williams on a stretcher and hurried him to one of the six trauma rooms; pulse, respiration, and EEG showed he was flatline, but the doctor said "We'll work him for three more minutes but if we don't get anything, we're gonna have to call it, because we have other people..."

Some agents stood silent against the wall, mourning their friend. "Most of the agents were, at the very first, real quiet. They were just shocked. And then they started talking about how they had no idea they [the Branch Davidians] were going to be so aggressive, and how they thought this was going to be just a standard, go in and get their guns, serve the warrants and get out of there kind of thing. And everybody's walking around trying to find their buddies, asking 'where's so and so?'

"One of the guys I helped treat (probably Bill Buford) had been shot in the leg; a big chunk had been taken out of his leg. It looked like it was more of an exploding bullet or something like that. And he was mad. He was just like, 'I wanna go back out and get 'em!' I saw a lot of anger and disbelief and a lot of just plain awe-struck."

And the carnage was awesome.

"People were shot at every place; any place you can think of, they were shot. There were shoulder wounds, arm wounds, everything from the little finger to the head. There was one ATF agent with an injury to her hand. She joked about how she hoped it didn't mess up her manicure, and she was real nice—one of the good ones who try to make some kind of humor out of it and calm the situation a little bit, make everybody feel a little better. But you know deep down inside, she's hurting for her friends, and maybe she's just trying to put it all way back in her mind so she doesn't have to think about it."

What will stick with Burton perhaps forever was not the scene inside the emergency room, but in one of the ambulances that had just brought wounded in and had to be prepped to go back out again. Since the ER was already incredibly overcrowded, Burton volunteered to go put the ambulance back shipshape.

"And I come back outside and I look in the back of this ambulance, and I see blood everywhere. It was covered in blood. Blood [was] dripping out the back of the ambulance. It was a massacre."

At about 6 p.m., Burton went home, changed into his uniform, went to the station where he was assigned an ambulance, and drove it out to the scene. He had just left the physically wounded. Back out at the closest safe approach to the compound, he found the psychically wounded—blood-covered men and women uninjured but still reeling from the day's events.

"You could just look back there [toward the intersection of FM2491 and FM2957] and all you see is this big glow, with these big things sticking up in the air. It was Satellite City, all right."

Already, the area surrounding the compound was turning into the place which would focus the eyes of the world on McLennan County for the next 51 days, and well beyond.

By mid afternoon that Sunday, more than 60 newspaper reporters and photographers and camera crews from 17 television stations had arrived, and the rest of the world media was either booking flights or already on the way. And the media covering the story became ever more a factor in the story it was covering.

The media's direct participation was by invitation, at least at first. After the shootout, the ATF, wanting to assure Koresh publicly—with the public as a witness—of their promise that he could come out without harm, contacted KRLD-Radio in Dallas and asked them to broadcast that assurance. KRLD replayed the announcement several times, starting at about 4:15 that afternoon. Koresh didn't come out—but he did smell some publicity, some sympathy, and some leverage, and started warming up, getting ready to ham it up rather broadly and to give the general public a taste of the kind of "I'm a mystery, figure me out" posing and the "I know something you don't" statements that had spellbound his followers.

He called KRLD that evening and did a live interview. "I've been shot," he said. "I'm bleeding bad. I'm going home. I'm going back to my father. Your weapons have overcome me this time. I begged these men to go away." And, with a baby squalling in the background, Koresh began to cry as he talked about a two-year-old child he claimed had been killed, and identified the girl as his own daughter.

"There are a lot of children here," he told KRLD. "I've had a lot of babies these past two years. It's true that I do have a lot of children and I do have a lot of wives."

The dead-baby story was never confirmed.

CNN also got him on the horn. Said Koresh to CNN anchor David French, "I never planned to use these weapons. The only problem is that people outside don't understand what we believe."

And he told CNN that he'd called his mother, to tell her goodbye: "Mama, they got me. Remember, I don't hold anything against you. You know, they just don't want to hear the truth."

And Koresh managed to further ensnare KRLD in the process by promising to release two children each time they played the messages he gave them. From the ATF's standpoint, this was the last promise he completely and unflinchingly honored: By Monday, 10 children had been released.

The messages were essentially Koresh's garbled gospel—harmless, meaningless doubletalk if taken in small doses with large grains of salt: "My father, my God who sits on the throne in Heaven, has given me a book of Seven Seals. In Rev. 10:7 of this sealed book, the mystery of God is to be finished as God has declared to his servants, the prophets. In Rev. 22, I come; my reward, which is the books, is with me to give unto every man the knowledge of the Seven Seals."

By late Sunday night, three other things had become clear.

First, it became clear to the ATF that this could no longer be handled as just another Texas gun raid. They called in hundreds of officers from the FBI and the Department of Public Safety and surrounding counties, and asked for military equipment from the National Guard. Bradley fighting vehicles began moving in the next morning, and soon, after Koresh told the negotiators he had "things that would blow them 30 or 40 feet in the air," these would be followed by larger and virtually invulnerable M1-Abrams tanks.

Second, it became clear to the media that the Koresh story was sort of like dying and going to Ratings Heaven.

And the third thing, at that point, seems to have been clear only to Marc Breault, who may be a prophet after all.

He told Mark England: "I have a hard time seeing him giving up. I don't see that. I think either Vernon will grow so weak that he knows that he doesn't have much time left or he'll believe they're going to storm the place.

"Then," said Breault, in the earliest hours of the siege, "I think he'll go out in a blaze of glory."

Chapter 12

It wasn't just a great story, it was an *easy* story, which is why the world wound up hearing so much about it.

If the ATF shootout and the siege were the steak, it was the *Waco Tribune-Herald* that, part by talent, part by happenstance, brought all of the sizzle to the table. Newsmen hitting the ground cold that first Monday couldn't stay cold for long if they had two quarters to drop in a news rack; to clearly stake out its lead and its journalistic turf, the *Trib* wisely opted to fill the entire Monday issue after bloody Sunday with the remaining installments of the whole exhaustive seven-part series, plus sidebars.

Out-of-town—and out-of-country—reporters could have spent days just finding out who the Branch Davidians were. And a few more days chasing around after who represented them? And then, they'd have to find out what the history was. And then, what was the big deal?

But there it all was, laid out in a sensational—but not sensationalized—smorgasbord of guns and girls, God and goofy prophets, clear and present dangers, and phlegmatic officials. And more than a good story, it was good journalism, with every fact documented and every contention corroborated, in many cases by sworn testimony. It was a turnkey job.

Even gutsier for a small-city gazette, the *Trib* had crawled way out on the limb of readership sensibility in terms of language and descriptions. This wasn't X-rated titillation, but it was certainly engrossing adult fare.

About all the newsman had to do, for the first several days, at least, was pick up a *Trib*, call his or her typesetter or producer, and just read the thing over the phone: Sex, God, and rock and roll. Nowhar but Waco. And the wiser editors and producers around the nation and the world immediately knew: Better send *more* folks to Waco.

And as the story continued to progress (and even more importantly, when it *failed* to) there was the *Trib* series with all the background, and, with each passing day, the best and fullest accounting of continuing developments—more, in fact, than any outlet other than the Davidian's hometown newspaper would care to print.

True, newsmen went to the press conferences, went to the press compound, hassled neighbors about what kind of difficulties they were having because of all this, bought drinks for sources (including each other), and so on. But the truth is that with the *Trib* for background, KRLD for breaking developments, and CNN just in case they wanted to know what something actually looked like, every one of them could have adequately covered the story in their motel room with the drapes closed.

With such a setup, especially with the tension of the first few days and maybe a week thereafter, dynamite couldn't have gotten them out of Waco.

Then there was the international angle. These weren't just a bunch of hillbillies from Texas holed up shooting at local deputies, these were hillbillies from all over the world, shooting at the U.S. government.

England. Australia. New Zealand. The Caribbean. South America. And sensing a story that would be hot back home because of their own local angles, here came the international press. The best example were the reporters from Chile, within spitting distance from Antarctica, and journalists from Israel, right next door to Armageddon, all looking for news of the polyglotally monickered Pablo Cohen, an Israeli citizen living in Chile before he became a Branch Davidian and realized that the world would end in Waco.

And once everybody was here, such is the nature of the news game that they had to stay here.

And such is the nature of the game that they had to have news, even if there wasn't any after the siege turned somnolent and seemingly unending.

There was one other element, too, though most were reluctant to talk about it much: Sure, the guy's crazy. Revelation is just an old book, who knows what it means or if it even means anything at all. On the other hand, what if... Yes, the end of the world would be one heck of a story to have missed. Wouldn't look good on the old resume when I interview at, uh, wherever one interviews for jobs after the end of the world.

And from that world eye trained on one little Central Texas town there would come great, and maybe even fatal, pressure. As in:

Hi. We're the whole entire world.

We're here. We're watching. We like to watch.

Now, make something happen.

Now.

Given the immediacy of the modern world and the fact that the camera routinely places one in such close proximity to events—very much like being there—it is easy for those who are not rooted, not grounded, who have no positive context in the scheme of things, to see themselves as integral to those events.

People who have no sense of belonging to the scheme of things—who have, in fact, no apprehension of what the scheme of things truly is, or even where to start looking for it—must invent one for themselves, and then invent for themselves a place within it.

The problem is, this definition, taken broadly, includes the whole of the human race: Let he among us who is without self-delusion cast the first stone.

Many of us, usually defined as the lucky and the "successful," invent for ourselves a scheme of things that, fortunately for us, generally overlaps and agrees with the self-delusional definitions of many others, even the Majority. This is what we have agreed to call reality.

But for others, the cast-off casualties of a rough, production-demanding, labor-surplus-driven and materialistic society, there is no acceptable scheme of things. Nor, for them, is there any place of honor within it, and no definition or meaning for them.

Unless one is willing to accept societal definitions such as: Useless. Redundant. Of no meaning. Of no worth. Grist for the mill. Dross. A waste of skin. An accidental creature unwanted and unneeded by the world, dust headed for the dustbin of history.

Ashes for the heap.

Few people are capable of accepting those definitions, not even when—perhaps especially not even when—they so clearly seem to apply.

So they must invent—or agree with a tiny minority who has already invented—some new scheme of things in which they may view themselves more favorably.

This new scheme of things is almost always apocalyptic, because only such a scheme offers ultimate redress for the unbearable lightness of being a nobody. Almost all of the apocalyptic philosophies have common themes, themes that in and of themselves explain their seductiveness for society's downtrodden.

First theme: The world is coming to an end. This, for most of them, is positively wonderful news: The world is the "other." The world is a thing of which they never received a portion or a place. It's not the world that's ending, but that world over there, the one that didn't want them.

Second theme: The world which has treated them so badly, the world to which they have been unable to accommodate themselves, to find a place within, is actually Evil, with a capital E. David Koresh called that world Babylon.

Furthermore, the fact that one has been cast out of such an Evil World means that one is de facto "good." And since one is good, chosen by God to be removed from the world, one is actually therefore much higher in the scheme of things than the Evil World can see.

One is, in fact, cosmically high in the scheme of things; so high, in fact, that, of all the world's teeming billions (and, for all we know, the galaxy's teeming quintillions), one has been chosen to serve right up there next to the Leader, among the Mighty Men, at the head of the Elect, at the Right Hand of God.

(You will notice: You never find an apocalyptic organization that has as its theme, "Hey, come join us! The end of the world is coming, and *we're* the ones God is gonna toss into the Lake o' Fire!")

Third theme: God will, by God, *deal* with those in the Evil World that have made His People suffer and served them such bitter bread. There will be revenge. Wrongs will be righted. The first shall be last, and the last, first. Heads will roll.

Once the self-deluded come together in a "body of believers," the strength of numbers gives way to mass delusions, and singular (and special) interpretations of random events.

If their enemy comes down with AIDS, it is God's will, God's wisdom that these abominations be dealt with direly; they are offenses to His—read "our"—eyes.

If members of the Body of Believers catch it, well, of course, we are being tested and purified but in the end God will—providing we've learned His lesson—rescind the sentence.

In other words: All things which befall the group are ultimately designed by God to be good. All which befalls others is bad— even their own apparent good fortune; it is easier to get a camel through the eye of a needle than a rich man into Heaven.

And if recruiting en masse was David Koresh's goal, he missed the opportunity of a lifetime after the standoff got rolling. If the FBI hadn't been blocking access, that compound would have been filled to the fences with teeming seekers of Truth.

Truth is, there are countless millions of followers—followers of anything that will purport to give their lives a larger meaning; people with the same sad needs and the same sad seeds of self-delusion that led Koresh and his Davidians on their foolish fatal trek.

There is no place for them at the world's head table, nor even the table by the kitchen door.

But David had gone before them. He seemed to have prepared a place before them. There seemed to be room at his inn.

And out into the bowl of sky went the word, Satellite City up to COMSAT 4 back down to Ground Control and into the radio headsets of the Spiritual Space Cadets and the Screaming Meemies for Jesus in off-the-wall holes in the woodwork all across this great land: "Heeeeere's *God*! God's *here*!"

And the schizoid antenna and Paranoid Delusion Decoder Kits get suddenly perky, warping up all the way from beerfuddled, bill-bothered brownout to Bright Throbbing Aneurysmic Red Alert.

Because the incoming message is ready-made to fit hand in glove, key in lock, neurotransmitter to neuroreceptor with exactly these drug-burned or just plain tangled synapses in the brains of the wasted souls wandering around way out there in the La-La Land of the Lord's Least Sane; it's the dope these Jesus Junkies have been waiting on all their lives.

They've been sitting slack-jawed on the cat-furry cushions of their butt-sprung sofas and all of a sudden out of the ether in comes the call: The voices in their heads now have a locus. God is no longer just Morse-coding mystic, garbled messages to them like he usually does, with muffled bangings and clangings on their rusty neuropipes, handing them vague bits and pieces of fragments of the overall Powers and Principalities Conspiracy Theory picture, No, sir.

There He is, right there on the Tee-Vee, right there in Waco, and He's holdin' off the revenooers this time, by God, and the tax collectors and the Pharisees and them Babylonians, and, well, it's got to be the end of the world, I mean, don't it?

Because this is a world they figure needs to end.

This World of Can't Pay the Rent and They're Repoing the Car and They're Revoking My Probation and I'll Never Get Ahead can't go on forever, can it?

And now it's like God has beeped them, right on their little mental pagers, called them right up on the old brain phone.

Everywhere, a special mission alert: The God of a Zillion galaxies reaching out special-like to impinge upon them His divine purpose for them: "Come to Waco! I'm in Big Trouble! I need ya! Bring lawyers, guns, and money!"

And the old muscle cars with the Bondo and the primer coats start cranking while those folks lacking jumper cables just set out walking, putting one foot after the other, thumb out, hitchhiking as fast as they can, gone to go help God in Waco.

And every goofy thing they've ever heard seems to be coming true.

It's a... test! Yeah, it's a test of some kind! And... the Elect, they'll be there! Yeah! And then, well, some things will happen, because, after all, he's the Son of God! And I'll be his friend!

No, wait! I'll be his specialest, bestest Friend! And when he sees all my troubles and all the trouble I've gone to to be here, why, he'll consolidate all my debts into one easy payment, waive all my back child-support, give me some beer money and put me in charge of Disneyland!

And so they came.

All across the country, the Wackos started heading for Waco. A lot of them didn't make it.

For instance, Jeff H. Terrell, 31, of Los Angeles. Jeff got only as far as Upland, California. That's where he came crashing through the living room window of Mrs. Fay Thacker's house, screaming, "I'm Jesus Christ, take me to Waco! Take me to Waco!" She just happened to be watching news programming about the standoff at the time, so it put the fear of the Lord right in her.

Terrell, with his long hair and black leather jacket, looked enough like Koresh to make Mrs. Thacker look twice, especially considering his grand entrance. Upland Police said he'd smashed the windows of nine other homes before arriving in Mrs. Thacker's living room. Terrell and a friend were driving east on I-10, headed for the cult standoff, when the friend began having second thoughts and turned the car back toward Los Angeles. Terrell went a little ballistic and accused him of being an FBI agent.

The driver pulled over; Terrell jumped out of the van and began searching—violently—elsewhere for a ride.

Police took Jesus to jail instead of Waco, booking him on charges of burglary and making death threats to a police officer.

But many more made the trip. What became more remarkable about each of them, over time, is that they didn't just come. They came with a specific and divine ordination to "save David." Each reported a call from God, but after a while it became apparent that God was using a party line, and had maybe even hired a whole boiler-room of Time-Life operators using the Publisher's Clearinghouse mailing list, because it got to be quite a crowd.

The two most famous members of this slightly off-center posse of David's Helpers were, of course, Jesse Amen and Louis Alaniz. (Amen was the visitor to the compound who was able to sneak in March 16. FBI officials complained he "made no sense" when they questioned him upon his emergence April 4.)

Jesse, briefly incarcerated on charges of interfering with the duties of a police officer after he walked out of the compound and into the hands of authorities on April 4, said the FBI didn't make much sense to him, either. "In their eyes I'm from another world, just like Jesus is from another world. They wanted to kill *Him* 2,000 years ago."

Amen further acknowledged that God had sent him, like Mr. Terrell, only Amen made it. He told the *Fort Worth Star-Telegram,* in a rare interview (because he usually doesn't stand still long enough to complete one), that "it wasn't hard to get through."

Amen, reportedly from California, said he traveled to Waco because "it was the will of the Father. God sent me in. The Holy Spirit. God is real. David is who he says he is."

He also proved to be, like Jesus H. Koresh, a master of what might best be termed "mystic crypticism."

He told reporters, "There's a real specific reason why I came out," adding that he would not divulge it until he was freed from McLennan County Jail. His M.O. changed little after he got out, however; he set up interviews, canceled them, then called reporters at 2 a.m. and wondered why they weren't happy to hear from him. He hung up on them. And he was working on his own book deal. Yes, book deal.

On March 24, Louis Alaniz got past federal agents guarding the Mount Carmel compound, peered into windows, knocked on the front door, and was allowed inside.

"Me and Waco did not agree," he told the *Fort Worth Star-Telegram* as he walked out of the McLennan County Jail dressed in a sporty paper jumpsuit, compliments of the county.

"I'm here being looked at as a person who is mentally insane for trying to help people out. I'd rather go back home where people know I'm insane," Alaniz said. He meant that he was going back to Houston.

But there were others. In fact, for each one who got in, there may have been untold numbers trying, or at least wanting to try.

After a while, at the ATF checkpoints surrounding the compound, the boys in camouflage would spot them coming a mile away. And they had a word for them. "Incoming." The ATF, not wishing to crowd McLennan County Jail or the local MHMR facilities just in case all the Davidians came out en masse, would usually just direct these Koreshian candidates on up to Holy Hill after they'd been allowed to rant long enough to wind down.

The press had a nickname for them also—Waco Wackos—though in fairness, the great majority of them were not from Waco but from the four corners of the country.

There were several "regulars" on the hill and at press conferences and, much of the time, inside the McLennan County Jail and MHMR, after they made local authorities exasperated enough to ignore the overcrowding.

Among the earliest to grace Holy Hill was the Halalaluyah Gang (that's how they spelled it on the handout).

As Waco Wackos go, they were quite tame.

The Halalaluyah gang is the family of Richard W. Schmaltz. He travels the country with his wife and five children getting out the messages, messages which are crudely painted all over the "gang's" ancient and battered Winnebago:

"Be pro-Christ now because Jesus *will* destroy the anti-christs when he comes again!" and "Prepare yourself with a G.E.D., God's Everlasting Dream" and "Repent of your sins" and "Follow Jesus" and "take up your cross" and... and... "Search the Scriptures for yourself! Obey the Whole Gospel."

Lots of messages.

"I can't fit enough on there," says Richard Schmaltz.

The Schmaltz family travels in a loose association with two other street evangelists, Philip Winger and Rick Long. Schmaltz and the other two men have ungroomed, chest-length beards. Talking to them is like talking to a box of Smith Brothers cough drops.

The beards are a "personal preference and a scriptural preference. In the Old Testament a scripture says 'Ye shall not round the corners of your head, neither shalt thou mar the corners of thy beard (Lev. 19:27)' So those of us who get into the Bible—like some people love cars and some people love computers, we get into the Bible—we just found that verse and said, 'that is a nice scripture, I think I'll do it.'"

Who are they with?

"Just Jesus. We are independent missionaries. Street preachers. We just got ahold of the Bible, I should say that the Lord Jesus got ahold of us and worked on us and here we are. We are out promoting Jesus Christ and promoting what the scripture says about events and what will happen. We are trying to get people into the Kingdom and let people know about what prophecy says about the coming of the end of the world, and various things."

Fill us in.

"Start at the beginning?"

How far back do we have to go?

"About 2,000 years."

Bring us up to more recent times. What is the significance of David Koresh?

"Well, the New World Order. According to Bible prophecy, there is a government system emerging into a single government of the world. The government system is against the things of Jesus. Now Jesus Christ being loving and compassionate and accepting of all those who came to believe in him, that's right. He accepts the weak and the downtrodden and the worst-off. But the problem with the government system is that they can only accept the efficient. So what happens is that the government has to kill off anything that is a liability, ultimately, and keep only those that fit into the mainstream of what they are trying to do."

If that is truly the government's purpose, it would have had a field day on Holy Hill.

Remember those Mexican jumping beans when you were a kid? Amazing, the way those things jump around—until someone explained that some kind of Mexican fly puts some kind of an egg into the bean, and after it hatches and starts to eat the meat inside, if it gets too warm in there, the worm just kind of pops around, moving the bean.

And now, here comes Maid Marian/Bathsheba, stalking up from the shoulder to the state-owned right of way that comprises Holy Hill. Quite some time back, judging by the state of things, one or more of those Mexican flies seems to have flown in her ear.

Some days, she is quite lucid and pleasant to talk to—or, more properly, listen to. Other days, she fancies herself Maid Marian to David Koresh's Robin Hood, and the FBI's Bob Ricks has become "The Sheriff of Shure-Wood Forest." She has to get into the compound to be at Robin's side, which will end the standoff and bring in the Kingdom of God (or perhaps Richard the Lionhearted).

Other days, she's off on some tangent about how she's the reincarnated Bathsheba to Koresh's King David. The common theme to all these varying theories is that her presence at David's side is the only thing that can end this standoff.

Whoever she is, when all those larvae get going, she just kind of pops.

With the prosaic old jumping beans, after the larvae explanation, the childish amazement wore off pretty quick. With Maid Marian, however, one's sense of awe just goes on and on: How can she *live* with all those things in her head? What's left in there for them to eat? So much is happening in there all at once—and yet every coheren*t, reasonable* thought is gone; are the larvae even now munching through the last of her Knock-Knock jokes?

Another more charitable explanation may come by way of Carlos Castaneda and Aldous Huxley and others who speculate that each of us is equipped with a sort of psychic reality valve that damps down the flow of psychic realities occurring in the 90 percent of the brain we don't use. Drugs, particularly psychedelics, are said to open up this valve.

In that case, Mariah is the poster child for Wide-Open Valves.

Here she stands amid the T-shirt vendors and psychic advisors and sundry other Waco Wackos on Crazy Hill; her arms are flailing like a scarecrow on speed and she's managed to corner a band of five Hispanic men. She's got 'em up against the barbed-wire for the lecture.

Her standard procedure on all occasions when she can gather an audience is to rant disjointedly and far-rangingly for several minutes, and then suddenly pause, cock her head, clench her jaw, ball her fists and lean threateningly toward her listeners, as if she's surely going to have to hit someone *this* time.

Over time one comes to realize that this is merely her means of collecting her maverick thoughts, which may at any moment go straying off Lord knows where. The boxer's pose is just a bit of stage business during which she tries to stay in character while attempting to corral all the things that her character, Marian/Bathsheba, was supposed to be so mad about, and herd 'em back up over by the chute.

She's wearing grungy, short shorts and a halter top; her legs are covered in dust, as is her stomach, but once upon a time, she was a very nice-looking woman; still has traces of it. Still you can see what she might have been like before the worms ate her control. Or the valve came unstuck and put the Psychic Reality Headlights on high beam.

Particularly out of her mental loop is that part of one's brain that prevents people from taking off from Kansas just because God has announced He's in Waco and has mentally phoned to say He wants to see you personally; that part of one's mind, in other words, that still has presence of mind enough to consider: He just *might* have misdialed. I might *not* be Bathsheba.

And her audience of Hispanic gentlemen standing transfixed in those high beams, have, in fact, been very quiet and respectful through all the lecture. Part of it is, they are gentlemen.

Part of it is, she looks pretty scary in this mode.

The other part is, they don't speak any English.

Some of these would-be messiahs are religious. Some are political. Many, however, are religio-political, like Curly Thompson. Curly Thompson ran for Governor of Montana. He also ran for the U.S. Senate. Oh, yeah—and president. And now he is uniquely qualified to end the Waco Siege.

Curly has brought down half a dozen followers from Montana who have, in turn, managed to attract a crowd of newsmen. Says Curly: "Once David Koresh knows that somebody is listening to him, from the inside out, I also know, based on what I believe in, based on my convictions, that I can win David over to this side. That a conversion will take place."

"What do you mean?" a reporter asks.

"Not a conversion so much in terms of theology, I'm talking about a conversion in terms of responding to what I believe the Lord is saying to me. The Lord is saying, 'Curly, you gotta do this.' If I could just get with this guy..."

Someone wants to know the name of the group he's with.

Curley kind of beats around the bush about it. It's called "The House of David," and it's a drug-rehabilitation organization with maybe 60 members—which also comprise the body of his political supporters. The House of David is not connected with Koresh, but the name alone seems to be enough to damage his credibility, such as it was.

Another name isn't helping him much, either.

A cameraman asks: "What did you say your name was?"

"Thompson."

"No, *first* name?"

"Curly."

And the cameraman, walking away, goes: Woob-woob-woob... nyuk nyuk nyuk.

Then there is Eddie D. McTwoHats, from Washington, D.C., an itinerant "street singer," who made his first Central Texas appearance in front of the Waco Convention Center—after the daily press conference, naturally, when reporters were looking for something to cover.

He'd come floating into Waco hoping to "sing" David Koresh outta there. And he hoped to get himself into the *Guinness Book of World Records* for singing the longest continuous song. The world record in the *Guiness Book*, says Eddie, "is one guy that sang 100 hours, 20 minutes and four seconds, but he sang different songs. I'm gonna sing the *same* song. Longest I've ever sung is seven hours. I made up a song about drugs one time—'It's Gonna Work If you Don't Give Up'—and I'm just gonna start singing and try to sing as long as I can."

And why does he think he can get David Koresh out of there?

"Lemme explain it this way. I'm a musician, and musicians have thinkin' minds. I know because I am one. All right. Now, it could be that I might be able to, by bein' a musician, *he's* a musician, it could be that I could communicate with him through music. And I was hopin', I didn't know what the situation would be when I got here, but I was hopin' that if I could get him to play *with* me..."

You want to go into the compound and sing...?

No, Eddie's got a thinkin' mind, but he's not *crazy*: "No sir. That was not my plan. I was hopin' that I could get a hookup where he could play with me, like remote. And he could play with me, he's in there and I'm over here."

Some cynical unbeliever suggests that he should take that idea and, first thing in the morning, go trotting right around to the ATF with it.

And so of course it isn't long before Eddie's retreated back up to Holy Hill, where he's singing his song, minus the accompanying hookup with David Koresh—though it's certainly David's kind of music.

The song, which God wrote in the first person on the loose-leaf tablet inside Eddie's head, is called "A Song to David (A Message in Song)." It goes, in C major, and as creatively spelled by the Author:

I am for peace David
I am for peace
Good health to all of you know that I–I am for peace
There is so much trouble down there in your world
For every man woman boy and girl
In the beginning it was not susposed to be
Susposed to be living in hormony.

I wrote it down in a book called Psalms
So every one would do NO harm
Psalm one-twenty and a verse called seven
I am checking it out from a place called heaven

Day in and day out
I am still in control let there be no doubt
Day in and day out
I trust you know what I'm talking about.

Now just when you think things are really going bad
Think about the blessings you've already had
Then think about the lives that's in your care
Deep down in your soul you know I'll be there.

(repeat intro two hundred times and out)

Eddie wowed 'em up on the hill, if not at Guiness. But Eddie's not the only one hearing voices in his head.

Over by the fence is a skinny little stickfellow who looks like an elder from a somewhat impoverished backwoods church—in other words, harmless enough, normal enough to stand next to for a moment, at least long enough to take another gander at the speck that is the distant compound.

And this man turns and says, "God tells me things in dreams and He's accepted me as His Son and He sent me here as G-God with a M-Message."

G-Go figure. This makes the second S-Son of G-God this m-month t-to come along with a stutter. (And the *third* Jesus Christ currently gracing McLennan County—the second was Christ Didymus Thomas who went around passing out handbills: "As my father promised, I am here! The invisible Christ spirit is the truth spirit.")

This double-knit Christ here on the Holy/Crazy Hill informs: "He sent me as a savior for the United States and for Israel."

How *thoughtful* of Him.

"M-Mount Carmel, the Holy Spirit inspired this. He set this up here and if it represents the United States it will be overrun by a great army. You know?"

Oh yes, thank you, *perfectly* well we know...

"I was led out of the W-Worldwide Church of God last August. The Scriptures, if you understand them at all, [really mean that] America is a part of Israel and Israel is supposed to fall, but since

God doesn't want America to fall, this here is the test," he says, leaning closer, "Right *here!*"

So we go right over *there* instead, a fair little piece up the hill—and darned if it's not right smack into another one—Gary.

Gary walks like he had a string around his neck leading up into the sky, holding him up. He is missing two front teeth, his shirt, and the 70s, 80s, and 90s. Gary and his Daddy just don't *care*. "Daddy" is God.

"He likes for me to call him Daddy," Gary explains, and then stands there grinning all snaggly, allowing listeners to try to appreciate Heaven's joyous tumult.

He's passing out some brochures that he doesn't agree with 100 percent, but hey, Daddy arranged things so he'd find 'em in a ditch, so, what the hey, "the knowledge that Daddy sends us just becomes newer every day, every day the rain's different from yesterday, stronger on a lot of days than it is on other days.

"I got robbed up in Parker's Crossing coming down here out of New York. I didn't have a... thing. I got down here... now I got money in my pocket and got all this stuff to set up here so I can talk to God's people when they come."

And what's Gary telling them?

"...I don't know. Whatever seems to wanna come out of my mouth when I speak. Whatever they want to know. My robes are gray and I desire to make them white, what should I use for cleansing the lamb? You know the ladder of knowledge is tall. What say ye that the top number of the rung is?"

Seven? For luck?

And Gary has us, now, waggling a finger and grinning happily because we're *wrong*:

"There *wasn't* any. It was infinity. The ladder of knowledge hath no top, we grow like trees..."

He came all the way from New York for this?

And Gary gets right animated, talking fast, kinda scary:

"I came down here because I had a calling from God. He said 'Get... to Waco.' I said, 'Daddy, wait until I get my crap straight and I get the herd straightened away, lost two baby calves, and got to get my brother shook up and nervous about watching the fold and make sure there was enough wood in the basement for momma and the babes.' But I got my crap squared away Sunday at 3:00 and I was down the line."

Gary spends his days on the hill, and his nights trying to get past the ATF and into the compound—when he's in good enough condition to try it.

And the ATF has snapped wise. They know who he is, and they know to be looking for him.

Gary lit out on a lengthy but unintelligible family history, something about his granddaddy's Masonic Bible, his grandmommy's satchel, Daddy's wooden staff, Iwo Jima, Shanghai, and Daddy "starting the herd" in about 1947; it's not clear whether the reference is to actual cows or to Gary's own family. Alas.

And then he's back among us for a little while, talking about how crazy everybody is on this hill.

"See that'n over there?" He indicates Marian/Bathsheba, who's flapping her arms like a pterodactyl at take-off while she harangues a perplexed T-shirt vendor.

"She's got a demon on her back," says Gary. "[If] God wanted us to stick chemicals in our veins, he'd put a spigot on 'em, wouldn't he? And that old boy right there? He's got a *hell* of a demon on his back. Yeah, he's charging people a dollar to look through his binoculars.

"And you. You got a demon, too. You got a bad back. Yep. Thought so. Here's what you do: Walk like you had a string around your neck leading up into the sky, like this. In a few days, no more bad back.

"And see that one laying over there, he was the one who slapped me in the face. Did you see the picture in the Houston paper?"

Missed it.

"Well… I wouldn't leave, I wouldn't bow down to him."

(Actually, says Linda Cox, T-shirt vendor, "That man punched his lights out because he was cussing in front of his wife, using very foul, nasty language. It was in the newspaper. It's a zoo out here, a three-ring circus. Some folks call it Holy Hill. We call it Mt. Carnival.")

T-shirts, hats, postcards and photos of Koresh. One dollar to look through a small and unimpressive telescope, and see not very much.

Barbecue stands, cold drinks for sale. Two shameless aggressive psychics, painted up like bargain-basement Rockettes, jumping in front of every TV camera and tape recorder they can find, and dragging poor old gawky boys with love-trouble over to the crystal ball on the card table to have their futures foretold.

Then there's old Woodie Lambert, wearing his "It's Never Too Late To Have A Happy Second Childhood" hat, has completely given up his other hobby, making birdhouses. The 74-year-old resident now spends all his time up on the hill, lending his binoculars while bending tourists' ears. He's here from early in the morning until well after dark, an old obscure fellow who's suddenly basking in the limelight of the world. Got hisself in the local paper and in the national news. "Yessir, I been around the world."

For a while, he carried a little clicker-counter with him; every time he loaned out the binocs, he'd hit the clicker. He hit 5,000 before he stopped counting.

Funny thing is that the actual local and long-standing name for this rise of land is Lamb's Hill.

And a lamb did in fact come here, wanting only to follow, not to lead, nor even to be near the leader. Not to take over the world, not to see the end of this one. Just to follow. She came following her shepherd.

She too claimed her shepherd was Jesus.

She went by a funny name, Atalmadad, which, she said, means in Hebrew "female disciple." "Forget all these other crazies," said Linda Cox, pointing past a barbed-wire fence at a shapeless little ball of blankets huddled under a tarp in the cold March wind: "I'm kind of worried about her."

Hey lady! Anything you need? You okay?

She turns and glares, jaw clamped, a little 40-ish gray-headed woman, road-worn yet sharp-eyed. And then she turns away to continue staring way out over the early spring fields of green at the compound miles to the northeast, and becomes a bundle of ragged blankets again. The stiff wind whips the blankets.

'Scuse me. We just thought maybe you needed something. Looks like you're kinda camped out...

She turns and glares again—not unfriendly, just very pointedly, as if to say, would you *please* get the message?

Oh. Vow of silence, huh? Sure'd like to talk to you...

And she finally gives up, maintaining her silence until she's clambered over the barbed-wire fence. She's only quiet on the Koresh side of the fence. That's part of her vow.

She takes vows very seriously.

She used to be a normal person, if there is such a thing. She had a job as a corporate secretary in Austin. Had a hair drier and hot-curlers and a TV and a stereo and an apartment and stuff.

And one day, she was walking down the street there in Austin, and—what do you know—she bumped into God.

"I can tell you exactly when. It was December 7, 1978, 7

o'clock in the morning. I got up to go to work, and I got one block from my house, and a voice just as clear as I'm hearing yours said, 'Go!'

"And I'm standing on a street corner at 7 a.m., and nobody was around, so I said, 'What do you mean, Go? I'm not going anywhere. In three months I'll have saved up $1,700. Why don't I go then? I'll need a backpack and I'll need a bedroll and I need hiking shoes and I need this and that; I'm not going.'

"And I walked another block, and I guess it was an angel hit me right there, right in the solar plexus. Nearly knocked me to my knees. And the instructions were very clear. It said, 'Go now. You'll never have another chance.'"

She went home, packed up everything she thought she'd need—big Army duffle bag, one of those old-timey hair driers with a cap, some books, clothes, and so on. And she just left.

She'd take all the pile that she could carry, walk two blocks, and go back for the rest, then walk two blocks, go back for the rest... Finally she left it all sitting on the shoulder of Highway 90. And she's been going ever since.

Her own egocentrism colors the 'signals,' of course, if signals they are. She finds omens. Sometimes it's just the chance glance of a stranger, or the destination of whoever she's hitchhiking with that tells her "what is meant to be." Once, she heard over the radio that there was going be a solar eclipse visible only in British Columbia, and she said, "This is it! I'm gonna go study with the Bear Tribe in Washington," but she never made it to the Bear Tribe.

"I made it to Portland, and I'm looking, and I'm just taking my finger and running it through the phone book feeling the energy," and thus she wound up working at a health-food store operated by two World Wide Church of Godders who taught her about the Sabbath...

God's vibes led her to some Mormons in California, and then to... it's a long story. But her most recent instructions came on December 4, 1992, when God told her to just round up her two big dogs and start walking, clear across the country, "proclaiming the coming of Jesus as I went, moving by faith and doing what the Holy Spirit directs me to do. And I was in Southwest New Mexico when the Holy Spirit began to move me to come here, when I first heard about it. I figured, 'Why? It doesn't matter.' And I just put it back on God. And He put it back on me. I said, 'Well, if this is You speaking, this is Your will, if You want me to go to Waco, then the next vehicle that stops has to offer me a ride and take me to Waco."

And did they? "Yes, all the way from New Mexico."

Well, not exactly. To Fort Worth. But the guy driving the car *was* a Seventh-day Adventist, which to Atalmadad was a sign. And the next person took her to just a little past Hillsboro, 30 miles up the road from Waco, which was a sign that, well, that she was getting closer.

And the next... until she got out of a car at Loop 340. She asked some woman where she was, and when the woman told her, Atalmadad concluded, "Oh. Well. I can't leave *now*." Because it was a sign.

And she built a big cross on the hill out of some scrap lumber. She found some corrugated metal and a plastic tarp and made a crude little shelter for herself and her two dogs. God had told her at the start of the journey to ask nothing of anyone, but to accept all that came her way. T-shirt vendors and journalists fed her. When nobody offered to let her come to their home to take a shower, she'd bathe in a chilly horse-pond just down the hill toward the compound. And was grateful for it.

One man, who seemed nice, took her to his apartment to let her wash her clothes—and tried to rape her. She got away, but for several days he stalked her on the hill. David Mevis decided to let her stay in his T-shirt tent, for which she was grateful, until the vandals—local punks—started coming up on Lamb's Hill at night, tearing down her cross, slinging gravel with their tires, and trying to tear down the tent while she cowered inside. The only thing that kept them at bay were the two big dogs.

When not being bothered by your basic everyday McLennan County rapists and vandals by night and the hundreds of thronging tourists by day, Atalmadad just sat at the fringes of the woods and prayed. Every spare moment, day and night, morning, noon, and evening, she prayed.

And it may be that, like the rest of the fools on the hill, she was only listening to the feedback from the circuits in her head.

And some as-yet-undiscovered ancient psychologist's old scroll near the Dead Sea may finally reveal what some suspect, particularly after reviewing the parallels with Mr. Koresh: That the same was true of her shepherd as well.

Daddy on the radio.

Circuits in His head.

Ghosts in the neuron machine.

Egocentricity writing checks that Reality can't cash.

The difference between the shepherd and the way he followed his God and the way that Koresh followed his may ultimately be just a matter of what action was taken after the signals were in.

Atalmadad, following her shepherd and his example, didn't rant, she didn't rave, didn't try to start World War III, and didn't see herself as the ultimate solution.

She just prayed. Just prayed. All day long, all night long, until she was blue in the face out there in the wind and rain and cold.

And that may have been the only reasonable course of action for the whole 51 days.

Chapter 13

After the number of "people released from the compound" slowed to a trickle and then was cut off entirely, the Groundhog Day routine began to settle into the pattern that would last for the remainder of the siege: long periods of apathetic ennui, punctuated by eruptions of mass panic.

No news isn't good news to a newshound, and as the daily bone tossed at the press conference got skinnier and skinnier, the dogs finally got hungry enough to come out from under the porch.

Most reasonable people, faced with the news that there was no news, would knock off and go play golf.

Part of the reason that the impermanent scene surrounding the Waco Siege began to seem as solid and substantial as city hall or the county courthouse was, that was the way most of them covered it—as a "beat."

The bar at the Holiday Inn, where many of the members of the ATF and the FBI were staying, was, in the evenings, filled with the big burly agents—and female reporters.

The same female reporters who, under other circumstances, would gladly knock you into the middle of next year at the most casual sexist reference in their presence, female reporters who would slap a sexual harassment lawsuit on you so quick it would make your head spin.

Except while "on duty" at the Holiday Inn, where the Women of the Press came to be "working girls."

One of the least abashed was C. H., a reporter for one of the big national newspapers. Strolling into the bar of the Holiday Inn, she laughed, "Wearin' my ATF jeans. They're tight; those boys'll *talk* to me in these."

These old boys, these cowboys and macho men wouldn't give a male reporter much more than a reserved glare and an ID check at a sentry post and maybe a field sobriety test just for good measure if you caught him in a bad mood.

But the little honeys... 'scuse, please, the Female Persons of the Press, why, they did real fine.

Slow Tuesday night, right after shift change at the compound. Male-female ratio in the bar: 18–3.

In bops the Jeans Queen, figuring someone will look. And someone does; he's wearing an ATF jacket. And pretty soon, they're talking up a storm. And in a few days, she will reveal—exclusively—that the FBI and the ATF did indeed have electronic bugs inside the compound, miniature electronic listening devices carried in with magazines, batteries, milk, and so on.

And a few days later, she will be able to regale her world readership with a medic's graphic account of the horrendous events on February 28.

Meanwhile, in flounces the girl from The Associated Press (AP). She's been cool as rainwater at the press conferences and unresponsive to the pleasantries of all but the most respectful of her male counterparts in the press corps.

But in here, all of a sudden, she's a regular bon vivant, a party girl, a barrel of fun as, pen and pad in hand, she flits from table to table for cozy cheek-to-cheek consultations with the feds. And when she gets something really *hot*, why, it's but 20 or so steps to the AP office, which has very wisely located itself in headquarters at the Holiday Inn, renting office space for $50 a day. From secret tête-à-tête to every reader in the world in a matter of minutes.

And then, in comes the bombshell. As Wayne and Garth would say, she's definitely Babraham Lincoln; a stone-cold *knockout*. If the FBI had just a little imagination, they'd have stood her right outside the Davidian compound for a minute and old Dave would have been doing somersaults getting out the front door.

She too has made it clear to her male counterparts in the press corps that she has nothing to say to a man jack of them, that she is strictly an equal opportunity-type businessperson with a high-dollar lawyer ready to sue at the slightest breach of propriety.

But now... into the bar she comes slinking. She looks very vulnerable, very in need of protection, very much like she needs something. And she does. And she finds it.

She takes up a position at the bar. She looks around the room, which in a few minutes is pretty busy looking back at her. Every ATF agent in that room is just dying to help her get the information she needs—but one old boy with thinning hair and a slight paunch looks as if he's ready to get a Bradley and drive her into the compound for a one-on-one with Dave, during which he will slip away to go get copies of all the FBI's classified files on any subject she cares to name.

And she goes over to him and kind of leans down, starts talking... then she's sitting next to him and his friends... then his friends, sensing his opportunity, leave the table to just him and her, and they're laughing, and talking, and drinking... free flow of information in a democratic society, the right of the people to know, and all that.

Ernie Kovacs had it pretty well in hand more than 30 years ago, with a skit involving the death of Julius Caesar, on the premise it had been televised. Julius gets wind of the cameras and as everyone is busily stabbing him, breaking things over his head, hitting him with everything that ancient Rome could muster, Julius is standing there doing Bogart imitations and Barrymore shticks, trying to break into the big time; no matter how many times they stab him, he just keeps on, keeps on, going for it, the brass ring.

The dynamics of a media feeding frenzy: The more little sharks there are, the less there is to eat, and the hungrier the little sharks are, the more aggressive the little sharks become.

The little sharks are not angry; they are not evil. They are just hungry, and fearful of not getting their share. And in order to get their share, there can be no sharing at all. There is only the getting of as much as possible of everybody else's share.

At the peak of it there were probably 1,000 reporters, cameramen, producers, on-air talent and so on, in and around Waco. The list of call-letters reads like someone blew up a can of alphabet soup. Behind each of them, in offices and newsrooms across the country, there was an untold number of editors, managers, news directors, and so on, each with the job of burdening the folks in the field with the urgency of how important it was to "get the story," whatever that was.

Get the story, says a man in Atlanta.

The field producer says, we're getting all the dang story we can.

And Atlanta says (and this is no joke; this really did get said): Why haven't we had a face-to-face interview with David Koresh?

And the field producer, only half-smiling, tells his reporters: If there's any way in hell, get a face-to-face interview with David Koresh. If you can't do that, get his mother. If you can't do that, get his brother. If you can't do that, talk to his dog. And we've gotta have it by 6:00. We're depending on you for this.

Meanwhile, there is only so much mother, brother, and dog to go around.

And, as mothers, brothers, and dogs begin to realize how

inordinately high has rocketed the level of demand for the chance to hang upon their every semi-literate, backwoods word, they begin to perceive that they can name their price for "exclusive access" to them thar words.

And it will be a tallish one, even to talk to the dog.

And the food floating around in these turbulent waters becomes that much scarcer, and the little sharks that much hungrier.

There are, at the top, the boys with the wide-open checkbooks. This strata is the tip of the reportorial pyramid. These are the made-for-TV guys, and the tabloid-TV fellows who, since they have no ongoing news budgets with which they must cover the entire world, can pick and choose their shots.

These guys fly first class. So do the folks they pay to get to interview.

Rights to Your STO-ry! Rights to your STO-ry! We *gotcha* rights to the story! Checks! Checks!

Here comes Warner Brothers, almost first day of the siege, Mark Sennet, checkbook in hand. People that reporters are sucking up to for the merest crumb of conversation—for instance, court appointed lawyers who thus have total control of access to their jailed Branch Davidian clients—well, Mark Sennet's got 'em. Riding them around in the big rent car. Wining and dining, plunking down for tabs, writing checks. Talking of cuts of pies bigger than bakeries. Mark has little lawyer eyes getting wider and rounder as visions of sugarplums dance full-figured and beguiling across bar napkins.

Balenda Ganem is, at this point in early March, still just being a mother. Her son, David Thibodeau, is still inside the compound. (Later on, after he's out, dollar signs will ring up in her eyes, ch-*ching*, and David's, too, ch-*ching* and in the eyes of their lawyer, Gary Richardson, ch-ch-ch-*ching*!)

But right now, she doesn't know whether her son is going to live or die or get life in prison, and she's scared. She's scared that the FBI is screwing up by not allowing her to talk to her son, and by not allowing other families to contact their relatives inside. It has become her cause and crusade.

And since she's flat broke, and, other than familial ties to the Davidians, a nobody, the way she forwards this crusade is by talking to the press in front of the Waco Convention Center after the daily press conferences.

She can usually count on a good size mob. If it's been a good press conference with Ricks and the boys tossing plenty of chunks big enough for everybody, the little sharks are content with what she gives them.

On days where the pickings are slim, there is a feeding frenzy. Because for many of these folks, Balenda Ganem is the only game in town.

She's been talking for maybe 30 minutes. Big-time cameramen swim up, nose their way into the crowd of mere radio microphone-feeders surrounding her, gobble off a chunk of what she's saying, and then swim away looking for someone else to glom.

And now she's winding down, trying to get away, trying to shake off the pack.

And here comes Robert Vito, CNN, and he didn't get his chunk, and he's mad. He's also jealous. "Good Morning America" had a pretty nice little interview with her—and nobody else had it, especially CNN. First he tries to bait her, just to keep her talking, to keep her from walking away. Balenda is accompanied by a youngish, pleasant and soft-spoken woman. They seem to be friends.

Vito: Balenda, you told us how your son more or less doesn't see David Koresh for what he it is. What's your opinion of David Koresh?

Balenda: My opinion of David Koresh is that David Koresh is in a very tough situation right now, and my opinion is that he needs an awful lot of care, an awful lot of counseling. I don't hate David Koresh.

Male: Is he an evil man?

Balenda: No, he's not an evil man. He's a very...

Vito (challenging, righteous): He killed four ATF agents.

Balenda: Armed confrontation is a very horrible thing and we don't know how it happened and we're not sure.

Vito (coldly, acting as if personally angry): Do you expect the general public to feel sorry for you?

Balenda: I expect the general public to get the information, to get the evidence, I expect the general public to keep their eyes and their ears open and then when the truth comes out, at that point, we can all, none of us can point fingers right now, because there is no evidence at this time.

(Balenda's friend grabs her by the arm, attempts to get her away from Vito.

Vito (barking): There are four ATF officers dead.

Balenda: There are four dead Koreshians, as well. OK, so there are dead people on both sides. It's tragic, it should never have happened. Let's find out how and why it happened first and then we'll go from there.

(Balenda and her friend again try to leave Vito behind.)

Vito (sneering): Early on, when you talked a whole lot to CBS and were very unavailable to the rest of the press, there were a lot of rumors that you were compensated by CBS to pay for your motel.

Balenda: No, no, they didn't pay for my motel. They did treat me to some lovely meals, but no, my brother paid for my motel.

Vito (conciliatory): How much has this process cost you?

Balenda: I don't even know, that's not a reality to me now, I can't even begin to think of that.

Vito (understandingly): It's been destructive to you financially?

Balenda: I'm unemployed now, so you're talking to one of the ranks of unemployed. It will be difficult to deal with, but again, what's more important to us right now is the life of our family member and there's no price attached to that, no price whatsoever, OK?

Vito (casually, smiling—even a tad unctuous): How can we *reach* you?

Balenda: You can't reach me until you see me around, because I'm staying at a small family motel, and it's run by a small family, and we lock the place up at night. You'll see me, I'm very available. I'm around, you'll see me.

Vito: Do you come to these every day?

Balenda: I don't come to them every day, but I do come on occasion when I need to say something.

Vito: Why did you come today?

Balenda: There are things that we need to say and things that need to be expressed, and when we get together and talk together and decide and then get the time to make a statement or express something, then that's the time to come out of the woodwork.

(And Balenda and the young woman, after this non-answer to what is basically a non-question, try to get away again.)

Vito (jumping forward): Are you going to your car now?

Balenda: No, I'm not.

Vito (officiously): Where are you going now?

Balenda: I'm just going.

Vito (walking up to within an inch of her nose): Where are you going? I would like to talk with you. I'd like to just take a walk with you. Can I just walk with you for a second?

Balenda (getting really tired of old Vito): I just talked for 20 minutes and I'm not... if you didn't get it, I'm really sorry, you'll just have to find a tape.

Vito: If you'll walk with "48 Hours," you'll walk with CNN,

right? I just wanted to find out where you're going, what you're going to do.

Balenda: I've done my 48 Hours of being in Waco before the public eye. Right now I'm just going to regroup myself.

Vito (taking another tack): Do you feel at all guilty from a parental standpoint, that this (her son's Davidian involvement) is something that maybe Mom should have seen coming...?

Balenda: No, not at all. If you're looking for that you're going to have to get that from someone else. I'm surprised to hear that from CNN. I would have expected that from a tabloid, not from you. No I don't feel guilty, but I feel very sad, so what I'm feeling is sadness. My son is in there. He's in a very difficult situation. He has a very long haul ahead of him. We hope that he comes out of it OK, intact. We're certainly prepared to put him back together as best as we can when its over and that's the long and short of it. So you'll have to wait for the book.

Vito: Are you planning to write a book?

She and the young woman finally just bolt, getting into the young woman's car. Vito scurries after them and sticks his head in on the passenger side, again an inch or two from Ganem's. The crowd roots for them driving off with it still in there.

They finally extract his head and upper torso and leave Vito standing there in the dust. It becomes obvious to a writer who has witnessed the exchange that the easy way to find out where Balenda Ganem is staying is to follow the car.

The young woman knows immediately she's picked up a tail. She drives up Fifth Street, hangs a hard U-turn, heads west, scoots through a couple of crowded parking lots and goes through some other subterfuge to shake the geeks in the old yellow Buick.

She finally shakes us. Boy, were we mad.

And she drives Ganem to the hotel in which she's staying— the Brittney, right across the street from the Waco Convention Center, and turns out it's maybe 20 yards from where Vito had been whining.

And the young woman later turns out to be Donna Vislocky, of "Good Morning America."

"We already had a special relationship," Vislocky explains later.

Good thing to have, in a feeding frenzy.

The impact made by the media pack was ubiquitous, all-pervasive, insidious, and unavoidable. It was present on every level. In terms of hard facts and information—for both Koresh and the FBI—the media was where most of it was coming from.

The FBI had neither the trust of those involved nor the resources nor the time to gather information at the same broad level as the media. The media did the FBI's work for them, gladly and for free, by sending out hundreds of people from news organizations around the world to gather background information on Koresh and the Davidians.

Of course the FBI could—and did—question individuals and pull in specialty consultants, but for the broad, sweeping strokes, the information was coming from the media, and the information invariably had its own media-serving spin.

By the end of the siege, it would be difficult for the FBI honchos to keep straight on what they knew, when they knew it—and where they knew it from.

And in terms of pure information, Koresh, as the siege progressed (or failed to), became *completely* dependent on the media for his view of the world, and his view of the world's view of him.

And thus the amplifier effect—news, then reaction to the news, then reaction to the reaction creating more news—was going great guns.

In the lull after a horrific event, particularly one that is the result of a conflict between humans, if the parties involved are left unmolested and unhurried, if there are no third parties to muddy the waters with their own agendas and urgencies, then just maybe cooler and wiser heads may prevail.

In hindsight, the strange dynamics of the Waco Standoff seem to have taken place in the space bracketed between two violent events, the shootout and, 50 days later, the inferno.

But in Present Time as it was back with each passing day of February, March, and April of 1993, there was only the one, the opening bracket; no conclusions were foreordained.

Somewhere in the middle, the violence of the initial shootout was absorbed, amplified, redirected.

Now that the medium has become the message, the message is technology.

And the technology of the media, reduced to its essential elements, is an amplifier. Not merely of images and sounds, but of emotions, conflicts, hatreds, misunderstandings: The fatal shots fired into it on February 28 emerged on April 19 as death for 81.

The emotional content and conflict was electronically sampled, re-reverberated, supercharged, re-mixed. It was manipulated for the high sharp notes (Ralph Vito to Balenda Ganem: Do you expect the American public to feel sorry for you?) and these were stepped up, distorted, and recirculated yet again as feedback.

Sad that the Great Communications Network should only amplify and then communicate mainly the miscommunications, the frictions of force meeting counter-force, pressure meeting counterpressure:

The contradictory needs and agendas of the three kingdoms, jostling, clashing. And furthermore, the jostling and clashing within each kingdom—interpersonal, interagency:

The competing needs of the media, and its various outlets.

The competing needs of the government, and its various agencies.

And, perhaps most important, the Messianic needs of David Koresh.

Chapter 14

They were called "press conferences," and they had all the trappings of modern mass journalism; the banks of big, tripod-mounted TV cameras, the still photographers strobing the speakers and the crowd, reporters scribbling furiously, the showboating TV reporters barking questions to show the folks at home (and their bosses) that they were on their toes.

But these were not really press conferences at all. They were not really for the press, and there was no conferring. And despite the fact that millions of people saw snippets and sound bites on television, the intended target was really a captive audience of one: David Koresh.

Just as some fundamentalist preachers use their pulpits to savage their enemies, denouncing the "Papist Conspiracy" rather than furthering the truth of their own faith, the press conferences were—as even the FBI would later admit—rigged events with three major agendas: Controlling the media; controlling public perceptions of David Koresh; and further inflaming the already beleaguered cult leader.

And toward those ends, the conferences worked like a charm.

Seldom have so many been manipulated so willingly by so few.

First, the daily tossing of the bone to the newshounds of pack journalism provided them with grist for their mills: Little blobules of Officialese from Official Sources which are the lifeblood of editors and producers, and make perfect raw material for soundbites for talk shows, voiceovers for video, and are a quick and painless way to wrap newspaper ads with 20 inches of copy with "lotsa good quotes."

Even the emotional undertones and nuances were carefully orchestrated, calculated, and stage-managed to get subtextual messages across the airwaves to Koresh, listening intently and with increasing frustration to the FBI's version of the gospel.

When the FBI, in consultation with its cadre of priest/psychologists from the Freudian Cult, determined that it was time for Koresh to conclude that the government's patience was wearing thin, the FBI High Priesthood's altar boys and spokesmen Bob Ricks, Richard Schwein, Dick Swensen, et al, would speak of Koresh in hard, even libelous terms, calling him a liar and a coward, and accusing him of using children as a shield.

And the reporters would dutifully report that the FBI was "frustrated, impatient and angry." Good copy, great manipulation—and, at the bottom line, somewhat cruel.

It was as though the already vastly powerful government had spitefully bound and gagged David Koresh and brought him on stage to relentlessly insult and abuse him, and make fun of him. For an hour every day for 51 days, the press laughed along with the verbal abuse, some of which was really funny—and dutifully and soberly recorded and rebroadcast, over and over again, that which was designed not to inform the public but to inflame and provoke the trapped Davidians.

It was a policy which would ultimately backfire hellishly— presuming, of course, that the FBI *did* want the Davidians to come out alive, and that the FBI *did* want the "crime scene" preserved intact, and that the FBI *did* want to take David Koresh to court.

The briefings, as a means of both communicating with Koresh and simultaneously preparing the public for "what may come" were too heavily laden with too many different kinds of freight. The FBI seemed to be trying to ship fresh herring, Limburger cheese, and lemon meringue pies all in the same boxcar. Those recipients who didn't get the wrong shipment altogether got at least too strong a whiff of the shipment intended for someone else.

At the same time—and often, in the same sentence—that the FBI was prepping the public for catastrophe by painting a picture of an irrational, mercurial, baby-raping sociopath who was capable of anything but always up to no good... they were trying to get the message to Koresh that the FBI would make good on its promises and do "nothing precipitous"?

Koresh had to be concluding: Hey, if *I* were up against someone that crazy, *I'd* have to do something.

The goofiest tack may have been the "nanny-nanny-boo-boo" routine, which was based on the assumption that if they insulted him often enough, he'd come on out fighting mad to defend himself in front of the world.

"Come on out and *prove* what we say is wrong," Ricks said.

This first presumed that Koresh was stupid enough to fall for playground tactics. Second, it was based on a misunderstanding about Koresh's love of publicity. True, he did love it—but not in any normal way. Koresh loved being the Big Mystery, the Occult Possessor of Wisdom, the One Who Knows Something You Don't

Know. When he *did* receive air time, early on, he proved exactly
that. Subsequently, he was content to settle for being the boy
everyone misunderstood. He'd take the Babylonian abuse because
it was, after all, attention, and he didn't expect Babylon to have
anything nice to say about him—probably wouldn't have liked it
if they had.

The only thing he cared about was making sure they spelled
old Vern's name right—K-O-R-E-S-H.

Every afternoon, Ricks (or his relief, usually Swensen, and the
occasional Schwein) would meet with consulting psychologists
and the negotiators, the FBI's Byron Sage, Jim Cavanaugh of the
ATF, and others.

He would not ask them what's new. Instead, he'd basically ask
them what he could say to the news weenies to help further the
negotiations.

And the answer was always some form of behavior
modification. Ricks' comments each day were designed to either
reward Koresh for being a good boy, or to punish him for being bad.

Good boy? Press conference, March 21, Swensen: "We are
optimistic. We spoke to Koresh last night for over four hours. We
think and are hopeful that this will lead to a resolution but we
have been down that road before, so we are not totally positive...
again, I think the thrust of where we are coming from is that he
is alluding to the final end of this thing and he is talking in terms
of large numbers, not this trickle thing of two a week which, as I
said before, will take over a year. He is addressing it ending, it
ending fairly soon. He is still waiting for various signs. But we are
not talking long-term, according to what he is saying. As a matter
of fact... the tone was more optimistic and tended more to address
a resolution to this thing instead of the various Bible discussions."

Bad boy? Ricks, April 16: "I think he's a classical sociopath, in
that his way of thinking is: 'One more day, the world's gonna be
better for me.' And that's his ultimate game, to keep it going one
more day. I don't think he can think beyond that: 'One more
day, maybe, God will strike everybody dead.'"

Be a better boy: "We're sending a message to him: 'You say
you're a leader, you're a man of God. Be truthful; be honest; be a
leader of your people.'"

Or we'll spank: "...we are going to get them...to bring them
before the bar of justice for the murder of our agents. They're
going to answer for their crimes. That's the bottom line to this
whole thing, they're going to come out."

But the agents—especially Ricks—seemed most preoccupied with getting the idea through everyone's thick head just what a *liar* Koresh was. That the man could under no circumstances be counted upon to tell the truth.

As the *Dallas Morning News'* Lee Hancock noted:
Repeating what has become a daily litany of what he termed the sect's bizarre statements, baseless pledges and outright lies, FBI Special Agent Bob Ricks told reporters that he is emphasizing the Branch Davidians' untruths to show why no credence can be given to their latest promise to give up.

...Agent Ricks said the 33-year-old sect leader lied to his mother (Koresh's, not Ricks'—Ed.) about being mortally wounded and lied to the public about losing a daughter during a Feb. 28 firefight in which four ATF agents died and 16 were wounded.

Yet, in spite of all the broken promises, all the lies, all the dashed hopes, all the reasons why "no credence" can be given to their promises, the FBI seemed to take Koresh completely at his word and absolutely on his honor on one subject: Suicide.

Negotiators asked Koresh on four occasions whether suicide was part of the plan. He said no, not in the cards. And he reassured his attorney of the same thing, and his attorney again reassured the FBI.

He said that wasn't in the plans. And they swallowed it. Hook, line and sinker.

It was also clearly Ricks' intention to cast Koresh as a crazy—to prepare the American public to "see" that any future action against Koresh would be justified. Because Ricks found it particularly frustrating, early in the siege, to learn that the public seemed to be of the opinion that the government should have ignored Koresh's guns and girlfriends and Godhood and just let sleeping dogmas lie. Their attitude was, that he was minding his own business in the middle of nowhere. What's the big deal?

So Ricks began to pester negotiators for the Koresh Nutcake Quote of the Day to allow him to make more extreme characterizations of Koresh and his danger to humanity.

The only problem with this approach is that it was laying the groundwork for the big question asked after April 19: if the guy was so completely bug-eyed and crazy, why'd you push him into a corner?

As early as March 9: "We have done everything in our power to downplay the negative side of his personality. I think it is important to you and the American public to maybe have a better understanding of what we are dealing with. As far as his religious philosophies, it is our belief that he believes his prophecies will be fulfilled if the government engages in an all-out firefight with him in which he is executed.

"We have portrayed the other side (of his personality), that he would wait for a message from God. I wanted to put that out here so that you understand that he has taken many steps that are very provocative and in fact is calling us to come engage with him.

"Our greatest fear is that he is so intent at times to provoke the situation to where our people are fired on so that we may feel it necessary to fire back. That is not our desire at all. We want to make sure that we are doing everything in our power to ensure that does not take place."

Asked if there was some critical point at which they would enter the compound to save lives, Ricks replied:

"At this point, we believe any effort to effect a rescue would be counter-productive because we would be playing right into his hands. And that is, we believe an all-out gun battle would ensue, and it would cause us to have to retaliate. His purpose would then be accomplished."

Amen. As Koresh would prove, with an assist from the Feebies, there's more than one way to skin a catastrophe.

The rules of the "press briefings" were also rigged so that the FBI would always win. No shouting. Raise your hand. And, more important, each newsman getting the FBI nod was strictly limited to one question and a follow-up—but only if he announced his intention of asking the second one at the start of the first.

And he never got another question, not the next day or the day after, if he asked one question the FBI or the ATF didn't much like.

(Our own experience in this regard was pretty amazing. We asked the ATF's Dan Conroy a pretty simple question: "Does the ATF have any reason to believe that Koresh and the gang are in there destroying evidence from the shootout?" It was the last question we were ever allowed. Conroy's comic-ominous reply: "Well, if they haven't thought of it before, they've thought of it *now*." Oops, our fault. They've got a Harvard-educated lawyer in there and more than a few ex-cons, and they're sitting in the compound by the radio listening to the press conference smacking their foreheads and shouting, "Eureka! Why don't we *destroy* some *evidence!*")

The format and the punitive attitude prevented any deep probing. Only rarely was the press able to engage the government in any true debate. What appears to have been the sole exception came in the wake of the FBI's confirmation that, oops, yes, one of its Bradley Personnel Carrier drivers had indeed run over a *Waco Tribune-Herald* vehicle, a Chevy Cavalier, that had been left at the scene of the shootout.

Reporter: "Can you tell us more about the accident involving the Bradley and the car?

Dick Swensen: As it was explained to me, it was a question of trying to push the car out of the way and it was moving, all right, but when they tried to turn it off the road, the Bradley rode up the back of the car.

Reporter: The car was crushed from the steering wheel back. Now, you told us, when we asked whether military personnel was going to be driving these vehicles. The answer was, 'No, we are fully qualified. We have qualified personnel in the FBI to operate these vehicles.' Now, one gets out of hand and squashes a car and you say 'we are not professional drivers.' Yet you see these vehicles racing back and forth across the compound on a daily basis. Which is it? Are you qualified or are you not qualified?

Swensen: The short answer is, yes, we are qualified to drive the vehicles. Obviously we were not qualified to be a tow-truck. I don't mean to be smart with you, but...

Reporter: But you did not try to TOW it, did you.

Swensen: We tried to push it and obviously if you know anything about tanks...

Reporter: Who in their right mind would push a car with an armored vehicle?

Swensen: Well, what are the options?

Reporter: Well, what was the RUSH?

Swensen: I'm not going to debate this with you...

Which probably should have been the FBI's policy overall. No comment.

The first question an individual, corporation or government agency must ask itself about press coverage is: Do we want any?

Will our interests be served? And the rule when dealing with a media feeding frenzy is, quit feeding them.

If there's nothing left to eat, they'll go away. A flat "no comment," issued often enough with no preamble or explanation, finally becomes a no comment. There would have been some public grousing from both the reporters and the pundits along the lines of "Why is the FBI being so secretive?" and such an approach would have fueled some paranoid conspiracy fantasies. But the other approach—the one the FBI and ATF in fact followed—had far more disastrous results.

And the press had largely exhausted the ancillary stories and sidebars—interviews with Koresh's cousin's dog's veterinarian, interviews with the girl whose teacher at school knew the convenience store clerk who'd sold him a six pack—during the first weeks of the siege. To say that if the FBI had quit holding press conferences, the story would go away, is unrealistic. But it would have slowly worked its way to the back pages. In fact, it already was.

And talk show hosts were already telling their listeners they could talk about anything they wanted—except the Waco siege.

Just when they should have shut up, the FBI began to bray.

And all those daily utterances—roughly 40 minutes of them, every day—gave the press something to shoot at; things to either disprove or expose as outright lies. It was also the prime locus of the amplifier. Would you respond to the *New York Times* report that... you are really a bunch of baby killers...

Reportorial rule of thumb: When people are failing to make anything actually *happen*, cover what they are *saying*.

The FBI began to perceive that this war between them and Koresh was a war that would be played out in the media—but they didn't see quite far enough. They didn't see that it wasn't a war at all. It was just a case of children and misled men and women unfortunately trapped by the rigidity of their beliefs. It was not a war. It was a rescue mission.

Rather than the FBI behaving honestly and openly behaving like the benignly secret organization they really are—by battening down the informational hatches, terminating the daily press conferences and cauterizing the leaks—they instead secretly and dishonestly tried to pretend to be open and honest.

They continued the "press conferences," hoping to use them to both malign and manipulate Koresh and reduce the nation's sympathy toward him, and thus lay the predicate for any "unpleasant action" should it become "inevitable."

This was not only dishonest; it was very, very stupid from the FBI's standpoint.

As each day progressed in a siege where nothing really seemed to happen, the public was beginning to express not only a lack of interest but downright irritation at the continued coverage and its domination of the airwaves, particularly in light of the fact that nothing was happening.

The pressure of public opinion seemed to say: Dammit, *make* something happen. Aren't you supposed to be the FBI? Where's Efrem Zimbalist, Jr.?

There is an unfortunate synergy in the competitive mass media. If one reporter shows up, he gets the story and goes away. If two show up, both stay until the other one goes away. If 200 show up, they almost never go away. And each organization reconsiders its position: Well, if all those other guys are down there, maybe we better send some MORE reporters...

Television is especially susceptible to the budget trap: We're spending $10,000 a day down there. So whatever is happening, it has GOT to be news.

The syndrome resulted in some scenes that were both silly and sorry.

Downright scary was the anchor who asked his field reporter if it was true that an undercover agent had been in the compound, and if so, had he managed to escape? That off-the-cuff reverie could have gotten an undercover agent killed—or, since by then they were all out, someone among the Davidians who just looked like one.

Downright hilarious was one poor newscaster, obliged by both budget and schedule to give *some* kind of an account of daily Davidian doings, who informed his listeners: "As the morning sun comes up, the shadows are getting shorter on buildings of the Branch Davidian compound," as shadows are much inclined to do until, well, along about noon, "and that's pretty much about it from here, Stan."

And so the Groundhog Day routine began to settle into the pattern that would last for the remainder of the siege: Long periods of apathetic ennui, punctuated by eruptions of mass panic, usually based on unsubstantiated rumors, which were sometimes nevertheless reported as fact.

Groundhog Day into Groundhog Night.

Nights, it's a bizarre cross between a Fellini film and *Star Wars*.

Beer-swilling producers in Bermuda shorts, some waving golf clubs, career insignificantly through what looks like a high-tech spaceport dropped in mid-prairie—the giant clamshells of the satellite dishes atop the bulbous trucks, all brightly lighted whited sepulchers against the utter darkness of the Central Texas sky.

These trucks cost at least $300,000 and rent for a couple of grand a day. Cost of the time "on the bird," as the techies call the unseen communications modules whirring through the airless void hundreds of miles overhead, costs at least $35 a minute— and that's for a sweetheart deal.

You can't see it, but this is a river of money, pouring skyward, and the nighttime scene is perhaps the quintessential snapshot of the late twentieth century and the current reality; these high-tech vehicles, surrounded by modernity and cynics, winking upward at eyes miles in the sky, while less than three miles away there are 80 people who are fervently, worshipfully believing the words of predictions made 2,000 years ago, and dating from a time when communication was on papyrus and transportation on camels, and the skies were full of gods.

Who's better off? Who's wiser, smarter? Sometimes in the evening, around 6 p.m., it's very hard to say.

At the end of the compound nearest the Davidians, right by the last DPS checkpoint and the barbed-wire fence, six pools of light, each a little island of brightness against the still chilly March darkness. At the center of each pool of light, a TV reporter, or, since this is still early in the siege, in many cases, a full-fledged big deal anchor, dispatched from the comfort of the news dais in the studio to actually *go* somewhere, to capitalize on the excitement of the moment (and, no doubt, to later wind up in a promotional ad about what a great job the anchor person does in covering the world).

And standing in the center of one of the light pools is an anchor from one of Dallas "big 3" network affiliates. She instantly calls to mind the Don Henley song, "Dirty Laundry." She's the "bubble-headed bleach-blond on the evening news" made into living, breathing, false-eyelashed flesh.

When it comes to a helmet of hair, Jillian Julian, or whatever her name is, puts Waco PD's Malissa Sims' Kevlar coif to shame. Witnesses report that when her helicopter landed a short while ago, she hopped out long before the blades had slowed. And, they said, the hair didn't even MOVE.

And she has this little irritating thing she does with her eyes, whether on the news dais or bravely stepping out from her luxuriously appointed Winnebago to face those cameras. The deal is, every time she finishes a newsy revelation, whether it's someone adopting a cute lost puppy or the outbreak of World War III, she flashes her eyes into the camera, as if to say, "This is serious, because I said it!" Flash.

And now she's waiting in front of the camera, warming up, waiting for the cue that she's on the air, and talking back and forth over the microphone with the boys in the control room. You can almost hear the chatter in her earphone. And in her head.

"Okay," she says, to unseen ones in front of other distant cameras. "Brett, my toss to you is going to be real *hard*. I'm gonna say, 'Brett...' Wait a minute, I cannot hear myself speaking. Is Brett talking??? Fix that. Okay, Brett, I'm gonna say, 'Let's go *live* now to Brett Shipp,' hard, okay?"

And the toss-to-Brett controversy being resolved, she now turns her attention to her own upcoming performance, rehearsing, trying various inflections of her lines this way and that, each rehearsal complete with various permutations of the Eye Flash Thing.

"Local authorities are in-cuh-reas-ingly concerned with David Koresh's *state* of *mind*," flash.

And again.

"Local au-*thor*-ities are increasingly con*cerned* with David Koresh's state of *mind*-uh," whammy flash.

And now the full, last walk-through: "John and Clarice, concerns here are increasingly growing about David Koresh's state of... Hey! My I.F.E is really hot! There's another audio feed!"

And some lackey dutifully barks into his walky-talky, "Okay, Jillian's I.F.E feed is *really* hot, see what you can do about it, okay."

And while they're pouring water on it or whatever they do after several thousand dollar's worth of hair, clothes, nails and makeup gets herself a hot I.F.E., one old print reporter, taking in the six such scenes proceeding simultaneously, with each Ken and Barbie stand-up increasingly concerned about David Koresh's state of MIND, uses the lull to announce:

"I'm leaving. I am going to try to get *in* to the compound. It just don't seem safe here."

The deep nights of the dog-watches are different. Being lost and lonesome out here under this small forest of microwave masts beaming standup Kens and Barbies up into the field of dreams would allow members of the media time for introspection, should they desire it. Time to ask, what hath Edison wrought?

Once, this media monster—this Beast—was described as an extension of the senses. But this is *over*-extension, recursive, becoming more "truth" than the reality in which we live.

Because it not only tells us lies which we believe, but tells us lies about ourselves, which we ourselves believe.

Three miles. In spite of the arbitrary, artificial distance placed by the FBI between David Koresh and the rest of the world, it's really not that far. The same stars shining on the media shine on the compound.

And old Dave can look out at the microwave antennae and the clamshell dishes of the entire world, pulled up as close to him as the law will allow. Some of these microwave masts are, gracious, from certain angles, clearly topped with crossbars. They are very cruciform.

In fact, over by NBC there are three of them, clustered together, two short and one taller one in the middle, a sort of microwave Golgotha. Is David Koresh at a darkened, shattered window looking out through the March wind at those crosses, his own personal communications Calvary?

Beneath the cruciforms, in their metal crypts, the technicians shape and mold and vivify the electronic soul of the world.

Occasionally, the blanched colorless night is broken by the opening of a door on one of the trucks, out of which spills the full 256 colors of the electronic rainbow.

Can David see the faceless engineers sitting staring at the rows of flickering monitors, these menlings who are both masters and slaves of the airwaves, spidery hands scuttling across the banks of knobs, switches, slides, and rheostats, cueing up this, fading out that, weaving our reality from the separate strands of the electronic spectrum?

We know that Koresh does *hear* the Word as the Electric Beast feeds it to the entire civilized world, and most of the time, at least early on, he hears what he's longed to hear all his life—that he's *not* Vernon Wayne Howell, some goofy, snaggle-toothed, jake-legged, rustic stuttering con-man from Chandler, Texas, with a name straight off "The Beverly Hillbillies" and a tiny following of the woefully gullible and the easily misled; no sir.

He's David Ko-*resh* and local authorities are increasingly concerned about his state of *mind*, because he is the Dark Man, the Man in Black that has always haunted man and the world from the edges of history; the Man of Dread risen up to fulfill the ancient prophecy... hey, *cool*.

Come *out*? Quietly? And leave all t*his*?

The man may be a child-molesting psychopath—but he's not CRAZY.

Chapter 15

It's easy to blame the FBI for lots of things, to second-guess them. They probably most feared what, in reality, finally happened: that the one someone who might've had a bona-fide solution for the crisis would get lost in such a huge shuffle of so many who *thought* they were that someone.

Because for every Waco Wacko goofing it up on Crazy Hill—or McLennan County Jail where the would-be "Saviors of David" population usually never fell below six, including the likes of Gary (one arrest) and Marian/Bathsheba (four, including once by ATF helicopter, which made her day), Jesse Amen, and so on—there were thousands more with "the solution."

Mostly, they just made phone calls and wrote letters—usually addressed to the FBI. It became a huge nuisance, and may have served to cause some of the more legitimate expertise to get lost in the shuffle.

The calls began the moment the media took the story to the airwaves, and within the first eight days of the siege, the FBI recorded more than 2,000 phone calls from around the world, many were from the countries in which Koresh had spread his message several years earlier—New Zealand, Great Britain, and Australia.

Some were from self-anointed "cult experts." Others were from people offering the One True Interpretation of Revelation. According to Themselves.

Some just called to confirm that, Yes, Virginia, it *is* the end of the world.

News outlets were encountering similar fun folk.

Perhaps the most sympathy should go to a Mr. David Oates, who, according to the *Dallas Morning News* was in contact with FBI negotiators to talk about theories of "reverse speech"—the process of listening to, in this case, Koresh's KRLD tape, only in reverse, to detect subtle subconscious messages (such as, perhaps "the Gospel According to Paul Is Dead").

The amazing thing is not the messages he found therein.

The amazing thing was that he was repeatedly trying to figure out backwards a tape most people couldn't understand when played forward.

The FBI may have made a genuine effort to sift through the volume of mail and faxes and phone calls, but the bigger the story became, the greater the volume. Which is unfortunate, because one person was listening to David Koresh's rantings very closely and insightfully indeed.

Dr. Phil Arnold seems to have tried to hand Bob Ricks and the FBI the key to the Seven Seals at least as many as seven times, and seven times they threw it away.

Arnold refuses to bash the FBI with the benefit of hindsight and heap dead children at their feet, because he feels that the truth is the agents themselves are probably even now doing more of this to themselves than is healthy or justified.

And it might have ended badly no matter what they did and didn't do.

The negotiators and the FBI faced a unique situation, circumstances which one psychologist called "a living laboratory"—after, of course, all the guinea pigs were dead.

There is, however, nothing unique about the way the FBI handled it. They brought old rules to a new game. They came in as blinkered and blinded and hidebound as any established religion, in fact: They brought in their own dogma and sacrosanct doctrinal assertions. They were playing by the book. But it was the wrong book.

And the only book that David Koresh would play by—*could* play by—was the only one he knew: Revelation.

Worse, by the FBI's scornful, superior refusal to play by it (or even take a long look at what was in it), they didn't just lose the game; for David Koresh and his followers (most dead, but some alive) the Federal Beast Incarnate confirmed everything that both Koresh and Revelation were saying.

If President Bill and "Atta-girl" Reno had gotten on the phone to tell them, "Boys, just go ahead and make it all come true," they couldn't have done a better job of it. And odds are good that that error will return to haunt them.

One can easily qualify Dr. Arnold as a major expert on apocalyptic thinking and the Book of Revelation (and we shall) but the ultimate proof is this: When David Koresh finally got his long-awaited and much-derided "message from God" and sat down to write his magnum opus on the Seven Seals, it was specifically addressed to Dr. J. Philip Arnold of Reunion Institute, and Dr. James Tabor of the University of North Carolina.

Drs. Arnold and Tabor, along with the world, will forever wonder just what it was he wanted to say.

Dr. Arnold was on the scene in Waco almost from Day One, heading to McLennan County from Houston the minute he heard Koresh talking about the Seven Seals. Dr. Arnold came simply because he presumed the FBI might be able to use him. And he wasn't being presumptuous.

In fact, he was bringing the two things that the FBI needed desperately, though they didn't *know* they needed them—an intimate, lifelong knowledge of both Revelation and the disparate interpretations of it by Apocalyptic groups such as the Koreshians, and mediation skills specifically geared to resolving religious disputes; it's what his non-profit Reunion Institute is all about.

More important, albeit in a subtextual way, though he's been a "cult" counselor who, since Jonestown, has aimed at reuniting families disrupted by these fringe groups, Dr. Arnold does not believe in "de-programming."

"De-programming is sometimes done against their will by kidnapping. And in the case of a minor, it may be appropriate to sit them down and talk to them for a few days, hopefully give them some food and water while they do it, though. But when you get to adults, it becomes a very difficult thing, you know; are you going to deprogram Jewish adults? Deprogram Seventh-day Adventists? People who convert to the Christian faith or Christians that convert to Judaism?

"So adults should not be kept against their will and tried to be persuaded out of their beliefs. Now arguments that the Davidians were brainwashed... well are they? How do you define brainwashing? Was Buddha brainwashed? Catholics? Who gets to make the final determination?"

The point is, no matter how wrongheaded a person appears, you can't reach in and change a person's thinking. You can only help *them* to change it.

Yet every "cult expert" the FBI seems to have consulted—the Cult Awareness Network, Rick Ross—seemed to offer nothing more helpful than shrill "leader's a psycho, followers are crazy" advice, plus public assertions to that effect which could only rigidify the Branch Davidians' resistance to the outside, and their ultimately clearly fatal terror of the FBI.

And, less pie-in-the-sky: Arnold had the key.

It was very simple. Find out which of the Seven Seals David Koresh thought he was on. And gently, ever so gently, without ever questioning his beliefs or his thinking, help him to see other alternatives, and arrive at less dire conclusions; help him to find *in* Revelation the clear way out of his predicament.

Again, the key here is that it doesn't matter what the FBI was thinking. It doesn't matter what the psychologists were thinking. The only thing that matters is what Koresh was thinking, and gradually helping him to change it.

The proof is in the pudding. Ultimately, Arnold and Tabor would achieve this rather irrefutably, acting on their own. They believe they effectively ended the siege. The FBI just didn't want to believe it. Or just couldn't seem to wait long enough to find out if it was true.

Arnold first came to the government's attention when he snuck into a press conference (non-press or even non-mainstream press being verboten). They were able to tell almost instantly that he wasn't with the media; he was too well-dressed, and he knew *way* too much about the Bible. And, as it turned out, way too much about Koresh. His only two questions told the FBI things it had not learned about Koresh in 10 days of negotiating.

He asked Dick Swensen:

"As a biblical scholar, I'm quite interested in this question. First, has there been any expression on his part, on Koresh's part, as to the significance of the Jewish calendar which he observes; Passover, Yom Kippur, these days; has he attached any particular meaning to the fact that Passover is coming up on April 6th?"

Swensen: "To the best of my knowledge it has not come up in any context. There have been hours and hours of conversation and I am unaware of that. I have not heard of that."

Second question, the one around which the entire standoff revolved: "Since he has talked about the importance of the Seven Seals, have you been able to listen to him to determine at what point in the script written in the Book of Revelation he is on today, this week?"

Swensen was dismissive, and a tad condescending: biblical scholar indeed. "The answer is it depends on what day we asked the question and we have discussed the whole Seven Seals at various times, at great length at various times, OK?"

Go away, kid, ya bother me.

He managed to buttonhole Ricks after the press conference.

Arnold handed Ricks a stack of material about Reunion Institute and what it had accomplished over the years. Ricks shoved it under one arm and stood there FB-eyeing him in his trademark deadpan manner.

"He's not an easy guy to talk to," Arnold recalled, but he persevered, telling him he'd been working with apocalyptic groups, particularly those obsessed with Revelations, for 20 years, and thought he could "shed some light on what Koresh was talking about..."

Ricks interrupted him: "There's *no*body that can understand what *this* man is saying," and stood there kind of breathing through his nose at Arnold while Arnold kept on trying.

"I wanted him to try to focus on the tact that the key to the whole thing was decoding the Seven Seals—not what they *meant*, but what Koresh thought they meant. It was like breaking the code in World War II: You break the code, you'll know what he's going to do next. And if you know exactly where he *is*, you can help him to get to somewhere else. We would know what we needed to do and say, in his language, in order to procure a result. The only way to do that was to understand the script that he was following."

And Ricks looked at him a moment more and walked away, only to be mobbed by reporters. Still Arnold persisted, following Ricks into the fray, trying to get in a word here and there to Ricks, but it was like water off a duck's back.

Arnold had a feeling the info he'd handed to Ricks might wind up in the nearest trash can. "I had a feeling that he wasn't going to get the information I'd given him to the negotiations team. He didn't seem to know any more about the Book of Revelation than I know about FBI weapons and tactics—which was *his* Seven Seals, *his* doctrinal assertion."

So Arnold took a packet out to the command post, and, after a 30-minute wait, assistant agent Tom Murphy took it off his hands. Arnold drove back to Houston.

And a few days later, Murphy called. Very cordial. Wanted to establish contact. Murphy said that since things were currently at a standstill and they were looking to get things moving again, they wanted to bring in some more expertise to help out.

Arnold told Murphy that he'd planned to be in Waco in the next couple of days. Murphy instructed him to call when he arrived.

And during that 30-minute call, based on what Murphy said, Arnold concluded that Koresh was indeed still "on" the Fifth Seal. But it was also about the time that the last two Branch Davidians were getting ready to come out, and since it looked as if there was "movement," the FBI wouldn't be needing him.

Said they'd call him, though, if and when they did.

And, though they didn't, Arnold wasn't finished.

Chapter 16

A few mornings after his last contact with the FBI, Dr. Phil Arnold consented to do a live, drive-time interview by telephone with KRLD. He talked at some length, and with some respect, about Koresh and the Seals.

Two hours later, the phone rang. It was the FBI, wanting to know, "Was that you on the radio this morning talking about the Seven Seals?"

"Why do you enquire?"

"Well, David Koresh heard you. The group was impressed, and it's created some movement. We'd like to get a copy of the tape."

The phone rang again, it was Ron Engleman from the Mighty 1190, a Christian radio station, wanting an interview. When Arnold had done it, he sent a tape of that one along to the FBI also, as a bonus.

The tapes did make it inside the compound to Koresh and the group.

"I never heard from them [the FBI] after that, though I called and left messages for Murphy twice. But I was just real happy to have been able to do what I'd done, happy that the tapes got sent in. But in hindsight: if a bunch of crazy people had taken over the asylum, and there was a psychologist on the outside who'd somehow demonstrated he had a solid connection with the leader of the inmates, I sure think I'd call that shrink back up and ask him to at least have lunch, or give a little talk to the negotiators..."

In short, Arnold believes, they'd written the whole simple theory off "as so much religious BS, and it turned out to be the key to the whole thing."

Given the FBI's attitude and some of the intractable noises its spokesmen were starting to make at the press conferences as March gave way to April, Arnold began to fear that the FBI was planning to rush into the compound before Passover. "And I knew Passover would play a significant role in the crisis. During Passover, Koresh would either come out, or decide never to come out, or receive the revelation that he was to come out. Which, as it turned out, was what happened.

"I decided maybe I could help out, forestall things by just talking up the importance of Passover to the Koreshians. I called some of the media, and I called the FBI. They didn't return the call."

And that's when he decided to try to talk to Koresh directly. He called Dr. James Tabor, a longtime friend and associate of Arnold's. As a specialist in ancient apocalyptic groups, he provides a complement to Arnold's almost encyclopedic knowledge of modern ones (Arnold, with a Master's degree in Colonial religious history, got his PhD from Rice University, where his specialty was sectarian religious groups of the first century).

Arnold suggested they try to reach Koresh via commercial radio. Tabor was intrigued. For three nights, Arnold and Tabor rehearsed over the phone, working out the details of what they would say to Koresh, how they would relate to him, how to get him to trust them, both Biblically and personally. And, most importantly, how "we could grant to him the presupposition that his prophecies are being fulfilled, and how, having given him that, we could show him that the prophecies he has predicted can be construed to mean that he may yet have to come out of the compound."

This was not just an academic parlor game for the two men, however. "We worked on it spiritually, even. We were concerned about these lives, and we took it very seriously. We made a commitment to do our best to convince him of another way of seeing the end result, of convincing him that the Fifth Seal didn't have to end in death and destruction."

Getting the air-time was the easy part. They called Ron Engleman, who, over the course of the siege, was party to some projects so ill-conceived that this particular project may have been his atonement.

"We further had the audacity to instruct Engleman that he *not* be on the show, except to introduce us. He understood the importance of it, and began promoting it on his show several days before we appeared."

Once on the air, Arnold said, "We gave the performances of our lives—but were sincere: we communicated to him exactly the message we had wanted to communicate in the practice sessions."

They warmed Koresh up first, talking about how "interesting things are happening as a result of David Koresh, and the whole world is suddenly looking at Revelation. We don't really know if he's what he says he is, but we'd sure like to talk more to him and find out..."

And then, to business.

The intention overall was to try to get Koresh to "see" in the

Scriptures that the Fifth Seal actually gave him more time and room to maneuver than he'd believed.

Rev. 6:9 And when he had opened the fifth seal, I saw under the altar the souls of them that were slain for the word of God, and for the testimony which they held:

Rev. 6:10 And they cried with a loud voice, saying, How long, O Lord, holy and true, dost thou not judge and avenge our blood on them that dwell on the earth?

Rev. 6:11 And white robes were given unto every one of them; and it was said unto them, that they should *rest yet for a little season,* until their fellowservants also and their brethren, that should be killed as they were, should be fulfilled.

Rest for a little season. And then more fellowservants, to be killed. And then, the bloody Sixth Seal.

Tabor and Arnold saw a workable loophole there, and are fairly certain that they were able to duplicate and then help Koresh change his own thinking.

"The Fifth Seal said—to Koresh—that after his people were killed on February 28, they were to wait for a little season and then be killed. That's what they were doing throughout the siege: Waiting. That's why they *couldn't* come out. Not wouldn't: Couldn't. It wasn't because they didn't want to, but because they believed God said not to, to wait a little season.

"And my part of the argument that morning was to show him that a 'little season' might be longer than he thought it was.

"I knew how long it was to the Koreshians, because I'd been on the phone with Livingston Fagan in the county jail for hours and hours. And after all those hours, I was probably the only person who understood their theology. It was clear that David Koresh knew what he was doing when he sent out Fagan as their master spokesman," Arnold recalls.

"Anyway, Fagan told me that they thought that since a season was three months, a little season would be somewhat less. Koresh believed that the Fifth Seal would close, and that he would be attacked. And since February 28 to Passover was about five weeks, six if you include Passover, Passover was probably about the time it would happen. Fagan said they were just waiting to see what would happen during Passover; that was their plan."

On the air, Arnold said, "Well, it looks to me like David Koresh may have lots more time than he thinks he does, time to do more prophesying, maybe for years and years, maybe even from jail. Because the Fifth Seal says 'A little season,' but the Greek word is 'chronos,' which can be translated as season, but more often means 'time.' It means, then, 'a little *time*.' And the word 'time,' as it is used in the Bible, as in Daniel, has more to do with at least a year—and it certainly doesn't mean 'less than three months.'"

Arnold was trying to allow Koresh a chance to buy himself some time, pure and simple: He was throwing him a lifesaver.

Jim Tabor took another tack, equally liberating for Koresh without invalidating his prophetic premise.

Said Tabor, "You know, there's a duality in Biblical things. Two paradises—the Garden of Eden and the Last Paradise, and so forth. And I think it's possible that in the microcosmic sense, in the life of the 100 or so people in his church, maybe the Fifth Seal *has* been opened. But in the larger, macrocosmic sense, the sense of the world, I think the world is only still on the First Seal."

Arnold spoke up, as per practice: "Before February 28, Koresh was an unknown, the world had never heard of him. I think that's when the white horse really started to ride, and Koresh may be the man on the white horse. I say, Ride, ride, ride, David Koresh, you're just beginning your ride. The next two or three Seals may come to pass, but now, the world is still in the first..."

And they read, over the air, over the same "Beast Network" Koresh had used to paint himself into the corner, several citations from Revelation 10:8—11.

And in those citations, were these words:

Rev. 10:8 And the voice which I heard from heaven spake unto me again, and said, Go and take the little book which is open in the hand of the angel which standeth upon the sea and upon the earth.

Rev. 10:9 And I went unto the angel, and said unto him, Give me the little book. And he said unto me, Take it, and eat it up; and it shall make thy belly bitter, but it shall be in thy mouth sweet as honey.

Rev. 10:10 And I took the little book out of the angel's hand, and ate it up; and it was in my mouth sweet as honey: and as soon as I had eaten it, my belly was bitter.

Rev.10:11 And he said unto me, Thou must prophesy again before many peoples, and nations, and tongues, and kings.

And Arnold said, "See? You must prophesy again, before many nations and tongues. Your mission isn't over."

Arnold believes in retrospect that Koresh got out his Bible, never far from hand, and began to think also about "the little book."

On the air, they talked more about writing—about how all the great prophets—Moses, Jesus, Jeremiah—had come out and faced their accusers and gone to prison. And we talked about how prison was where Paul had produced his letters, and how it is important for a prophet to also produce a literature.

"And we suggested that he could do it after he'd surrendered, that he could go to prison and write it there. But, the way I put it together now, he feared he would be killed in prison. He decided to write it before he surrendered, to be safe. Where it says it shall make your belly bitter and your mouth as sweet as honey? I think that part came true. It must have felt very good to be writing that book, to feel the words—and very bad to know that he was going to prison, maybe for a long time."

By complete though fortuitous accident, six days before Passover began, on April 1, the day before the tape was to have aired, Phil Arnold met Dick DeGuerin in Waco. DeGuerin complained that, Biblically speaking, he didn't have the foggiest notion of what Koresh was talking about.

Phil said he thought he could help him there, and they wound up spending four hours one evening going over Koresh's world-view per Revelation. During the conversation, Arnold wondered aloud if Koresh would be listening to the broadcast.

DeGuerin went into the compound again the next morning. When he came out, he told Arnold that they'd been listening to it when he walked into the compound, but that he'd interrupted them.

DeGuerin arranged with the FBI to have a tape of the broadcast sent in.

"And the next thing we know, we're into Passover. And David Koresh did his very best to count up the days to know when Passover began, which is a very difficult thing to do; it's very involved. And then they observed it.

"We all believed he would get some kind of revelation at Passover. And sure enough, he claimed he did—claimed he'd gotten some kind of word from God.

"And the funny thing is, that's what everybody—FBI, press,

Davidians, everybody—had said they were waiting for him to get, waiting for it almost since Day One. 'Would he ever get the word, the word?' everybody wanted to know.

"And finally, he says he got it... He said the word was that he would come out, after he wrote down the meaning of the Seals. And immediately, everybody forgot that this was the word we'd been waiting for."

Here it was, in writing, and to his lawyer. He'd said he was going to do things before, but reneged. This was in writing. This was the word:

As far as our progress is concerned, here's where we stand.

I related two messages from God to the FBI, one of which concerned present danger to people here in Waco. I was shown a fault line running through the Lake Waco area. Many people here in Waco know that we are a good people, and yet they have shown the same resentful spirit of indifference to our warnings of love.

I am presently being permitted to document in structured form the decoded messages of the Seven Seals. Upon the completion of this task, I will be freed of my waiting period. I hope to finish this as soon as possible and stand before man and answer any and all questions regarding my activities.

This written revelation of the Seven Seals will not be sold, but is to be available to all who wish to know the truth.

The four angels of Revelation, Chapter 7, are here now ready to punish foolish mankind. But the writing of these Seals will cause the winds of God's wrath to be held back a little longer.

I have been praying for so long for this opportunity to put the Seals in written form.

Speaking the truth seems to have very little effect on man. I have shown that as soon as I am given over to the hands of man, I will be made a spectacle of and people will not be concerned about the truth of God, but just the bizarrity of me in the flesh.

I want the people of this generation to be saved. I am working night and day to complete my final work of writing out these Seals.

I thank my Father. He has finally granted me this chance to do this.

It will bring new light and hope for many and they

won't have to deal with me the person. The earthquake in Waco is not to be taken lightly. It will probably be the thing needed to shake some sense into the people.

Remember, the warning came first and I fear that the FBI is going to suppress this information. It may be left up to you (DeGuerin).

I will demand the first manuscript of the Seals be given to you.

Many scholars and religious leaders will wish to have copies for review. I will keep a copy with me.

As soon as I can see that people like Jim Tabor and Phil Arnold have a copy, I will come out and then you can do your thing with this beast (by which, Fagan says, he meant his fleshly being).

I hope to keep in touch with you through letters. We are standing on the threshold of great events. The Seven Seals in written form are the most sacred information ever.

Arnold reflects for a moment. And there is both sadness and anger in his voice when he says, "He was coming out. I know he was coming out. He was sincere. He wasn't trying to con us. How do I know? That business about the dam bursting."

Why?

"We know that dam wasn't going to burst. But he believed it was, and said so. He wouldn't have put down something so easy to disprove—time would disprove it—if he hadn't believed what he was saying. He was coming out. He was seeing the prophecies of Revelation in a new light. I don't mean he ever said, 'Gee, Phil's right and I'm wrong.' There is no right or wrong in interpretation.

"But he was able to see that, even within his own interpretation, he had more room in Revelation than he thought. I think he probably prayed about it until he got this sense—from God, he thought—that he would be able to write down the Seven Seals, something he'd never done publicly before. Write his 'little book' and come out. He would have done that. But then..."

Chapter 17

What a mixed-bag lawyer Dick DeGuerin turned out to be. In fact, he embodies a sort of an oxymoron: a talented, aggressive lawyer and, though it's well hidden, a good guy.

Not a great guy. But a good one.

That he is a lawyer, and a good one, is not in dispute; the 50-year-old, benignly fox-faced barrister learned the tricks of his trade under Percy Foreman, the highly successful and arguably sociopathic trial lawyer who became a legend both in Texas and in his own mind.

DeGuerin, like his predecessor, understood the basic rule, the bottom line in considering whether to attach oneself to suspects in criminal cases: Always get the money up front—unless the resulting publicity is worth more.

And when Bonnie Haldeman, though devoid of any substantial assets, asked him to represent her son, David Koresh: Ch-CHING.

It didn't take much convincing. CNN, NBC, the *New York Times*, Larry King... swimming pools, movie stars, y'all come back now, heah.

Before the siege was over, without having once entered into a courtroom to defend his client, DeGuerin had made off with maybe a million dollars' worth of the priceless, intangible publicity stuff, with the ink and the airwaves carrying him and his reputation around the world. And he'd almost inked a $2.5 million book deal for himsel... his client.

Why good guy? Two reasons. He almost became The Man Who Got Koresh Out—and could further console himself with the notion that, if it hadn't been for FBI impatience, he almost certainly would have succeeded, with just a little more time. Regardless of his motives, 78 or so more people alive than dead looks good on the résumé.

And second, fiduciary concerns aside, over time he seems almost to have come to *care* about Koresh and the folks trapped by their religion and painted into a corner by faith, the ones who had to live in that rank-smelling compound.

DeGuerin made his grand entrance on March 11, showing up with Bonnie Haldeman at the ATF checkpoint near Loop 340 and FM2491 and "trying" to get in to "see David," not to mention the much more likely result—getting those TV cameras turned his way.

As soon as he had them, he began to do the "jes' a po' country lawyer, trying to do what's right" routine, telling the *Dallas Morning News*, "I'm only here because David Koresh's mother has asked me to be. I think that he needs some independent counsel that he can trust."

The ATF told him he could take his mighty nice and noble self on back up the road, and DeGuerin did, following that road straight to the federal courthouse, to file a writ of habeas corpus.

DeGuerin was by no means the first lawyer on the scene, however. Events in Waco had already attracted a fair-sized gaggle of them, some just looking for business and others with a political axe to grind.

North Carolina lawyer Kirk Lyons appears to fall in the latter category. Lyons, who has represented KKKer and former "America's most wanted" Louis Beam and other far–right-wing and white-supremacist figures, is also executive director of Cause Foundation, which presses rightist "civil liberties issues."

Lyons and his cohorts were active on several fronts, rousing a rabble and raising a stink—and a pile of legal briefs—concerning the standoff and events related to it. For instance, Louis Beam himself, who also writes for a right-wing rag called the *Jubilee*, assumed that his credentials with that publication entitled him to attend press conferences. And most observers, whether they loathed Beam or merely hated him, subsequently agreed that they probably did: credentials are credentials and press is press, regardless of slant or cant—political correctness could be the death of the system it purports to protect.

But after Beam waited politely for his raised hand to be recognized and then asked whether the country was indeed witnessing a fascist takeover, the government by its actions seems to have said, well, yes, sort of, because he was instantly whisked from the convention center, credentials notwithstanding.

And when he attempted to return to a subsequent briefing in the middle of March, he was arrested on charges of criminal trespass. Lyons and CAUSE filed a half-million dollar lawsuit against the government.

Lyons was also kicking up a furor over the fact that the arrest and search warrants for Koresh and the compound remained sealed and thus unavailable for public inspection.

Lyons, CAUSE, et al, seemed to have a valid point, in that these "unavailable" documents were the basis for the government's "probable cause" in raiding the compound, which was very much like saying, We're attacking this citizen, but won't tell the other citizens why, and maybe we can do the same to *you*.

U.S. District Judge Walter S. Smith contended that the cultists did not have any legal rights under the circumstances—a ruling which seems to suggest that you don't have rights as a citizen until you get arrested; that in the period between the time the government decides it wants you and the time it actually gets you where it wants you, all bets are off.

Federal prosecutors were also behaving in an unusually secretive manner, conducting hearings inside the jail house instead of the public courthouse, and thus alarms were going off not only in the minds of the right-wingers, but, increasingly, the public at large.

Early on, the government had seemed rather firm when it said No Lawyers Allowed at the Koreshian Klubhouse.

But as time went by, the FBI became increasingly uncomfortable, or at the least, irritated by the large numbers of right-wing, pro-gun, fundamentalist church and Libertarian Party groups coming out on weekends to protest the raid and decry the government in general at the Convention Center and also at Fool's/Holy/Lamb's Hill.

And though Judge Smith had been very sympathetic to government concerns in his rulings, there was always the chance that an appellate judge somewhere up the line might see things differently, and, with the stroke of a pen in New Orleans, put a Kirk Lyons and a Louis Beam into the Waco equation—or even into the compound, where they could do some serious *cheerleading*—and grief like that the government didn't need.

The government seems to have concluded that DeGuerin, at heart at least, a reasonable man, was the least of several evils, and that allowing him into the compound might defuse some of the ardor over "violation of Koresh's constitutional rights," and that he might even get old Dave to come out.

And for a while there, it looked as if he would.

On Monday, March 29, a long-lensed cameraman spotted Dick DeGuerin sitting in a chair in the yard of the Davidian compound. It looked as if he were just sitting there talking to himself. But he was actually speaking to David Koresh, behind a door a few yards away.

DeGuerin did not reveal what was said during this first meeting, but results were swift, and FBI officials were more optimistic than at any other point in the siege—encouraged enough, in fact, to stop blasting the compound with obnoxious Nancy Sinatra tunes.

    And DeGuerin met with Koresh for three hours the next day.

And twice on Wednesday.

And after almost every meeting, out of deference to the public's right to know what a crucial kind of guy he'd suddenly become—he held a press conference.

DeGuerin would come floating luxuriously up in the big silver Mercedes (so inconspicuous among Waco's old El Caminos and '77 Buick Limiteds), slide out of that luxuriously appointed interior and, in front of the Waco Hilton, tell the world and the press at some great length all the things he wasn't going to talk about.

"Good evening. Well, I've been in the compound this afternoon and I've made some more progress. I feel good about it. David is kind of weak from his injuries and that's kind of impeded the talks a little bit, but I feel very good about it. It's going to take a while. That's about all I've got to say."

But then, he doesn't turn, and he doesn't walk away.

And the newshounds commence their barking.

High-pitched news poodle: What do you think will finally be the thing that pushes him to make a decision?

"I'm not going to discuss what we're discussing or what he's discussing."

Big TV Doberman: Are you running into any resistance from Schneider?

"I'm not going to discuss the various personalities or who I've talked to, what's been said by anybody on either side."

Friendly, tail-wagging radio beagle: Can you comment on his injuries?

"No, I can't."

A pause, while the newshounds cock their heads to one side and raise their ears lopsidedly in puzzlement, trying to think of a question that will at least get an answer from the man who *still* won't turn and walk away.

Great Radio Dane: Dick, are you more hopeful tonight than you were last night?

"Well, I'm always hopeful. I don't know that I can compare last night to tonight. I don't intend to do a blow-by-blow account or an inning-by-inning score either."

Oh.

Newspoodle: You said he is weak. What are you talking about, like how weak? What's his physical condition?

"Well, his physical condition is not good. I'm not a doctor. I don't intend to go into it any further, except to say that it has slowed down the discussions a little bit. It's become a bit of a problem."

Irish Typesetter: Is he bedridden?

"I'm not going to discuss the details of it."

Beholden News Retriever: Sir, can he only go a few minutes of time basically?

"I'm not going to discuss the details."

Why hasn't Koresh come out before now?

"Well, I don't want to address any specifics."

Has he been preaching to you?

"I'm not going to get into specifically what our discussions have been." And so on... ad nauseam.

As long as they stand there asking, he's willing to stand there not answering, grist for the mill of the Beast, because what works is this: It's not what you say. And it's not even what you *don't* say.

It's whether or not the cameras keep rolling.

Dick DeGuerin—and to a lesser extent, Jack Zimmerman, now representing Steven Schneider—continued to ride the Koreshian wave—but in the first week of April that wave began to crest, then to break.

Part of that was due to that Recalcitrant Deity, Dave. Some of it was due to the government, ever quick to become impatient about remaining patient.

As early as April 1, Ricks, perhaps only following "strategy," had already begun to carp again at the press conferences. "It does appear there's a kind of stretching out" of the time preceding a surrender, and it looked like Passover would play an increasing role in the timing of a surrender.

And so, the next day, the government cut off its end of the negotiations, and resumed the sound-blastings. And allowed FBI Agent Dick Schwein, sort of mean-mouthed-cop to Ricks' righteously-but-professional-outraged cop, to mount the press conference podium on April 2 to bark loud and mean about "this man who we want for murdering federal officers."

And, as Passover neared, the excitement over DeGuerin declined, and it began to appear that the Davidian's celebration would delay a surrender at least one more week, so also loomed the return of the thing most dreaded by all Koresh's "hostages" *outside* the compound, still stuck in Waco:

Groundhog Day. *Again.*

In New York, however, for the guys with the pinkie rings and the big cigars, things were getting hot hot HOT!

When Dick DeGuerin decides he's gonna look out for a client's interest, he apparently looks after all of them. While he was not in the compound talking to Dave about legal matters, he was burning up the phone lines to the Big Apple and using his prayer breakfasts to pray for a Power Lunch regarding Dave's *literary* career.

On the other end of the hot-hot-HOTline were Manhattan lawyermen Michael Kennedy and Kenneth David Burrows, who were busily "packaging" Koresh for a big, big deal. A book deal.
How big?
Somehow the *New York Times* latched onto a fax from Burrows to several publishers in which he breathlessly announced he hoped to auction the Koreshian Kaper—as told from the holy horse's mouth—for a "floor" price of $2.5 million.
If that's the floor, where's the ceiling? Odds were good that the publishers just might talk them down a few steps closer to the basement—nevertheless, big bucks for Koresh and, perhaps more important to DeGuerin: to DeGuerin.
To the government, spending about half a million a week on helicopters, tanks, paychecks and per diem—figure about $3 million, total, not counting state and county expenditures—about all it could hope to get would be taxes on the same.
Because, juicier still, the judiciary had overturned some recent laws, such as the Son of Sam Statute, meaning it is officially okay for bad guys to turn a profit on the recounting of their bad deeds—though Texas law requires defendants to deposit such blood money into an escrow account that is distributed in accordance with judgments on behalf of the victims (remember them?).

Oft-outraged *Fort Worth Star-Telegram* columnist Debbie Mitchell Price reported that DeGuerin wouldn't comment (Hey, no kidding; see above press conference) on any book deals, "but didn't seem too worried about the government confiscating royalties."
Slice'em-Dice'em Price quoted DeGuerin: "It would be improper for a government or a state to prevent an accused from paying for a lawyer from legitimate funds. We're facing a monster of a trial and a monster of an investigation... It's going to take years out of... the life of any lawyer that is involved. That means tremendous legal costs, even at... minimal hourly rate, and I don't charge by

the hour. If I thought there was any kind of deal afoot for profiteering, I wouldn't have anything to do with it. Nobody is going to make any... money off this."

Price hotly suggested that Dickie Baby should take his Pro Bonificence and tell that to Amy Fisher. She summed up her towering miffedness in a manner worth repeating:

A lunatic can stockpile enough firepower to arm the militia of a Latin American nation. When federal agents try to serve warrants, he and his mind-controlled pals can engage in a gunbattle that leaves four ATF agents dead, 16 wounded and who knows how many culties killed.

He can hole up for six weeks and refuse to come out while hundreds of law officers sit on a country road running up the taxpayers' tab.

And then he can sell his life story to pay his lawyers.

It's the American way.

Ch-CHING...

It was only after the contract went up in smoke along with Koresh and the compound, after much hope of any major recompense for time and trouble disappeared, that DeGuerin began to show what may turn out to be a less mercenary side.

There is not much profit in defending a dead client, nor really much to defend but a memory. Nevertheless, DeGuerin fell to the task with a vengeance—an energy and devotion that makes one wonder whether, beyond the usual lawyerly posturing and knee-jerk crying of "foul," DeGuerin had also stumbled onto something genuinely troubling and deeply wrong in the government's self-serving account of Koresh and the Koreshians, and their ending.

It was only natural, lawyerly, and adversarial that, at first, immediately after the fire, he would embrace the stories of those surviving Koreshians claiming that the big bad government had started the fire by knocking over some lanterns with its tanks.

Such, in fact, would have been a natural shysteresque exit line:

No way. *You* killed my client. My client was a *good* man. I rest my case. Now, I'm outta here.

But now, clientless, he's more "all over the place" than he ever was before, still grinding that "lantern" axe with enough vehemence and consistency to make one wonder.

Perhaps more compelling, however, is how diametrically opposite DeGuerin's picture of Koresh and the Koreshians looks when compared to the government's.

As far as the master of mind control leading a flock of brainwashed zombies, DeGuerin told CNN's Larry King:

"...In fact, we talked extensively with Steve Schneider, Wayne Martin—two very intelligent, well-educated individuals—and they were individuals.

"They deferred to David when David spoke about the Bible, but they were both individuals and they both had their own thoughts. We talked to a number of other people, not to the extent that we did to David and Steve and to Wayne Martin, but they all seemed content, they seemed peaceful.

"They weren't bowing and scraping to David or following his every word. They seemed to be individuals who were exactly where they wanted to be."

As to the contention that Koresh was never coming out, DeGuerin told King:

"Well, I think David had his own timetable that he was abiding by, a more important consideration to him than the laws on the outside. He understood how important it was for the truth to get out, and the only way for the truth to get out would be to go to trial. And he understood how important it was that he come out peacefully. He wanted to do that. But he also had spoken to a higher law. He had deep religious beliefs. He was very sincere about those religious beliefs. And whether you or I would consider them to be ordinary religious beliefs is judgmental. He felt them very deeply. That's why he was listening to his own drummer and had his own timetable.

"But I believe that he would have come out, and would have come out peacefully. And all it would have taken is just a little more time."

Perhaps more puzzling, in a way, is the tape that DeGuerin made of his first, hour-long phone call to Koresh.

DeGuerin, who said he was now interested only in getting the truth out, made that tape exclusively available to the *Houston Chronicle*. The tape contains several stunning assertions—that the government shot first, mounting the assault even as he opened the front door, that Peter Gent was killed by machine-gun fire from the helicopters, shot in the top of the head, and that he was most fearful that the government, upon his exit, would begin planting evidence around the compound.

The most worrisome thing is that, on this candid and casual tape, Koresh sounds completely normal, given the circumstances. On the possibility of a surrender, the *Chronicle*'s copyrighted story quotes him: "Every avenue that is going to give me the legal rights and the protections and the safeties and the security that our opponents are not going to plant something on us, is making moves to a better end. Once I do go out of here, I want to go out walking," here, according to the *Chronicle*, talking about his loss of several pints of blood.

"I'm in the dragon's mouth and whatever happens to me happens to me. God is on my side and truth is on my side. I want to have my head clear. I want to be able to stand on my own two feet and go through this like a man with a straight face."

The most startling revelation of all was that was the only mention of God. And it was in the third person.

However, at about the same time during the long, dull Passover lull as DeGuerin was winding up business in Manhattan, the Living David Koresh was also on the horn trying to settle up his accounts with God.

Yes, he finally got his message. But it wasn't one that the FBI or anybody else especially cared to hear. Because it looked like maybe six more weeks of Groundhog Day.

Chapter 18

As a major story, the siege of Mt. Carmel was slowly dying. Dying, in fact, of boredom. There had been all the fitful starts and false alarms throughout the siege. Some children had come out. Some adults had come out in little short-lived and rather unpromising trickles, and the trickle was shut off after March 24.

Koresh had broken the negotiations. Koresh had resumed the negotiations.

The sheriff went in, talked to Dave. The sheriff came out. Sent Dave a letter promising some stuff. Dave didn't like the stuff. Sent the letter out.

FBI says, no lawyers allowed. And then let Dick DeGuerin and Jack Zimmerman go in.

And go in again.

And again.

And now, everybody is supposed to just be sitting around on their thumbs, waiting for Koresh's "book" to come out, and him to follow it.

But the biggest disillusionment, the one that initiated the decline in coverage, was "The Passover Thing." Koresh and his lieutenants had said things to DeGuerin and Zimmerman that encouraged them and, initially, the FBI, to believe that they would be coming out sometime after the end of Passover.

Passover came. Speculation continued.

Passover went. Stalemate continued.

What gives?

On April 8, Steve Schneider got on the horn to the FBI and said that, gee, well, Dave "never understood what was the big deal about Passover," and that he was wondering why everyone was putting so much stock in him coming out after it was over.

Ricks said he was disappointed, but added that on the other hand the cult had a history of back-tracking on promises.

The media had noticed it too. And they started leaving.

The story had not changed in any important essential since Day 1. Reporters had completely exhausted those primary sources who were still talking for free—and the secondary and tertiary sources as well. And with nothing happening, there was way more media present than the story required—so they were covering each other.

There were features on Satellite City, sunbathers, golf, Saturday night ditch dances. Reporters were actually, seriously doing interviews with Satellite City's rival mayors—Clint Houston of KRPC, self-proclaimed mayor of the Northside (north of FM2491) and only slightly more legitimate Joe Duncan, a freelancer for NBC who was elected to the Southside post by a handful of reporters—many of whom worked for Duncan's *Satellite City Daily News* (motto: If It Happens, It's News To Us!).

There were many, many rather recursive, self-referential scenes like this: A Channel 8 reporter from Dallas, doing a standup. Cameraman Tom Lovelass filming her monologue. *Dallas Morning News* photographer David Woo photographing Lovelass. And a writer standing there writing about Woo, and about the fact that he was writing about Woo, who was in turn photographing a photographer, who was filming a standup, who was talking about other newsmen...

David Koresh no doubt divined—by looking out his window— that with each passing day that the siege continued with no foreseeable end in sight, Satellite City was getting smaller.

The world was going away.

The foreigners—the BBC, the Chileans, the Australians, and New Zealanders left first. A week or so later, the smaller-budget and the more-distant radio and TV operations quietly began to pack their tents. Then, in anticipation of getting good footage from the riots expected should the Rodney King trial result in unpopular verdicts, and from the Bosnian situation, should it result in war, even the big boys—NBC, ABC, CNN, and the major-market stations like WFAA in Dallas and KHOU in Houston—began reducing their presence, cutting back to... well, to about what they should have been in the first place.

As the standoff wore on and the FBI's patience wore thin, on April 8 the FBI announced through Ricks at the daily non-news briefing that if Koresh didn't come out pretty soon, "We're going to have to regroup, and we'll have to decide what other measures we can take. There are other weapons in our arsenal."

Ricks, of course, didn't elaborate. And the FBI never released— if it ever even recorded—the name of the person who came up with the really hot idea of gassing the compound, women, children, and all.

There is some circumstantial evidence that it was Billy Walker.

Now it's late in the siege. A slow Saturday night. At honky tonks and gin joints everywhere within a hundred miles of Waco, everybody has a plan, knows just exactly what they ought to do to "make them people come out of there."

Some advocated just building a fence around it and treating it like a prison until they came out, whenever that was going to be. Just wait. (That one had occurred to Janet Reno as well. "I kept thinking we could create our own prison," she said later, and trotted that idea past the FBI. They didn't like it. They told her that it would pose an unacceptable threat to their agents, on account of those .50 mm rifles.)

Some of these barroom philosophers, admittedly a small minority, thought the FBI just ought to wait for a little while longer. (The FBI thought about that, too. As Sessions told Congress: "We do not normally in our criminal justice system allow a criminal to set their own timetable on when they will submit to authority." In fact, the FBI didn't like any of the ideas it had been getting. "We examined every offer of advice," Sessions told Congress. "Most of the cult experts told us that law enforcement should leave the area altogether, in essence ignoring Mr. Koresh and others, regardless of their crimes.")

You don't get to be where Sessions is today—wherever that is—by being the kind of guy to go around ignoring crimes.

The other thing was, Sessions said, the FBI was afraid that letting them have more time might also present them with an opportunity to *kill themselves.*

Never mind the obvious question of, Who's more likely to kill himself: A man with time on his hands? Or the one with federal tanks knocking holes in his house and hosing him down with tear gas just because he doesn't want to go spend life in prison?

When it came to tap-dancing around the subject of suicide and whether or not Koresh and Company would commit it, the ATF and the FBI were Ginger Rogers and Fred Astaire.

Or maybe it was just indicative of the holes in the line of command between the FBI on the ground in Waco—and Sessions, gone to ground in Washington.

Sessions and Reno told the Congressional committee that they went in there with the gas on April 19 for the same reason that the ATF stormed the place on February 28: Suicide—because they, like the ATF, feared that the cultists would commit suicide at almost any time.

But here's that pesky Jeff Jamar, roaming around well outside the loop and *way* outside the official story, in spite of the fact that he was in charge down in Waco. Here's Jeff telling the press: "Our best estimate was that he was not going to commit suicide, and mass suicide was a possibility but not a probability."

That much can be said for people in *any* compound, from Elk to Camp David to Kennebunkport to Club Med. Added Jamar, somewhat confusingly: "The only way to stop that was to gas them with enough speed to break communications so people might think for themselves." Among them, presumably, were all the people who were not sitting around thinking about suicide.

Further roiling these already-muddy waters was the report of Dr. Murray Miron, a psychology professor at Syracuse University who was on the team of psychologists analyzing Koresh's mental state. It was Miron who, at the request of the FBI, consulted with his colleagues and delivered the verdict: Koresh was *not likely* to kill himself because he was a psychopathic personality. His report also alleged that further negotiations would only lead to more stalling tactics from Koresh. His report was dated April 16, three days before the tanks rolled in—and into—the compound.

Essentially, what they were saying was, Koresh isn't going to commit suicide, so let's go in and stop him from killing himself just to be sure.

And, oops, here's the ubiquitous Bob Ricks, at a press conference on the afternoon *after* the fire, telling reporters that Koresh had been talking pretty seriously of suicide since March 2.

"On the day he was supposed to surrender [after his radio broadcast] on March 2, the plan was, he was going to walk out. He had grenades. When the FBI approached him, he was going to pull the grenade pins and was going to kill himself. Everyone knew that this was the plan."

(Make that, "everyone—*except the press who were at the press conference on March 3 and thus the public at large*—knew that was the plan." Just another case of the news media being the *used* media.)

Ricks said that after the hour-long KRLD broadcast, Koresh "kissed the kids goodbye. He was going to go outside and commit suicide in front of the TV cameras. And at the last second, he chickened out."

The same is true of the majority of suicide victims. A couple of false starts and failures, but then one day—ka-blooie.

As earlier noted, the idea for the gas seems to have been Billy Walker's.

Billy Walker wasn't in the honky-tonks, though. Billy is a man who likes to do his drinkin' and thinkin' where the action is, and so he managed to do some of it out there on Lamb's Hill. He'd gotten into the ice chest pretty often as afternoon turned to evening and then into night.

Billy, thanks to the beer, is rubbing two brain cells together as hard and as fast as he can, trying to get a little mental fire going.

And now he's starting to "catch," so he pours on a little more Milwaukee Bafflement to help it along.

Stuff is starting to come back to him, like how he used to talk when he was in the service. And that there's something wrong with the world, something he was mad about, but to save his life and his liver he can't remember quite what it is, so he lights out after those folks who are trying his patience and cluttering up his TV set—those dadgum Branch Davidians.

"...I wish they would end this... one way or the other. The state of Texas is going busted and yet you look at... [what] they are spending on this...

"I mean, it don't make sense."

Amen, Brother Walker, amen! Walker tears the pop-top off another one. He's really starting to tie a thinking cap on.

"...I believe this way, this is how I believe, this is the way I was raised up and the way I will always believe: If the United States is doing good and we have plenty of money and plenty of food and everything else, send it over and help them a little bit."

Billy Walker puffs out his chest and says, "I told one woman that and she said, 'boy you are cruel and you are going to Hell.' And I says, 'Well I might, Lady, but I will sure go to Hell believing what I believe in.' I told her we got people in the United States, elderly people that ain't even drawing enough Social Security, getting the heat cut off and dying in the winter time because they don't have enough money for heat."

And now Jack the Giant Killer is getting to the top of his beanstalk.

"I hate to say it, cause I don't want to see any little kids lose their life, but he has brainwashed those little kids so bad that they are not going to be good for anything anyway. It is going to stick in their brain from now on. He has had them since they were born."

Then, with profanity sprinkled like salt all over his words, his brain sharpened by copious amounts of alcohol, he outlined a plan to get the Davidians out of the compound. They ought to use tear gas!

Whether or not word was passed to the FBI about Billy's plan remains to be seen. Maybe they just sat down, got drunk, and came up with it on their own. "Great minds," and that sort of thing.

Anyway, the FBI started mulling over Billy Walker's plan in late March, and briefed U.S. Attorney General Janet Reno on it the first week of April. Ms. Reno balked initially, and asked the FBI for other alternatives, including bringing in the military, but finally approved the Billy Walker Plan, she said, because the FBI kept telling her that conditions were getting more and more "unstable."

Who was the more unstable, the government or the Davidians, was not a topic she addressed. It is clear, however, that the government had no real desire to ever "stabilize" the Davidians.

As early as March 14—a Sunday—the government had begun shining high-wattage lights at the windows of the compound, turning it into a blaze of brilliance most nights. This, they said, was to protect their officers from possible snipers.

Then they wired up giant loudspeakers and trained these on the compound. At first, in the middle of March, these were, the FBI said, used to broadcast messages into Mt. Carmel. They were later used to deprive the Davidians of peace by day and sleep by night. Recordings of screaming rabbits, dial tones, and busy signals, Buddhist chants, Mitch Miller Christmas carols, Alice Cooper songs, and Nancy Sinatra's "These Boots Were Made for Walkin'" were blasted sporadically into the compound at all hours. The only song that even the hardest hearts in the FBI refused to bring to bear on women and children was "Achy Breaky Heart."

The sounds and the lights, like the praise or censure of Koresh offered by Ricks in the press conferences, were used as punishment and reward.

At a March 22 press conference, after another lull in negotiations, Ricks said the government resumed the boom-boxing to increase the pressure on Koresh. He had disappointed the negotiators. "We're disappointed. The proof of the pudding is in the eating and we want to see that there is [sic] in fact positive steps taken by them. We did get some expressions of annoyance with regard to the music..."

And when Dick Swensen was asked at a press conference on March 25 whether he thought the psychological warfare of noise was having a negative effect on Koresh's health, Swensen said that he would certainly hope so.

According to Louis Alaniz, there were other irritants brought to bear of which the public was not aware. He told Mary Garufullo of "A Current Affair" that the government seemed to be showing two opposite faces—one to the public it purported to serve, and another, darker, one to the Davidians—such as government officers "mooning" the Davidians from their Bradleys.

Said Alaniz, "The negotiators, I just don't understand. They tried to get them out by offering food, freedom, and 'When you come out you can tell the story, just come on out, we won't do you any harm'... but what you see is these Bradleys running around and the guys in them shooting the finger at these kids, and one incident where they actually mooned some of these girls. These people were scared. The only thing they saw was a bunch of people coming and shooting at them."

The press conferences were further enflaming the Davidians and magnifying their view of the U.S. government as an evil empire, a "Babylon." Alaniz said that there were generally four to six people either taping the radio broadcasts or taking notes from them. "Every time there was a press conference," he told Garufullo, "they were listening. What really got them is they constantly heard the story changing—another lie, another lie, another lie. These people were saying, 'Why are they saying all this about us?' I didn't see anything that they [the FBI] was telling the press that was true."

Especially disconcerting to the Davidians was the FBI intimation that they were holding children up to the windows and using them as "shields."

"That hurt everybody inside there. There was one young man who looked out the window and there was someone with him, but it was just to show him what they were doing to everything out there—bulldozing the go-carts and bicycles, pushing cars all over the place, tearing up the trees, and running over a man's grave, constantly."

And then there were the "flash-bangs," the term the FBI uses for its diversionary grenades: low-powered in terms of destructive force, but very bright and very loud, designed primarily to startle and frighten victims.

They were used several times during the course of the siege for a variety of reasons—but usually to scare someone into going back into the compound.

The FBI made clear on numerous occasions that it didn't want anybody coming out of the compound without prior announcement and federal permission—which is tantamount to tacitly agreeing with Koresh that nobody could leave without his permission, since he was in complete control of the lines of communications.

"Uh... Dave. Need to use the phone."

"What for?"

"Uh... to order a pizza?"

To underscore its resolve to keep people inside the compound, the FBI and ATF also began stringing razor-wire. As Ricks explained it at the news briefing: "We've had, unfortunately, too many people in the last few days who've violated our instructions [concerning exiting the compound]. It seems to be that they are more emboldened in their attempts to come out and test the control of our perimeter."

This was very like the FBI cooperating with Koresh to help prevent what they should have been trying to encourage—a mutiny. Worse, it may have left the Koreshians on Day 51 still believing that the policy, rigidly enforced up to that time, was still in place.

As Rep. John Conyers of Michigan would later ask Janet Reno, somewhat rhetorically: "When in God's name is law enforcement at the federal level going to understand that these are very sensitive events, that you can't put barbed wire, guns, FBI, and Secret Service around them, send in sound 24 hours of the day and night, and then wonder why they do something unstable?"

Chapter 19

At about 6 a.m. on the morning of April 19, Day 51, Groundhog Day finally gave way to Da Big Heat.

A watchful cameraman, who'd been staring at next to nothing off and on for nearly two months now, finally hit pay dirt.

A few minutes earlier, a DPS trooper had come by and told the photogs and early arriving news folk, "It's going down." And now there was finally something to see looking across those dark fields through the huge telephoto lens of the camera.

At about 5:55 a.m., the FBI had called into the compound and reached Schneider, who, in Ricks-speak, "was telephonically advised that the FBI would begin shortly to insert tear gas into the compound." Schneider slammed down the phone, tore it out of the wall, and threw it out the window.

At about 6:05, a huge, tank-like vehicle equipped with a special boom emerged into the early morning light and began knocking a gaping, eight-foot hole in the compound and blowing tear gas into the buildings, 15 bursts per hole.

The loudspeakers were booming, echoing crazily, asynchronously around the complex:

"This is not an assault. Do not fire. If you fire, your fire will be returned. We are introducing non-lethal tear gas. Exit the compound now and follow instructions. You are responsible for your own actions. Come out and you will not be harmed. You will be provided medical attention. Come out and you will be treated professionally. No one will be injured. Submit to proper authorities. Do not subject yourself to any further discomfort."

But one survivor later said it was almost impossible, because of the echoes and the time delays between the loudspeakers, to make head or tail of these robotic, Orwellian marching orders. It was just a lot of amplified noise impossible for them to understand: This-is not-ot an ass-ass-ault-ault...

Inside the compound, even as the building shuddered and shook, even as the choppers thundered *thuppa-thuppa* overhead, even as the air where there was CS gas became stinging, intolerable, as if filled with bees, some Davidians were shooting back at the big M-60 combat engineering vehicles, volley after volley.

Branch Davidians who weren't shooting at tanks were busy attempting to take care of routine chores, in spite of the early-morning nightmarishness of the situation. Those who weren't doing either were reading or remembering their Bibles—Revelation.

Now *this* they understood.

Rev. 9:9–10 And they had breastplates, as it were breastplates of iron; and the sound of their wings was as the sound of chariots of many horses running to battle. And they had tails like unto scorpions, and there were stings in their tails: and their power was to hurt men five months.

Babylon and the Beast that Koresh had so sold them on had been knock-knock-knocking for 50 days. And now, on Day 51, it was going to just come on in, right there in front of God and everybody, with the very Eyes of the World watching.

And David Koresh may have grinned his last grin and smiled his last smile: It's *show* time.

On the other hand, he may have been just a man, and scared to death.

About 30 minutes after the gas attack began, cult members briefly raised a white flag. The phone was reportedly retrieved after the white flag signal, but the line remained broken.

The *New York Times* reported that agents, listening over one of the eavesdropping devices delivered with food and equipment, heard someone saying: "Don't shoot until the very last minute." Another voice, believed to be that of Koresh, was heard on an eavesdropping device saying, "Stay low, stay ready and loaded."

At about 9:05 a.m., the Davidians unrolled yet another banner from a window of the compound. It read: "We want our phones fixed."

"We tried to figure out a way to get a line," said Jeffrey Jamar, agent in charge of the Waco operation. "But we couldn't figure out a way to do it safely." Several dozen rounds had already been fired at his officers in the tanks. "They had automatic weapons," Jamar said, "and had demonstrated a willingness to use them."

Jamar described the compound's "inmates" as being calm and "very disciplined, putting their masks on and gathering in a central area where the effects of the gas were limited," in the above-ground structure located inside the main building and known as the concrete bunker.

The battering continued until about 9 a.m., when the vehicles withdrew. There was a two and a half hour lull before the battering and gassing resumed. During that time, President Clinton says in Washington that he'd given the go-ahead for the long-awaited tactical operation. And Bob Ricks once again mounted the lectern at the Waco Convention Center.

It was 10:30 a.m.

He seemed to be standing a little taller. "Today's action is not an indication that our patience has run out."

Apparently the theory was that if you could tell people, while you bashed in their homes with tanks, that it was "not an assault," perhaps the patience thing would fly, too.

Said Ricks, "The action taken today was the next logical step in a series of actions to bring this episode to a conclusion. Dozens and dozens of rounds have been fired at FBI agents. We estimate that on each hole in the building we were subjected to 10–12 rounds after the initial volley. The FBI, in an effort to demonstrate its extraordinary restraint, has not returned fire thus far.

"We will continue to gas probably all of today. The information we have is that those inside the compound have tear gas masks available to them. Those gas masks have limited life associated with them. We will continue to gas them and make their environment as uncomfortable as possible until they do exit the compound.

"What is the status of the children? We do not know if they have gas masks as well. We have gone to extraordinary steps to ensure that the dosages being utilized are well below the minimum lethal ranges of CS gas. We would not use dosages that would harm those children, nor would those dosages cause damage to their lungs or other types of injuries. We are using a non-pyrotechnic type of tear gas which does not deprive them of oxygen."

Why not wait on Koresh to finish writing the Seals?

He wasn't writing them fast enough.

"The First Seal has not been completed yet. Mr. Schneider said as of yesterday, he has not even seen it and he is responsible for getting it out. They've also, through the intelligence we've gathered, considered the meeting with the attorneys a fiasco, that this was strictly a stalling tactic, that the attorneys did unknowingly go along with that, but that they had no intention of coming out."

As to the potential for suicide:

"Obviously, we have a step-up in pressure taking place. Is

suicide a possibility? We thought that this was probably the best way to prevent that type of suicide pact from taking place. That is, to cause confusion inside the compound; also, we hoped that their instincts, their motherly instincts would take place and that they would want their children out of that environment. It appears they don't care that much about their children, which is unfortunate. But we have continually quizzed those coming out and they, as a general rule, state that suicide, they believe, is not a possibility.

"At this point, we're not negotiating, we're saying 'Come out. Come out with your hands up, this matter is over.'"

As the M-60s resume the battering, the gassing, Balenda Ganem tries to stay informed on the progress of the tanks as she goes about her chores at the Brittney Hotel, where she is exchanging labor for rent. She never allows her chores to carry her far from a television set, however. What she sees on the set in the lobby is deeply alarming, but not particularly surprising. She'd been hearing for nearly a week through her grapevine of family members and former Branch Davidians that the compound could expect a gassing soon. In fact, she'd sent one of her many faxes, this one to the President, attempting to warn him of the possible serious health effects the gassing of children could produce.

"There's a good possibility of death or brain damage. And I seriously doubt that Aisha [Gyarfas] is going to get through her last month of pregnancy now.

"Anything could happen at this point. I just can't believe it. I just can't believe they weren't willing to wait out the Seals. They would have had so much more just cause to go in if they'd waited until he finished, if he still wouldn't come out. To do it right now is just unbelievable.

"And I don't think it has anything to do with their not wanting to spend any more money. I'll tell you honestly, I think it's the macho thing. I think, you got two macho factions, the FBI and the cult leaders.

"I am real scared. I am also very angry; we went to the FBI yesterday and gave them a stack of tapes, long ongoing tapes that we family members had made. We were begging them to put some family voices into the compound to help break David's control. Everybody sends this stuff to me and I send it directly to the FBI, from the moms, the dads, the brothers, the daughters. But almost nothing has gone into that compound.

"I've sent messages to the White House and registered letters to Janet Reno saying 'Please, please give us a chance—give us a chance to fail. If we fail we have to step back, but let us try.'"

The next day, Jeff Jamar will find himself at a press conference trying to explain to 70-odd families why the FBI didn't let them communicate: "It's a matter of judgment, of what would have been effective negotiations. We think there were 70 or 80 families that would have been involved. Who do you choose? With the control that Koresh had, I don't think it would have helped us at all."

The phone at the lobby desk rings. It's a relative of Steve Schneider. And Balenda picks up the receiver and tells her, "Better come. Better hurry, because all the flights are gonna be booked because all the press is coming back. It's gonna be over today. Either they all come out, or they all die in there..."
It is not yet noon, and already there is crying.

In the Fox truck, the TV folks are busy as bees and happy as clams because Groundhog Day is over.
One of the face-boys, with a name like Harris Spradewell, is keeping one eye on the videos and the other on his checkbook, trying to figure out the logistics of how he's going to get all his bills paid back home.
A TV field producer, Cathy O'Dray or some such, chatters happily back and forth over a cell-phone to Washington—happy because it's not so boring around here any more.
Stu DiAmonitor works the console.
Spradewell explains to no one in particular, "Man, I'm in trouble, Gold Card–wise. My creditors have been banging on my door, and I promised I'd be home and have the checks out on Monday. And now this happens. Looks like we'll be here for several days more."
Asks O'Dray, "Is there any way we can get someone into your house to Fed Ex all that stuff to you?"
"Yeah, that's what we'll have to do." Turning back to the bank of video screens, he says, "You can't see it from this camera, but they've put some great big holes by his bedroom."
Laughs DiAmonitor, "How do you know where Koresh's bedroom is?"
Laughs Spradewell: "We're real close."

On the screen there replays a tape of one of the morning's more aggressive M-60 thrusts; the huge machine goes crashing right through the compound's front door, taking out an eight-foot chunk of wall with it. There is no sound, but the imagination automatically fills in the gut-thumping crunch and the scream of tearing timber, popping nails.

Says Spradewell, "I can just hear the driver of that thing going 'heeeee-he-he'... Man, that's got to be the Video of the Year. Maybe the Video of the Decade."

No.

Just the video of the morning.

In the background, coming from one of the car radios, is KRLD, which has also shaken off the ennui of Groundhog Day. Steve Coryell at Hillcrest Hospital, Tina Nelson at the FBI-ATF command post, and Mike Rogers at the media compound watching the M-60s, all sound positively glad to be alive again.

Things are happening.

Business is good.

Bob McCormick in the KRLD newsroom is providing the perspective: "To set the stage for this assault: David Koresh had told the FBI that he would come out after he finished the manuscript on the Seven Seals, but authorities had discounted that, saying that they didn't really believe much of what they'd heard from David Koresh, that he'd broken so many promises in the past that they didn't put much stock in this one."

Rogers is watching the tanks, providing the color:

Says Rogers, "This may be something that takes them a few days. You've seen this compound many times over the past few weeks, it's a very large building. Even punching holes in it at the rate of two or three an hour, as they have been all morning long, it would take them a long time to bring the whole thing down."

No.

Actually, not very long at all.

Up at the very front of the media compound, those reporters and photographers wearing hats had to hold onto them. Winds were gusting to 35 miles an hour, prompting some to wonder why the FBI was even bothering. Wouldn't that wind just blow the gas right out the windows and the holes? This just couldn't get any crazier.

But it could.

First, a ghostly, pale waft of smoke. "Must be tear gas,"

someone by the last barricade remarked.

Then a white and yellow cloud. "That's a hell of a *lot* of tear gas," another rejoined, his piqued interest turning to mute astonishment as the smoke suddenly billowed wider and darker and the cameras clicked, autowinders whined, and telephotos zoomed. And satellite trucks buzzed and microwaves towers crackled to carry the special, dreadful, indelible image into the planetary mind: The smoke darkening slowly to black, and then, beneath the blue spring skies and above the miles of Kelly green fields, almost *pretty* in a direly, severely colorful way, the compound's first bloom of bright orange flame. Something in there explodes, perhaps ammunition, perhaps propane tanks, and one lone billow of flame flowers above the rest to form a burning bouquet.

And everyone standing there in that field two and a half miles away became very, very quiet.

The Seventh Seal was opening.

Rev. 8:1 And when he had opened the seventh seal, there was silence in heaven about the space of half an hour.

And another angel came and stood at the altar, having a golden censer; and there was given unto him much incense, that he should offer it with the prayers of all saints upon the golden altar which was before the throne.

And the smoke of the incense, which came with the prayers of the saints, ascended up before God out of the angel's hand.

And the angel took the censer, and filled it with fire of the altar, and cast it into the earth...

Government snipers watching through their scopes or binoculars say they saw an unidentifiable figure inside the compound make a spraying motion, then light something, and then throw it down, with flames whooshing outward from that point. Heat-sensitive cameras revealed two other hotspots where the FBI maintains cultists started their own funeral pyre, using lantern fuel.

Behind that wall of bright orange flame—pure hell, as pure as it gets on Earth.

There are two possibilities for the sources of that hell, one likely and human and sad, the other eerie, unlikely, and chilling but strangely beguiling, particularly for reveries on a lonesome, moonless midnight.

The first is that this was just the handiwork of a madman whose "specialty," madness-wise, was religion and Revelation, and that the fulfillment of this hoary ancient bogey-man mumbo-jumbo by Koresh resulted mainly from the fact that there were plenty of fools stupid enough to follow him.

The second possibility is more seductive to the morbidly contemplative: That this was indeed what the ancient prophets foresaw, that the inner eyes of the prophets of Ezekiel, Jeremiah, and John the Divine did somehow slip the shackles of Time and move for an awful while amid the flames behind that bright wall, and though they reported in the language and the symbolism of their age the horrendous, confusing things they saw in this one, they spoke truly—even if only by their telling of it, it may have been fore-ordained.

Eyes from the childhood of man would have seen chariots, and scorpions, and kings and powers and principalities in the conflict, and multiple faces and horns calmly watching from that compound two miles away. John's eyes, confined to Mt. Carmel and the perspectives of that "world," might have seen...

First, as the flames first took hold, mass panic, with the terrorized Davidians running from one room to the next to escape both the flames and the gas. Coughing, choking, moving en masse into a crowded central hallway, scrabbling their way blindly through the smoke and feeling their way along walls until they either found an exit, or, impelled only by the heat and the smoke, moved by instinct until they found some corner. Then, with nowhere left to go, began curling up, covering themselves...

Only John the Divine knows whether the occupants of the compound began to kill themselves as part of a pact, or because they *couldn't* escape and thus suicide was the only reasonable alternative to the flames. But kill themselves they did, many of them—and mercifully also killed each other.

Koresh met a quick end, dispatched by a rifle bullet between the eyes. No gun was found near him, leading to speculation by the *Houston Chronicle* that it was Steve Schneider who leveled that rifle against Koresh's forehead. If so, what a moment, what a cusp that must have been.

The Lamb of God.

And the man who stole Schneider's wife and, knowing Koresh, no doubt rubbed it in.

As Schneider looked at Koresh, sweating there in the heat and smoke and darkness:

Love and hate, love and hate.
If you love him, can you kill him?
If you hate him, does it feel better to kill him? Or to let him burn?
Which thought pulled that trigger?

One blast amid the roaring inferno, and the skull of the Lamb of God shattered like crockery—indeed, like the skull of a lamb in an abattoir—leaving only the snaggled, imperfect teeth of the Godly Sinner to help identify the crackled remains.

The teeth in that smile on the cover of *Time*—of an exultant Koresh rising toward heaven—told the forensics experts what to look for. Imperfection.

Schneider then turned the gun on himself. Though unconscious, probably comatose, he didn't die instantly. Carbon monoxide and the smoke finished him off.

One might say that Judy Schneider Koresh, the woman who reluctantly left behind the man she loved because the Lamb had declared she must, died literally of a broken heart—of massive injuries to the chest from a high-caliber gunshot wound. It is not known whether she killed herself there in the bunker, or someone else administered the coup de grace. She did not die alone: The bodies inside the bunker were so intermingled that many had to be removed en masse.

Seventy-eight bodies were found in the rubble, but that figure is by no means absolute. So bad was the commingling, so devastating the damage to the human form, that in 12 cases, no heads could be found.

Above her, on top of the bunker, David Michael Jones, the postman who'd alerted Koresh, and son of Perry Jones. David Jones died of a gunshot wound to the head. He may have gone into Koresh's bedroom to kill himself. Because many of the victims found on top of the bunker had in fact been in Koresh's second-story bedroom when they died, tumbling to the top of the bunker when the floors beneath their burning bodies collapsed.

Wayne Martin, the loyal lawyer, died by the stage where Koresh had held sway, where God had rocked and rolled. He was probably overcome by smoke before the flames came.

On the second floor, as smoke and heat reaching through the floorboards warned of the fast-approaching flames, mothers clutched their children.

The fire spread with a ravening, maniacal fury, due in part to the kerosene, the ramshackle nature of the construction, a possibly ruptured propane tank, bales of hay and other material placed around windows as protection from government guns, and that relentless wind.

There was some speculation by survivors that women and children were trapped on the second floor because the M-60 had knocked out a stairwell. Others on the government side suspect that Koresh locked them in.

Either way, quickly the tenor of the screams turned from terror to agony. And then, as the last flammable shred of the compound went up in flames and tumbled down in rubble, silence.

Twelve of the youngest of the 25 children who died in the compound remained wrapped in the charred bones of their mothers' arms—even after the second-floor burned away and tumbled down, and the watchtower's glowing skeleton listed, swayed, and tumbled in atop them, burying them in the lake of fire.

Chapter 20

Arlington Police Department chaplain Harold Elliott, for most of his life a Baptist preacher, does not use the word "hell" lightly. But hell is the word he uses to characterize life in the bowels of the Tarrant County Medical Examiner's building, when the bodies started streaming in after April 19.

Hell reached out through the air before you even got inside the building, reaching out to the nostrils with tendrils of the odor of burned flesh—an overpowering, sickening, indescribable smell.

"That's the first thing that anyone is going to notice when they first get there—that tremendous odor. You are greeted by it before you even enter the door. Whew. I can't even describe that odor. It's an overpowering, sickening smell. Of course, up to that point, you haven't personalized the magnitude of this thing. You know intellectually what's beyond that door, but it's not emotionally real for you. But once inside..."

Inside, yet another hell of Koresh's creation waits to assault the eyes and ears.

Elliott, after 20 years as a chaplain with the Arlington PD, is familiar with death and suicide—so familiar in fact that he's written a book about his experiences with suicide victims and their families (*Ripples of Suicide: Reasons for Living*, WRS Publishing).

He has worked two major airline crashes, countless fires, and innumerable murders and suicides. But nothing has ever hit him like this, and his sole assignment is to look after the psychological well-being of those who were having to reach into the body bags and deal with the bodies, body after body, bag after bag, day after day.

Elliott considers himself the luckiest of the workers, in this regard: He was free to leave. In fact, he made it a point never to stay in the room much longer than an hour before leaving for at least as long as 30 minutes. Longer than that, and he would have become so affected as to be useless to his charges.

The task ostensibly facing the small army of technicians, anthropologists, forensic scientists, fingerprint experts, and radiologists was to identify all the bodies as quickly as possible—but their real war was with their own reactions to them.

The battles were waged on three fronts: The workers had to prevent the bodies from affecting them because of their ghastliness. They had to prevent the bodies from getting to them because they were once human. And they had, in spite of the resulting aloof professionalism, to remain human.

Elliott considers it good news that they lost on the first two fronts, and thus won on the latter.

The stress felt by the crowd of sometimes as many as 40 experts all toiling simultaneously over some of these Koreshian horrors is implicit in its grisly yet simply stated mission: identify 72 people— 17 of them children—who have been *burned beyond recognition.*

(Put a roast in the oven and then broil it on high for two days, and then you will start to get the picture.)

Every last drop of moisture boils away from the tissue. Long after the owner is dead, because of the heat and the loss of moisture, the muscles slowly contract, so that the bodies bow and contract inwards, a sort of slow-motion convulsion through the glowing ash towards a final, fetal position. And then the tissues, bone-dry, begin themselves to burn, and bones to snap.

Put a man the size of Koresh in a fire like the one at the compound, and he emerges about the size of a slender six-year-old girl.

Put a slender six-year-old girl in there...

Now imagine that you have to look at the blackened, charred, crisped remnant of her for 10 hours a day. You have to reach out and touch her. Cut into her. Examine her teeth. Poke around in her for evidence of past injuries that may be useful in finding out who she was. Because, of course, her little face and perhaps much of her skull are burned away.

And you have to try not to care for her, try not to imagine what those last minutes of life in hell were like for her... and that is the thought, sooner or later, that caused almost everyone to lose their war.

Says Elliott, "If anyone went into that carnage at the ME's office strictly for curiosity's sake, their curiosity was completely satisfied in the first three seconds. After that, you don't want to look any more than you absolutely have to. I feel real sorry for the ones who have to spend long periods of time with them."

Elliott, a longtime friend and admirer of Tarrant County Medical Examiner Nizam Peerwani, is, because of his job, intimately familiar with the ME's office. "I've been there many, many times, and have a close working relationship with them. They are, of course, human beings, and many times I've laughed and talked with them over the years. But now there's a different atmosphere, a silence that just permeates the place. There's a different attitude, very somber and professional, almost a highly over-courteous atmosphere. It's very formal."

That is one sign of too much stress. Elliott's job was to watch the officers for other signs, to be ready to pull them outside for fresh air, or a change of scenery. And to be there to listen, to let them ventilate when it was getting too much for them.

The signs were varied. Some would get the thousand-mile stare, just sitting very quietly and passively, overcome by it all. Others would undergo temporary personality changes, developing hair-trigger tempers and a tendency to jump at the slightest obstacle.

The ones who showed absolutely no emotion were the ones who worried Elliott. "If they don't show anything at all, you know that it's all inside, and they're a walking time bomb. Because you don't see that kind of hurt and pain and damage without it affecting you.

"And they can't help but think about what those children were going through. I've heard that everywhere I go, from the ME's office to the site itself. This is my personal feeling, and I keep hearing it from others as well: The children. They didn't have a choice. They did not choose to die."

It didn't hit Emily Craig for a long time, but when it did, it hit her hard.

Emily Craig is a graduate student in forensic anthropology at the University of Tennessee, and was among those who volunteered to help identify the victims of David's inferno. She was, in fact, one of the ones responsible for the identification of MC-DOE-8.

"She's a strong person," says Elliott, in whose home Craig stayed for the two weeks she was in Texas. For the first several days, she was businesslike as she went about her duties, in spite of the fact that much of her work was on the bodies of the children.

She's seen "bad" bodies before. In fact, the forensic anthropologists at the University of Tennessee see perhaps more than any one group in the United States. They are the recognized experts in this dreary domain, working death scenes around the country—and deliberately exposing as many as 40 donated cadavers a year to the elements to track the phases and the timing of human decomposition.

She has also worked more than her share of fires, including those with multiple fatalities.

"You never really get used to it, but you do get so you can deal with it. In every case, you have to steel yourself all over again," she says.

Inevitably, part of the way you do that is to set aside the humanity of the victim. "I dwell on it as a science—determine the age, the race, the sex, the trauma. We try not to ever deal with names or personal habits. Each case is assigned a number, and even in cases where we know the names, we deal with the assigned numbers."

And, of course, she had a time identifying the children—had worked on so many that she'd lost count during the 10- and 11-hour days of her first week at the ME's.

She was in the conference room one afternoon, using the phone.

And for reasons unclear, some investigators in the conference room began playing a videotape from before the fire—one of the videotapes that Koresh had made and sent out to let the FBI know that the children were all in good condition. As, at that point, they were.

"I didn't intentionally see it. I was on hold, and I glanced over my shoulder... It's hard to put in words what... it was a shock. I just glanced over my shoulder, and saw this child, and I immediately looked away. But that image is burned in my mind forever."

She refuses to describe the child—although there was nothing extraordinary about it, other than it was a child. "It was a young child, and I had been working on the remains of young children, and all of a sudden, all of the children were *real*. It was not that specific child. That child was Everychild.

"I was able to finish the phone conversation. As I started to get up and leave the room, I was suddenly overcome with, I guess, sadness. I realized the magnitude of what had happened. I wasn't grieving for that one; I was grieving for all of them."

Days later she would replay the rush of emotions and find something that disturbed her even more.

"In order to make you understand, I guess I have to do a little bragging. I am a medical illustrator and sculptor by profession. And I have a kind of almost unique, uncanny ability to transform three-dimensional objects into two dimensions [by drawing] and then transform them back into three dimensions again through sculpture.

"I started out in forensics with facial reconstruction. And I had been working with all these tiny skulls and faces and bones and teeth. And what affected me so much with the incident was that, when I saw that video, my instinctive reaction was to compare the skeletal remains with the face I saw on the screen, trying to do almost a mental superimposition. And that's what got me.

"It got me in terms of how clinical I was being. I couldn't just look at that child and say, 'What a tragic waste!' I instantly went into the mode of forensic anthropology. So I was suddenly as sad for myself as I was for the child. That's what tore out my insides... When I really stopped and realized what I was doing, I was inconsolable... I went to Dr. Peerwani's secretary and asked if I could go into his office. I thought if I could get away, I could catch my breath... but I didn't. And once I got started, I couldn't stop."

Elliott was summoned. The first step, in such cases, is to remove the person from the environment; Elliott asked her where he could take her to make her feel better. At the ME's you could not get away from the sights and smells of death, so she told Elliott, "Right now, I need to go where there is grass and water and trees, and things are alive."

Elliott took her to the Fort Worth Botanical Gardens where it was quiet and clean. It smelled good, there was fresh air, sunshine—and lots of children, alive.

They walked and watched the water, the ducks, the birds, the trees—life—and, when Emily was finished crying for a while, she was ready to go back. Not eager, but ready.

Like everyone else, Elliott himself was working hard to maintain his own composure and peace of mind amid these horrors.

"First thing, if you're involved as a chaplain or a counselor in critical incidents such as these, you don't *ever* get down and participate in what the others are doing. You always keep yourself separated from the process; you don't ever touch anything. I was never asked, but if they had asked me to help, if they'd needed a body bag lifted or moved, I wouldn't have done it. Once you do that—get involved in the process—you become, psychologically, part of the problem. You are no longer the solution." Elliott, however, lost his battle against being emotionally affected, and he lost it in the same manner as the rest of them; he just got to thinking.

First, about Koresh.

Harold Elliott was straightforward. "There's a general rage, a disgust with him. I had it, and I haven't talked with anyone who hasn't felt that way, who hasn't thought, 'This didn't have to happen.'"

And then, the children.

"You look at those little things, and you realize their innocence.

You wonder about what they must have thought. You wonder about their fears. You wonder about those last moments—and you try to imagine them.

"You can't spend much time in there. I don't think we *dare* allow ourselves to spend much time in those last moments. It's like with any child that is murdered: The first question from the family is always, *Did they suffer? What were they thinking? They must have been so frightened...*

"And once you start doing that, you've lost it. You can function at your job, but you aren't going to be the same. Many times through this I've wondered: Who's going to debrief *me*? I've been in more of a somber, heavier mood. And I've had to cancel some speaking engagements, particularly the ones where humor was requested. I'm still doing some of them; did one this morning at 7 a.m., where they'd said 'Come make us laugh.' It's not that I can't do it, I can still make them laugh. It's just that I don't feel like laughing with them.

"I guess I just don't feel the same sparkly way that I used to. And I don't know when I will again."

A chaplain in Arlington, 100 miles from Waco. A brigade of pathologists, forensics experts, and dentists from all around the country. An anthropologist from Knoxville, Tennessee.

Still more victims of David Koresh, of presumption.

Chapter 21

———————————

Whatever you think, it's crazier than you thought.

Very little of David Koresh's written material survives.

In the first place, beyond the transcript of that one wild-eyed rantfest on KRLD, there wasn't much of it. His stock in trade was disjointed religious ranting and rapid-fire Scripture, a technique which does not lend itself to a flattering exposition in print.

Therefore, accounts of the teaching—and of the method of teaching, and thus many of Koresh's tricks—survive only among his followers. (Why does that sound familiar?)

Chief among these surviving followers is Livingston Fagan, released from the compound on March 23, and now preaching the Gospel According to St. Vern from the McLennan County Jail, where he is being held as a material witness.

Fagan, 33, is believed by many, including the FBI, to be the only Branch Davidian to walk out of the compound with a purpose higher than relieving Koresh of one more mouth to feed. That purpose was to represent the Branch Davidians to the outside world, to carry "David's Message." (Why does *that* sound familiar?)

If in fact Livingston Fagan's logic, thinking processes, and theology are truly representative of Koreshianism, it answers many, many questions. Talking with Livingston Fagan may be as close as we'll ever come to having a conversation with David Koresh.

In one conversation with him you'll find enough loopy logic, apples-and-orange comparisons, generalizations, non sequiturs, contradictions, special cases, pseudo-intellectual demagoguery, special dispensations, and questionable corollaries to make your head cave in.

Keep in mind the scariest thing of all: It may be catching. Koresh taught him all this stuff—and Livingston Fagan believes every word of it, is parroting, mainly, what he's been told, with an occasional embellishment of his own that is, nevertheless, firmly based in Koreshian theology.

The reason Fagan loves this Wiser and Holier Than Thou flapdoodle, it becomes clear, is the same reason that Koresh loved it: it makes him feel really, really powerful.

It is also delivered in the Koreshian method—that is to say, at about a hundred miles an hour so you can't see where you've been, through hairpin curves and mountain passes so you can't see where you're going, to sudden and unexpected stops, so you can't tell where you *are*. And have to take Fagan's word for it.

Any elisions we have inserted are there only to keep the ride from being any bumpier than it has to be. So strap on your seat belts.

Says Fagan:

"When I was going through college, trying to find meaning in the Scriptures, you could see the limitations, because a lot of the context has been lost, in terms of the meanings of words. [As Koreshians] the stress we saw to facilitate meaning was Inspiration itself—going back to the One who wrote the book. You just need Inspiration."

If at this point you guessed who the One was, give yourself a Davidian Dispensation:

"What David did was, in his approach, given the fact that he was the person that was opening the Seals anyway, and, as we saw in Revelation, the Lamb, and the book was a revelation of Him, so, really, all authority in terms of meaning was invested in the hands of the Lamb."

A little shorthand, to help this incomplete sentence along: David said he was opening some Seals. The Bible said that only lambs open Seals. Therefore, since David said he was opening Seals, he must be the Lamb. And, if he's the Lamb, all authority is vested in him. So whatever he tells you, it's the Truth with a capital C for Circular.

Onward, further into the pseudo-intellectual semi-scriptural fog.

"There is a limit to textual criticism, as you can see. Because you still have to decipher meaning in what the scripture has to say in the *divine* frame of reference."

In other words, in what the Scripture says to God?

Yeah.

"So what we're saying is that someone had to come from Heaven, from the divine, to facilitate the accuracy of what was being stated in the text."

And the one who "had to come," that's Dave? Facilitating up a mess of accuracy?

Yeah.

And Fagan can prove it.

"For example, Paul, remember, had much insight into the realities pertaining to the end of time. He was the one that above all the apostles sought to document these things. A lot of Paul's writing picks up on these issues. But he only makes allusion to this. Remember in Corinthians where he talks about things unutterable?"

Yep. (Cor. 12:4 How that he was caught up into paradise, and heard unspeakable words, which it is not lawful for a man to utter.)

Says Fagan: "Well, man could not utter them until the Lamb himself had actually come and begun the process. Through all Paul's writings, he makes allusions, but he doesn't give the details, because it wasn't given to him to do that. So when Christ comes, or when the Lamb comes and starts to speak on these subjects, then they become open. And therefore, such as like myself, we can discuss them."

Let's briefly review.

1. Nobody knows what things are not supposed to be uttered, which is fortunate, because uttering them is against the law.

2. Some guy comes along and says, "Hey, I'm-a uttering them, *trust* me, what I'm uttering is really those things."

3. Since they are unlawful to utter, and he's not in jail, that means he's, by golly, the Lamb.

4. Such as like ourselves, now we can go around uttering them too. Baaaaa.

Explains Fagan: "See, what we've seen here is just the pursuit of a line of thought, and it spans several groups, several organizations. But the benefit of that is that it solidifies the thinking at each stage, so that the person can come in and he's got a culture he can be in, so that he can come into and grasp certain things."

You're talking Millerite to Adventist to Davidian to Branch Davidian to Koreshian, right? We're going from a guy who predicted the world was going to end in 1844 to one who predicted it would end in 1959 to another one who said 1990 to one who said 1993, tops, and I'm gonna kick *everybody's* hiney, who's now also dead and we're not, right?

Are we having *solid* yet?

"But David, really, the gap between David and the rest of them is too incredible, so incredible that, as we pursue the Scripture and the teaching that David has shown to us, you can see that all the others just pale into insignificance."

Yeah. See that. See that for sure.

So, guess David Koresh was Jesus Christ, right?

Says Fagan: "Naw."

No?

No???

This is your captain. Please return to your seats. The captain has turned on the no-smoking light. You will notice to the left of the airplane, and to the *right* of the plane, well, just some of the dangdest stuff you ever saw.

Says the Fagan Man: "Remember: from a theological side, the issue was, 'Who is worthy to open The Book?' And the book is in effect the Bible. Now, if only one is worthy, the Lamb, then what are all the other religious bodies in the world doing with the Scriptures?"

Can't stand it. By Livingston's previous logic—"since only the Lamb can utter it, and therefore Koresh, since only he uttered it, is the Lamb"—no other preacher on the planet should be able to open that Bible even with the help of a tire tool, a blowtorch, and six sturdy deacons.

Yet there are those unworthy preachers, those rascals, opening it all the time. So, *what*, already?

"They're just making money out of it, which is part of the Seventh Seal. The Seventh Seal brings this to view. If the Lamb is the only one that can open the book, and all the other religious denominations are basically making money out of it, and their congregations came to this knowledge, what would their congregations do?"

Reveal this wisdom, O Rhetorical One, lest we perish unenlightened!

"Evidently, they'd stop paying the money, because they'd realize they don't *have* to pay the money. And they'd start listening to the Lamb!"

There it is. Plain as the nose on the face of a clock. Just never thought about it that way before.

"So you see, from the religio-political standpoint, it would not be expedient for the message of the Lamb, of the Seven Seals, to get out. But, why?"

Open mine eyes!

"Because... What are you—a Baptist? Well, you'd no longer *be* a Baptist."

Well, been trying to quit, and doing pretty good by many estimates...

"You see the point? Because the Baptists aren't teaching the

Seven Seals. All they're teaching is the dogma, the doctrine of baptism, which is basically their foundation for being an established religion. I'm not trying to be derogatory."

Us neither. Comes naturally. Heck—we're not even trying to be *Baptists*.

"But any established religion takes a particular aspect of Scripture for its foundation, and then incorporates all the rest that are common to all religions. And that little difference, like in the Baptists or the Adventists, is the means they use to justify being a separate religion, and in the absence of that, they're all the same."

And now, your captain suggests that, whatever your persuasion, you make your peace with the Maker of your choice and fill out the life insurance forms conveniently located in your seat back, because here comes the Theological Haymaker, the Holy Mother of All Wind Shears.

"It's incredibly significant that, when *we* came on the scene, whenever we were confronted with another religious group, we showed them the truths of the Seven Seals. And we showed them the relations between the one person, the *only* person that was able to open the book, and everybody said, 'Oh, yes, it's Jesus! Jesus!'"

You mean you're gonna tell us the Branch Davidian's Lamb and the Book Opener and the son o' God *isn't* Jesus?

"You know as well as I do that the concept of Jesus is actually Zeus Christos, in the Greek. It's referring to Zeus, the Greek war god."

By Jove! Jumpin' Jupiter! Mercury and Uranus! Goofy and Pluto!

"And the *true* name of the person who lived 2,000 years ago was Yeshua, which, when translated, into English, is actually Yahshua, or 'Yah Saves.' So this Jesus which the Catholic Church gave to Protestantism was in fact Zeus, ha ha ha ha, the war god. And you see this is the United States, the warring nation."

Yah don't say—it's the Greco-Americans! *I knew* it! No more gyros for us!

"Do you see what I'm talking about?"

It's as clear as... as clear as... metaphors fail here.

"So when you go and look at Daniel, Chapter 11, for example, when it speaks of this king of the north, in fact, let me just read the text to you. Daniel 11 is an appropriate prophecy right now, let me just relate to you why."

Italics in parentheses reflect Livingston Fagan's ongoing parenthetical interpretation:

Dan. 11:32. And such as do wickedly against the covenant (*that's the Seven Seals*) shall he corrupt by flatteries (*we're dealing with those individuals like Marc Breault*) but the people that do know their God shall be strong, and do exploits (*That's referring to us* [*Koreshians*]).

Dan. 11:33. And they that understand among the people (*those that understand the content of the Sealed Book*) shall instruct many: yet they shall (*listen to this*) fall by the sword (*in this day, that's bullets*) and by flame, (*you know, like April 19*) by captivity (*you know, like I'm talking to you from the jail*) and by spoil (*you know, some of them sold their birthright to the movie companies. And we've had some offers ourselves, but we're here for different purposes; and all the things they are offering to us belong to us anyway, and one day we will take them*), many days (*and we're in that waiting period, many days*).

Dan. 11:34. Now when they shall fall, they shall be holpen with a little help: but many shall cleave to them with flatteries (*you sent me a Bible the other day. You're* cleaving *to me*).

Dan. 11:35. And some of them of understanding shall fall, to try them, and to purge, and to make them white, even to the time of the end: because it is yet for a time appointed (*which is why we're still in this waiting period, it's not the end yet, it's a time to come. So what you're seeing here is the purpose of our being here, it's part of the purification. And then it goes on.*) And the king shall do according to his will; and he shall exalt himself, and magnify himself above every god (*so this king regards no god. He did not regard the God of the three Hebrew captives. This God does not regard our god, the one who sits on the throne, and gives the book to the lamb. Follow?*) and shall speak marvelous things against the God of gods (*and he has spoken marvelous things*), and shall prosper till the indignation (*you see? there's an indignation against us*) be accomplished: for that is determined shall be done.

Dan. 11:37. Neither shall he regard the God of his fathers (*you know when this nation came into being, and the Constitution was set up, the fathers of this nation regarded the God of truth, didn't they? This king does not regard this God*), nor the desire of women (*now, who is the desire of women? According to Romans 4, it's supposed to be Christ, right? Married to Christ? So we're dealing with David, right?*), nor regard any god: for he shall magnify himself above all (*and the United States has certainly done that*).

Dan. 11:38. But in his estate shall he honour the God of forces *(the military men, right?)*: and a god whom his fathers knew not shall he honour with gold, and silver, and with precious stones, and pleasant things *(how much is actually spent on the military now? And it's by these forces that he's been able to overcome the whole world? Right?)*.

DAN 11:39. Thus shall he do in the most strongholds with a strange god, whom he shall acknowledge and increase with glory *(in truth, it's* incredible *that the technology has been developed for war. This Greek God, Jesus—Zeus Christos—is what we're dealing with here. They all pray in the name of Jesus. Jesus Christos—the anointed Zeus. This is what's going down. Now, the Christian world is ignorant to this reality. And without the knowledge of the Seven Seals, they would not know. And this is why we can't stand on the part of this Zeus Christos. He can take our lives, but forget it. He can do whatever he... likes with us. We know our God! He sits on the throne! He gave the book to the Lamb. We're talking about the Seven Seals, and only he is worthy)*.

So—just a sec. Crash, boing, clang, clatter, sproing, tinkle, and finally, sound of hubcap slowly teetering to a standstill—excuse us, our heads just caved in.

It was probably the "desire of women" thing that got us.

No, it was the whole blame thing.

So this, then, uh, explains why we never hear any Branch Davidians talking about things from Matthew, Mark, Luke, or John?

"Right."

So what to the Mormons is a great angel, and to the Moslems a great prophet, and to the Christians a great savior, this Jesus Christ guy is, in fact, a great demon?

"Precisely."

So that's why nobody in the Branch Davidians prays in Jesus' name?

"You got it."

And that's why sending religious negotiators to the negotiating table the last two months was less than useless?

"Precisely."

So you'd have been better off with just a regular old atheist FBI man?

"Well... regular atheists might have been useful. But you know, these FBI men, they were Catholic, Baptist, right? They all had their own backgrounds in this Jesus stuff. So we've got a situation here that was indeed a religious battle. It was a false God who had the *name* of the real God.

And people believe that the name is not important.

"But the name *is* important. God has a name, and the name is Yahweh Koresh. The Alpha and the Omega. And it goes on time after time. So it is for His name's sake that this is done. The notion that people have that the name of God is unimportant is absolute foolishness. It's like me calling you John. What's gonna happen there?"

Dunno. We could try it. But probably, nothing much.

"God's name is important. And God's *son* has a name—David Koresh. It means 'Beloved Death.' And Yahweh Koresh is the beginning, the beginning of Life, Death. Now the reason why it's 'Beloved Death' is that the time is going to come that this fleshly reality is going to be destroyed, to give birth to Life, the true reality. Although the name may appear in its apparentness to be a negative, it's extremely positive. But you have to overcome the stumbling block, and that's the challenge of faith."

Well, we feel challenged faith-wise. We've mulled it around and squinted at it every which way, and can't get around to seeing "Beloved Death" as a strongly positive concept. Certainly not without a hangover.

"The truth about it is if God appeared in his Glory, all humanity would be destroyed. He has to appear in his humiliation, like us [Koreshians]. But the truth is if you were to give Him time, so you could understand where He was coming from, just like all men should afford other men time, to explain where they're coming from, then you would see the truth.

"But if you're not going to afford the time, then unfortunately, you're not going to see the truth and you are not gonna benefit by it. It's really that simple, and I think it's only fair."

So, uh, why was April 19th a surprise?

"To whom?"

To anyone in the compound, but especially someone like maybe his eminent omniscience, Beloved Death his own self?

"Well, David had been *telling* us about these things for such a long, long time, but you know how the human mind works, it blocks those things that it doesn't want to receive?"

Oh, yeah. Like, the guy's deader than Julius Caesar and, moreover, it doesn't look like he's getting back up. And instead of saying, oops, wrong about the guy, let's finally face up and admit it, *you* say:

"Well, it's just like the disciples 2,000 years ago. Christ was telling them that he's got to go to Jerusalem to be killed. They didn't receive it, did they? Until the event. And then it was a shock. Nevertheless, it was already placed in their minds, and was a shock, but they didn't fall. With this April 19th, some of us may have stumbled, but we didn't fall. Here we are, still. The Seven Seals were able to uphold us. It really wasn't such a shock to us as people perceive it to be.

"The thing that we were holding onto, that most of us were holding onto, though we didn't appreciate the specific details, was that no man but the Lamb could reveal the Seals, and they knew from their experiences in there that the Seals were revealed to them.

"So they knew this person [Koresh] to be true, irrespective of what happened. It showed that the strength of our faith can endure whatever is shown. Whatever happens.

"So, someone like yourself, who has not had the opportunity to know what the Seven Seals teach, but you can know the sayings of the Seven Seals, the revelations.

"And that would be strong enough for you to endure certain things. At best, all I can bring your attention to is the sayings. But there's a blessing in Rev. 22:7 to those who *keep* those sayings.

"If you went back to the Book of Revelation you would see that everything I've been saying about the sayings is true. It harmonizes squarely with what the Bible says. It's just a narrative. It's not something that is subject to interpretation. It's clear. John was on the Isle of Patmos, he was taken to Heaven. That's not interpretation. That's what the Bible says.

"And that's strong enough so you could believe that if I was the one that showed you that, the rest of the thing must also be true."

Pause for review, and rewind:
Livingston Fagan says something.
Livingston Fagan exists.
Therefore, whatever Livingston Fagan says must be true.

Okay, continue:
"So on that basis, you can hold on, you have a faith that you can hold on to. And in truth, I think that you will agree with me, that your church, the Baptist Church, has never taught you this doctrine."

That we should believe in Livingston Fagan? No. Catholic friends haven't mentioned it, either, and not a Jew one. And atheists *certainly* don't believe in Livingston Fagan until they see him with their own eyes and hear him with their own ears, and then it is too late, Yahweh bless 'em. Crash, sproing, their heads cave in!

"All right, seeing Revelation, in light of how it's been shown to you, it also shows the insufficiency of your own doctrine. That's very clear."

Again, metaphors for clarity elude us.

And now for more dire warnings about those who don't believe in Koreshian Faganism.

"Remember Revelation, Chapter 3: The key of David opens, and no man shutteth. All right, now what you're seeing is certain things that have been opened to you. They will be in you. The thing is that you can't shut them out. They will be in you. The thing is that you can't shut them out."

The thing is we can't shut them out. They'll be in us... As Dave said to the FBI: "Hey! Y'all are using hypnotism on us! We know more 'bout hypnotism than you do!"

"Which means that when you go back to your own denomination, you're going to be faced with a problem. And you can't forget this. You're responsible for it. And that's what I tried to tell you right from the beginning, when I started to talk. If you go against this, and you know it's true, you can see it: So you're in a problem.

"And I did not want to set that up knowing the fact that you were going to go against it. And quite frankly, at this point, I kind of like feel that I don't want to go any further. Do you want to go any further?"

We beg. We beseech. Don't!

"I prefer that you didn't if you're not going to want to recognize that accountability, I suggest you do not go any further. Because believe me, God's judgment is not going to be something to play with. Lives were lost around this. This is serious. You may call this your mind being brainwashed, ha ha, that's up to you."

We are past brainwashed. This brain has been fabric-softened, washed, rinsed, wrung, spun, and hung out to dry. A bird just landed on it and he had a newspaper under his wing.

"But quite frankly, if you're being brainwashed, you've got to believe that the *Bible* is brainwashing you. Because what I've shown you is coming directly out of that book.

"You're going to have to make that decision, because quite frankly, I'm not prepared to go any further. In fact from this end I'm thinking seriously about just making a statement to people that does not at all touch on the Seven Seals."

Amen. Do the folks a favor, Liv.

"We're not dealing with just your life. We're dealing with your soul, your spirit. And if you go against that, you have to bear the consequences. I don't want it on my conscience. I want individuals who want to know truth for the sake of truth. That I can speak with them in that context. But this is dangerous stuff."

True. Boredom kills. If we'd been talking on the car phone, we'd have already gone right through the guardrail. We use this escape route he's offered us, telling Fagan, "Why don't we leave that part right now until we have a better understanding of where we need to go?"

Whoops! We almost got away! Fagan rewards us with a little slack.

"In that case, you've gotten enough so far for you to be able to ponder that this is serious. Initially you were saying to me that you would *absolve* me of that responsibility, but as it has become more apparent to you what this is, I think you should get to the stage where you can review that."

Ah, glasshoppah, you are but grass in the path of Fagan's mighty spiritual lawnmower, a mote in the eye of Yahweh Koresh. And, moreover, everything you know or think you know is dead wrong:

"As far as the other basic stuff, that doesn't really have a direct impact, the human-centered stuff (*like, the reason we called? To find out why they all killed themselves?*), you can get that from books. There has been much reporting in the press."

And we offer Livingston this opportunity to enlighten us: "We're not sure how much of that press stuff is accurate..."

"Well," says Fagan, perhaps the second most irritatingly smug, self-satisfied, two-bit double-talking mystic of a Koreshian to ever live, "That's what I'm saying. You're not going to know what is true unless you go in the light of the Seven Seals. Which then carries responsibilities. So then I can't really address those questions outside of that truth.

"And so, if you want to come into that knowledge of what is true, what is *true* about what has taken place, you have to know the Seven Seals.

"And knowing the Seven Seals, you're accountable. So the

situation is, do you want to know truth? Truth is not separate to the events, what the human eye saw, centering around Mt. Carmel in the past few weeks. It's not separate. Even my communications with you. It's not separate. So it's a matter of me not saying anything to you at all, or you taking the responsibility and being responsible for the truth that I reveal. Mt. Carmel is Truth. To understand the context, this is it, that's the problem. We are reaching a stage where what I'm saying to you, you should be clear: Do you want to go? Or don't you? Do you want truth, or don't you?"

Here is the crux of what made Dave tick, and what may keep Koreshianism ticking now after he's gone. Here is why men handed him wives and wives handed him children, and all of them handed him their lives.

It's the oldest trick in the book. The trick question. By pure force of noise and non sequitur, pompous intonation, blustery threat, and pretense to knowledge of forces unseen—mystic knowledge, or, better still for the unwary, *Biblical* mystic knowledge—one manages to appear to be on the moral high ground, even if there's no real ground at all. And then one asks the trick question.

Do you wish to attain Divine Wisdom? Or remain forever stupid, blind, wrong, and destined to fry like a Tater Tot in Hell?

Are you going to quit beating your wife?

Uh, guess so... I obviously don't know what I'm doing, so here. *You* beat her for a while. You're better at it.

But we try to be honest and forthcoming with Fagan: Gee, Liv, see, it's against everything we believe and have been led to understand, you know?

And Fagan just dies laughing, sitting up there high atop his Judgment Throne at the McLennan County Jail.

"Ha ha ha ha—do you think that David was in harmony with everything that *I* was raised to understand? When I first received The Knowledge? Each time I studied it, it was clear to me that it was Scripture. It depends on how honest and open you are prepared to be, and I'm afraid I was honest and open, and I'm being honest and open with you. That's where the situation stands."

Open and honest as a Chinese puzzle. But, thank God, at least he's winding down. We finish the sentence for him by advising him earnestly: *If* this is as far as we can go, we want you know the Bible was given in good faith...

But Livingston is so high up on the mountaintop admiring himself in his majesty that he can't even say thank you. And it was a $70 Bible. Twenty-seven translations...

"Ha ha ha, I certainly wouldn't condemn you. We're about mercy. Whatever part I have to play in the judgment!!! (exclamation points ours), my objective is to save, to participate in that saving process, and not to destroy."

How many deities did they have rollicking around at Mt. Carmel?

"I think that is an activity that only the Devil takes on, and not the people who are concerned about Light. But eventually that Light will be the source of the destruction of those who continue to go on in error. The thing about it, whether one pursues this Light or not, it's going to break upon you at some point anyway. I want you to be appreciative of that.

"I *know* what the Seven Seals teach; I can go through all the books pertaining to the Seven Seals. I can give you a knowledge of what the prophets have written. I can blow your mind. But it's not about blowing minds, it's about saving souls. It will blow your mind if you're not interested in the salvation of your soul. As will be the case when all these things are made manifest in their truth, rather than the shadow that is currently taking place.

"My body shields the light. As Job 38 talks about, the light is hid in the clay for the sealing. And so, here it is. Okay, so it's been nice talking to you."

Yeah. Nice as all hell talking to you, too, and hearing the echoes not only of David Koresh but of every self-absorbed, self-promoting, self-important sheep-misleader of a cheap preacher who ever lived, in every church you can name.

Slap a piece of clay on it, Liv, on the whole crazy thing. Seal it up. Let it go. Give it a rest. It's over.

Chapter 22

David Koresh committed an unthinkable sin: He threw away his life and the lives of his children. He threw away the lives of his followers, and the lives of their children, and the lives of their children by him. And nothing could be worse.

But skittering impishly around the edges of the tragedy is another much more cosmically *ironic* aspect, from Koresh's standpoint.

It's the list of all the other things he threw away.

From the standpoint of his own greed, his own desire to attain his own definition of success, and his stated desire to proselytize the world, he threw it all away in that fire on April 19, 1993.

He threw it all away so big-time and so foolishly: Perhaps the sudden shocked and belated recognition of it entered his brain an instant before Steve Schneider's bullet did, perhaps even as his mind formed the phrase "Oh, *no...*"

If he'd started the fire on March 9, or March 19, other than his life and the lives of his followers, he would not have lost much, forum-wise. In fact, on March 3 or even 13, whether he immolated himself or came out like a good little boy, the results would have been the same. He would indeed have been the Flavor of the Moment. He would indeed have had his Warholian 15 minutes of fame.

And, dead or alive, that would have been it. Jim Jones (remember him?) would be telling old Dave, wherever they both are: Way too *fast*, man.

But 50 days is a long time, subjectively.

Fifty days is enough time to allow people to think, even reflect. Even for those wholly unaccustomed to thinking, 50 days gives plenty of time to try.

It's plenty of time to play out the usual role, thinking the ordinary thoughts, then notice the attitudes, and begin to re-examine them. It is, in short, enough time for thinking to *change*.

From every walk of life, from every political and social orientation, people were starting to think thoughts that they would not ordinarily have entertained.

The first few days of the siege, the right-wing, *America—Love It Or Leave It, God Save Our Flag, My Country, Right or Wrong* crowd of law-and-order buffs screamed for Koresh's head, Koresh's blood, and the heads and blood of his followers. These religious crazies had *broken* the laws of this *nation* and should be shot down like dogs, pure and simple.

It was their normal, first-blush reaction.

And then, there was this curious and lengthening lull. And time to think. Which laws? And, in the breaking of them, what harm? To have a stockpile of weapons? Now, that's a threat!

But what constitutes a stockpile? The pistol you keep by the bed? The high-powered deer rifle in the closet? And isn't what we get to keep in our closets becoming increasingly arbitrary? And... what constitutes a religious nut? Is a Baptist or a Catholic or a Church of Christer any more or any less nuttier than anyone else? And, most important question of all: A threat to whom?

There was sympathy, rightly or wrongly, building there. And, rightly, a desire to at least hear him out. True, he'd usurped the national spotlight—but after 50 days, he had suffered some to do it.

The left-wing gun controllers? They at first decried to the heavens this obvious threat, and shouted "told you so!" Guns R Evil was the initial cry. If the people didn't have no more of them guns, there wouldn't be no more of them killings.

And then there was this lull.

There had been a very obvious, heavy-handed demonstration of what the government will attempt to do when it believes it has superior firepower. It will sneak up and kick down your door. And if today you *like* the policies of the government, and you like the doors it elects to kick today, well and good—but what about tomorrow?

There was time for knee-jerk, dogmatic Christians to ponder the chilling similarities between Christianity and Koreshianism. There was time for hard-bitten atheists to start to wonder about what it is that everyone is reaching so desperately toward, and if maybe they might be missing something. There was time to examine the very nature of belief itself. Ranch Apocalypse had become a sort of socio-religious philosopher's stone, a mental bone to gnaw and worry, and the siege provided time to think, time to try on opposing viewpoints.

As the lull wore on, people were hearing unlikely comments from unusual quarters, and making unlikely comments themselves. People were beginning to cease thinking stereotypically. They were beginning to dis-presume.

From the religious arena, almost all the major denominations had at first come out predictably foursquare in prayer for the brave men of "our" government, praying for the speedy and expeditious downfall of the Heathen.

Then they started to ask themselves: *What* heathens? By a great leap, the Davidians were Christians. By a far shorter leap, they were believers in the redemption of man by God.

Or, at least, believers in the redeemable nature of man.

Or, at least, believers. In something.

And thus even the varied Bodies of True Believers, in whatever local denomination or planetary faith, were starting to make murmuring sounds of shy and highly conditional solidarity with people in the compound, but solidarity nonetheless. And they were starting to voice some sharp concerns about the government's motives, and some willingness to at least listen to Branch Davidian theories and theologies. Theories and theologies which, minus the distinction that antiquity and tradition accords the "established" faiths, were, at bottom line, not much more outlandish than their own.

Because the bottom line of all these theories and theologies is, after all, that someone is the Only Begotten Son of, or the Anointed Prophet of, or the Divine Revelator of, or the Designated Driver of, the One True God.

They were starting, in each of their minds, to kick around the differences and similarities between the followers of Allah and Jehovah and Vishnu and God Almighty and Jesus Christ and Mother Mary and Mohammed and Buddha and Brigham Young and William Miller and Edna White and V. T. Houteff and Ben, Lois, and George Roden and, yes, even Vernon Wayne Howell.

The similarities were there. In the case of all the followers of each, someone had told them something, and events had been interpreted for them in a certain way, and they believed these interpretations, and thus they had become believers.

And the difference? People of faith of every stripe were starting to take notice of the fact that, other than the fact that each camp thinks all the others are crazy heretics, the only truly distinctive, dangerous difference between them, from the Middle East to Yugoslavia to Ranch Apocalypse, is the difference in numbers.

And most people of faith were remembering the old, hard-won, oft-forgotten lesson—that the safety and security of each of these ultimately unprovable assertions is dependent upon one thing, and one thing only. Not the fervency or the firepower of those who believe it, but upon the benign if not respectful tolerance of those who patently do *not* believe it.

The media, the Beast, in spite of all its shortcomings—rabid lawyer-chasing, sensationalist survivor-hounding, official-version toadying, and bumbling, unintentional intrusion by sheer force of presence into the evolution and outcome of the Greatest Story Ever Told This Decade—had itself over the course of 51 days begun to digest the situation and even think about some of the questions it was asking.

The media, which determines that which all who listen will hear and thus believe, had at first been there only to cover the juicy details, get the tabloidy scoop about Koresh's sex life, his gun collection and how well and how often he paid his bills.

During the first week or two the press had itched only to photograph Koresh when he left the compound all wild-eyed and crazy-looking, hair sticking up, and then to be there again at the courthouse to shoot him some more as he walked in all showered, subdued, and humiliated in his orange uniform and chains.

But they, too, had a lull. During the lull, there was time for production of time-filling, thumb-sucking "thought pieces"—the overviews, analyses, backgrounders, seeking of alternative voices, and so on. And at some point, with this much time, even the Beast started to think. Or the discrete, individual cells of it, at any rate.

And their thinking started to change along lines like these:

"This man is obviously, to all intents and purposes, crazy. But instead of doing what I usually do—prove the obvious, and get paid for it—I think that I will instead make it a part of my personal mission to maybe see that this crazy man's rights get preserved."

Of course, it was never stated out loud in these terms, these plans for preservation of David Koresh's rights, and the rights of his followers. But it popped up more, in late March and early April, in conversations between "mediaheads" out at Satellite City, conversations like this:

"What do you think his odds are? I mean, in court."

"Well, probably 70–30 that Koresh walks. At least on any major charge. I mean, after all, that compound was not exactly a single-family residence, was it? And if somebody is kicking in one person's doorway down at the other end of the apartment complex and shooting off stun grenades or whatever they were, and at the same time, there's somebody coming in *your* window, *your* sleeping quarters, what do *you* do?"

"I tell you this, and I mean it. If I were on that jury, based just on what we've seen so far, I'd have a hard time convicting them of anything serious. Illegal weapons, maybe, but how in the world are they going to prove murder? That many people shooting from that many angles? And they've had plenty of time to get rid of evidence, haven't they? And can they prove who shot first, and who? And what is the difference between the sound of a stun grenade and gunfire? And how do the people at the back of the compound tell who shot first? Who in that compound is going to testify against Koresh—and won't it just be that person's word against 80-odd others?"

"Sex abuse? Those girls aren't going to be much inclined to rat on the son of God. So what does the government do—*beat* it out of them? Furthermore, almost all of them had the blessings and consent of their parents."

David's odds were getting better every day.

Even among those observers most obsessed with observing only that which may financially profit them, there was a growing obsession among the journalists with each doing their small part to ensure justice, at least a fair hearing, for this mysterious, obsessed man, and for the followers who were obsessed with him. Stated simply, their mission was to be a witness, and if something went wrong, to cry foul.

And the desire to be there had become as much a personal as a professional one. There grew within each of the members of the press a conflicting interface of dull, mundane, motel-room misery, and exhilarating expectation there in that cow pasture in the middle of April in Elk.

There were the bills unpaid back home and the desire for one's own soft, familiar bed. But there was also the expectation that, by remaining one day longer, just one more day, one might be on hand to be part of a process that would result in something... new.

Go home as one must, for a day or two, to shave legs or face, but then quickly return, to Groundhog Day, just in case it stopped being Groundhog Day.

Be there, to observe and report the utterances of any emerging Branch Davidian. And remain there long enough to cover the trials: To finally fully learn the contexts—religious, legal, philosophical, and personal—that had taken each of the Koreshians into that compound, and brought them out again.

Suddenly, rather than to sensationalize, they were there to learn. Not the loopy lessons that a David Koresh or a Livingston Fagan would try to impart, one on one, God forbid, but the larger lesson of how each of these personalities, each of these Believers, would wind up. To learn how The System would deal with such a deluge of a kind of people it had never encountered before, and to learn how the always competing and equally legitimate interests of Freedom vs. the Rule of Law would duke it out to a compromise this time.

Koresh would walk out to the hushed and undivided attention of the entire world. Whatever his shortcomings, whatever his sins, he had held the greatest nation in the world at bay for 50 days. And that was worthy of some major attention.

This ever-widening war was going to slog into the courtroom, bringing with it the advocates for every conceivable conflicting point of view.

Church-state separation was facing its wildest free-for-all.

No question that in most minds the things David Koresh liked to do with little girls, "teddy bears," was a pretty sick and pedophiliac proposition, morally.

Legally:

If it is truly one of the tenets of the "church" that the members freely offer up their daughters to the Deity (in effect, parents giving children their consent to marry) and the Deity beds those daughters in the interests of furthering and "enlarging" the church, has a crime been committed? It might be possible to prove the parents unfit, but tough to nail Koresh on statutory rape.

Polygamy? Only one woman, Rachel Koresh, bore his name. There is no law against marital infidelity. Even when it's blatant. Look at Hollywood.

What about the right of the people to keep and bear arms?

Any lawyer worth warm spit could further embroil these already muddy waters. The government could prove they possessed the *means* to make those weapons automatic, but with what most people have in their garages one could make a fairly "destructive explosive device."

There would, of course, be no change of venue; no defense attorney in his right mind would try to take it out of gun-toting, Bible-believing McLennan County. And to satisfy a jury there, the government would need to be able to show that the weapons were rendered automatic *before* the ATF assault (rather than *after*, a point at which many a Wacoan would think such modifications only reasonable and prudent under the circumstances).

Both inside the courtroom and out, there would be an all-consuming dialogue over constitutional intents.

Did the Founding Fathers guarantee the citizens the right to keep and bear arms only so they could protect themselves on the now-historic frontier from the odd passing rattlesnake or newspaper editor? Or were these guarantees intended to protect them and their constitutional rights in perpetuity from the abuses and excesses of the very government itself?

What about the right to be secure in one's home, and protected from unlawful search and seizure?

Does the government have the right to kick every door and climb in every window in an apartment complex housing 80 people just because it believes that everybody there knows everybody else, and thinks some of them may have broken the law? Does suspected illegal activity in Apartment 104 give them the right to come a-boiling in the window of Apartment 228? It would be easy to paint this one as a government fishing trip, and the *amicus curiae* briefs alone would have been most entertaining.

The world's mouth was watering.

What about the right to free association?

What about...?

These and a zillion other questions, and the pile of questions getting bigger every day, stockpiling themselves for the future.

And then, crazy, disorienting, unbelievable: smoke. Then flames. Then, craziest of all, after a little less than an hour, nothing. A hot, flat, black spot in the middle of a spring meadow.

It took a bit of pondering for the cameramen at the fence and the viewers at home to fully comprehend all the things that were suddenly disappearing in those flames, and to assess the depth and sources of the shock each was feeling.

Yes, deep shock, for the people.

Yes, most of all, for the children.

But also for the loss of a future, one that had seemed substantial. It was suddenly disappearing, becoming a future past.

For both the professionally curious and the amateurs at home, the viewers whose bottomless curiosities they presume and then satiate, out there on the empty prairie, in less than 20 minutes, all the answers and all the answerers were going, going, gone— disintegrating into gas and steam, dry bone and ash, infernal death and eternal silence, in that bright hot dot of orange under the question mark of smoke.

David Koresh had reduced to ashes both the answers and the

futures; all of his, and his children's, and a fair-sized portion of ours.

And in a little while, even the smoke was gone, lost on the wind, far-flung molecules commingling with those of the first volcanoes, first campfires, first burnt offerings, first gunfights, first railroads, first airplanes, first A-bombs.

And then the sky was blue. And then birds sang, and cows grazed, and grass grew. Life went on. New futures were unfolding in spite of the end of a world.

Postscript

*When it comes to facts, there's not a scholar
or theologian that can stand against what I have. If you
don't know the Seven Seals, you really don't know Christ,
so who are you to promise someone else that they'll
be saved by accepting your opinion?*
                                        —David Koresh

The centerpoint of David Koresh's convoluted theology is the mystical power of the one who can "open" the Seven Seals mentioned in the book of Revelation. Once the Seals were opened, Koresh taught, he and his followers would be martyred. But they would someday return and slay all Babylonians—Koresh-speak for nonbelievers.

The Seven Seals are only briefly described in John the Revelator's sweeping apocalyptic landscape. Mainstream Christian theology teaches that the events destined to follow the opening of each Seal applied both in Roman times and as a prophecy for the End Times—the days leading up to the Second Coming of Christ.

Seventh-day Adventist thought maintains that Jesus Christ opened six of the Seals in Heaven after the Ascension. The Seventh Seal will be opened with the advent of the Second Coming.

The number seven is the dominant number mentioned in The Revelation of St. John the Divine. There are seven candlesticks, churches, trumpets, thunders, vials, Spirits, and stars.

In Chapter 5, the opening of the Seven-sealed Book is accomplished by the Lamb, the singing of the New Song, and the universal worship of the Lamb. The first six seals are opened in Chapter 6:1-17. Although it is difficult to say with any degree of certainty, it appears that this is a description of an event that has already taken place.

John's fifth vision, which is chronicled in Chapter 8, describes the opening of the Seventh Seal, but it too is unclear whether this is an event that has happened, or is yet to come.

Taken as a part of the entire enigmatic fabric that is the Revelation, the opening of the Seven Seals is but a single thread running through one small part of the narrative. The Seals are not unimportant, but they are not even the central thrust and message of Revelation, much less the entire Bible.

About the Authors

BRAD BAILEY, a native Texan, is an award-winning police reporter and feature writer, and a freelancer living in Dallas. At the age of 33, Brad "retired" from daily journalism to pursue a broader range of projects, especially those concerning both the good and bad aspects of religion in America. He has a particular interest in offbeat cults and the abuses of televangelism. *Ripples of Suicide*, which he co-authored, will soon be published.

BOB DARDEN, lecturer, author, and magazine editor, has written a dozen books on a number of topics, including *Into the End Zone*, *Drawing Power*, and *The Option Play*. He is also the editor of the world's oldest and largest religious humor and satire magazine, *The Door*, and has served as gospel music editor for *Billboard* magazine since 1984. Bob and his wife, Mary, live in Waco, Texas.